WINDOWS 95
GAMES
PROGRAMMING

WINDOWS 95 GAMES PROGRAMMING

Stan Trujillo &
Al Stevens

M&T BOOKS

M&T Books
A Division of MIS:Press, Inc.
A Subsidiary of Henry Holt and Company, Inc.
115 West 18th Street
New York, New York 10011

Library of Congress Cataloging-in-Publication Data

```
Stevens, Al,
    Windows 95 games programming / by Al Stevens and Stan Trujillo.
       P.   cm.
    ISBN  1-55851-448-1
    1. Computer games--Programming.  2. Microsoft Windows (Computer
file) I. Trujillo, Stan.  II. Title.
QA76.76.C672S75  1996
794.8'15265--dc20                                          96-1748
                                                             CIP
```

10 9 8 7 6 5 4 3 2 1

Associate Publisher: Paul Farrell	**Managing Editor:** Cary Sullivan
Editor: Debra Williams Cauley	**Production Editor:** Maya Riddick
Copy Edit Manager: Shari Chappell	**Copy Editor:** Betsy Hardinger

Dedication

To my mother, Bonnie Coppock Trujillo
 S.T.

To Jerry Cozzi, who knew all the right changes
 A.S.

ACKNOWLEDGMENTS

We would like to thank the following authors for letting us use and distribute their software:

Gary Maddox—Blaster Master

David Mason—Dave's Targa Animator (DTA)

Paul H. Yoshimune of Handmade Software, Inc.—Image Alchemy

Lutz Kretzschner of SoftTronics—Moray

Jim Conger—Midi Sequencer

Neosoft Corporation—Neopaint Version 3.1

Owen Thomas—Astrofire

Chris Young—POV-Ray

Bob Powell—WinModeller

J.C. Pollman—Polywin

Rob McGregor—POVCAD, and Raw to POV-Ray Converter

John R. Wind—PolyRay Preprocessor

Alexander Enzmann—Polyray and Moray–> Polyray Converter

Contents

CHAPTER 10: THEATRIX TECHNICAL SPECIFICATIONS 205

CHAPTER 11: A C++ RAY-CASTING ENGINE 223

PREFACE

This book is the second in a series of two about writing computer games on the PC in the C++ programming language. The first book, C++ Games Programming, addresses games that run under MS-DOS. This book is about writing game programs that run under Windows 95.

The premise of these two books is that programmers can build professional quality games in C++ by exploiting the wealth of shareware, freeware, and public domain graphics and modeling tools that are readily available and that support game development. Inexpensive tools and libraries—some of which are free, and others that are shareware—are available for these purposes. The CD-ROM that accompanies this book includes many of such tools. The book goes one step further by introducing and providing the source code and documentation for three separate C++ class library frameworks that encapsulate the behavior of game programming in three different environments—conventional games developed with the Windows 95 GDI API, ray-cast games, and games that use the Microsoft Games SDK.

No one knows for sure who played the first game on a computer or what that game was, but from at least the mid-1950s, perhaps earlier, people have been using the computational features and storage of computers to simulate worlds, universes, and the rules of game play. For many years access to computers was limited to those who worked with them. However, due to the size of those early computers and their operating costs, personal and recreational use were mostly discouraged, and game technology did not advance much. The personal computer revolution changed all that.

There have probably been more different game programs developed and distributed for personal computers than programs of any other kind, and that circumstance continues today. But most such programs fade quietly into obscurity for one or more of many reasons: Perhaps a game fails to interest users; maybe the author does not adequately market, distribute, and support the game; in many cases, the game's implementation is simply amateurish, unreliable, inefficient, or some combination of the three. Our books cannot tell you how to design the concept for a successful game or how to bring it to market, but we can provide the tools with which you can build games that exhibit the professional touch—animation, photo-realistic scenes and characters, integrated sound effects and music, fast displays. Lights, camera, action—and that run efficiently and effectively under Windows 95.

The evolution of PC game technology and the complexity of PC game software has kept pace with the advancing technology of personal computer display, storage, and processing speed. Until recently, however, the evolution of game development did not track advances in programming technology. Object-oriented programming languages and graphical user interface operating systems were not among the serious game developer's options. As effective as those tools are for developing commercial software and hosting its operation, those environments were traditionally far too demanding of the computer's resources to support games of any consequence. Most games were written in C, assembly language, or a combination of the two, and they "took over the machine," which means that all the computer's resources had to be dedicated to the game while it was executing.

All that has changed. Contemporary mainstream desktop computers possess sufficient internal memory, removable mass storage, and processing speed to support not only the operating systems of today but also applications with heavy resource demands, and those applications include games. The work represented by the contents of this book and its accompanying CD-ROM reflect this revolution and its consequences.

INTRODUCTION

Windows 3.1 is not a good games platform. The games that were written for Windows 3.1 (or the lack of them) serve as evidence that 3.1 did more to get in the way than to help. The term *Windows games* conjured images of games such as solitaire and poker. Late in the life of 3.1, Microsoft released WinG, which helped, but it was too little and too late. Windows 3.1 had not been designed for games, and it showed.

This shortcoming was not lost on Microsoft, which promised that things would be different with Windows 95. Many promises were made. Windows 95 was supposed to be bigger and better—a more mature operating system than any before it. And this time, Microsoft promised that games would be well supported.

The support came in the form of the Microsoft Games SDK. The SDK provides support for input devices, network play, multichannel sound, and graphics performance that has never before been available on PCs.

Even if you decide not to use the Games SDK, you'll find that Windows 95 is a strong games platform on its own, providing support for sound, music, graphics, and networking, along with an ever-growing base of customers eager for new games. Windows 95 is a strong games platform.

Games programming has also been upgraded. Games development has been merged with modern software techniques and development tools. No longer is assembly language a requirement. No longer is it necessary to understand and reprogram the PC's timer chips or read terse descriptions about proprietary sound card interfaces. Games programming is now about object-oriented techniques, C++, class frameworks, device independence, and letting the hardware and the operating system do the dirty work for you. In other words, if you know C++ and have a PC, you can be a games programmer.

This chapter introduces these subjects:

- Class framework technology
- Objectives of a games class framework
- You, the game programmer
- What to expect from this book

Class Framework Technology

This book is about writing games for Windows 95. Our approach relies heavily on *class framework technology*, the science of building application frameworks from C++ class libraries. We include three separate class frameworks in the software that accompanies this book. Framework technology is useful for separating details from concepts. Using frameworks allows you to write games quickly and easily. The book serves two purposes, depending on your needs. If you simply want to write your own games, you can use the frameworks that we provide. If you want to write your own framework, you can use the ones in this book as models.

Frameworks are not new to Windows. The Microsoft Foundation Classes (MFC) have been an invaluable tool since the first release and are an integral part of Visual C++. Readers who are familiar with MFC will see similarities between MFC and the frameworks we provide. Readers who are not familiar with MFC will find MFC easier to learn after using the frameworks in this book. Three frameworks are included on the CD-ROM: Theatrix, Raycast, and GDKapp.

Theatrix

Theatrix comes from our previous book, *C++ Games Programming*. We ported Theatrix to Windows 95 so that the application programming interface is virtually the same. Consequently, games written with the DOS version of Theatrix are easy to port to Windows. We ported Marble Fighter, Shootout, and other games from the first book. Theatrix uses a stage metaphor for games development. Games are described in terms of a stage performance involving actors, directors, and cues.

Raycast

The Raycast framework supports *ray casting*, the technique used in games such as Doom and Heretic, and allows you to create environments complete with walls, ceilings, floors, doors, props, and moving creatures. The framework comes with a demo called Tubas of Terror.

GDKapp

GDKapp uses the Microsoft Games SDK. When GDKapp games run on hardware that supports the Games SDK features, incredibly smooth graphics and sound result. The TankTop demo runs at 60 to 70 frames per second on most 64-bit video cards.

That's Not Everything

The CD-ROM included with this book contains many of the tools and utilities that we used to write the demos. We've included ray-tracers, modelers, paint programs, and bitmap utilities.

Framework Objectives

A good class framework can make writing software an enjoyable and organized activity. A bad class framework can make matters worse than they were before frameworks came along. What follows is a discussion of what makes a framework good. These are the items that were used in designing the frameworks for this book, and they apply to games frameworks and to frameworks in general.

Details: What to Know, What to Hide

In the old days, a computer games builder had to know and do it all. You needed an intimate understanding of the computer's video, keyboard, mouse, joystick, and sound-generation hardware—an imposing scope of knowledge, to be sure, but not nearly as daunting then as it is today. The typical computer game of yore was written to run on a particular suite of hardware; the programmer had to master only one small set of configurations. Not only do the PCs of today have various and incompatible hardware options, but also their architectures are arcane and esoteric.

Today, Windows insulates you from most of these details. You don't need to know every detail of such things as video cards and sound devices. Understanding the Windows application program interface (API) is a daunting task; the API is legendary for being hard to work with. This difficulty spawned the success of MFC, which hides many of the API's details from the application programmer.

It is possible to write games directly using the API, but you will find yourself spending more time managing the API than writing your game. Writing games is hard enough. A Windows games framework allows you to concentrate on your game and ignore the nuances and vagaries of the API.

Levels of Abstraction

How much you must understand about low-level details of implementation describes the *level of abstraction* at which you operate. You may view level of abstraction as an imaginary line somewhere between the hardware at the lowest level and the application problem being solved (in this case, the game being developed) at the highest level. As the level of abstraction falls, it exposes more details of implementation. Furthermore, the lower that line gets, the more complex the details become. As the programmer, you must understand everything from the highest level down to your particular, personal lowest level of abstraction. It follows that the higher that line, the fewer details you have to deal with and the more details you can forget about.

People who understand details of implementation have built detailed functionality into libraries for others to use. By using these libraries, we raise our level of abstraction. The higher our personal level of abstraction, the fewer details we need to be concerned about. It is, therefore, advantageous to use these libraries.

Consequently, an objective of a class framework for games is to raise the game programmer's level of abstraction as far as possible above the details of implementation.

Encapsulation

The games frameworks encapsulate the details and interface of a game-construction metaphor. Their objective is to provide an interface that hides the details of bitmap management, memory allocation, animation, sound and music generation, and message dispatching. The Theatrix and Raycast frameworks are implemented with the Win32 SDK and allow its use without demanding that you know the SDK. The GDKapp framework is implemented with the Games SDK and hides the sometimes ugly details of the SDK from you, the games programmer.

The Framework Metaphor

A metaphor is like a parable. It tells a story that uses an analogy to make a point. The analogy associates something that we already understand with the lesson that we are about to learn. The familiar helps to explain the unfamiliar. One of Theatrix's objectives is to provide an intuitive metaphor through its class design. By associating game construction with more familiar human activities, Theatrix helps programmers understand and remember what the components are, how they relate to one another, and when it is appropriate to use each one in the development of a particular game.

The Theatrix game-construction metaphor equates the components of a game with the participants in a theatrical production. There are directors and players. The directors manage scenery and direct the actions of the players. The players control their own movements and originate their own voices and sound effects. There are conductors that generate music. This metaphor is modeled in a class hierarchy. A game program derives game-specific classes from the Theatrix classes and instantiates objects of these game-specific classes. The objects register for and receive cues from each other and from Theatrix—keystrokes, mouse events, timer events, and game-defined messages.

Theatrix is the only one of our three frameworks that employs the stage performance metaphor. The other two accomplish their tasks with more literal terminology. The GDKapp framework, for instance, uses terms such as *scene*, *sprite*, and *application*.

Performance

For a game to be taken seriously by the game-playing public, it must perform well. It follows that a class framework that encapsulates game components must likewise perform well. We used performance as the major criterion for the selection of our tools, and we kept performance in the forefront throughout the development of the frameworks.

A Comprehensive Toolkit

A games developer needs good tools for building graphics, sound effects, music, and video. There are expensive commercial packages that support these activities. If you like them and can afford them, then by all means use them. But we did not want to limit the use of this book to people who can afford high-end tools. So we went in search of and found quite acceptable tools that support all our requirements but are within the budgets of most independent developers.

You can use the tools on the CD-ROM to test and experiment with the example games, and you can use them to begin development of your own games. We selected tools that are available and supported. In some cases, the tools are free for you to use as is. Others are shareware, and, if you expect to continue to use them, you should pay the nominal registration fees to their authors.

Extensibility

We designed the frameworks to be extensible. If you want to incorporate new features into the frameworks, you can derive from the existing classes. All the source code is included, so you are free to extend or modify the frameworks.

Who Are You?

Building a killer Windows 95 game involves many skills and much imagination. The best games employ the talents of conceptual designers to create the game's premise and objectives, creative writers to write the scenarios and design the levels, graphics artists to design the scenery and sprites, musicians to compose and record the score, sound technicians to create effective sound effects, and computer programmers to write the code that bring together all these elements.

You may have these skills, but you are definitely a programmer, and this book assumes that you have a working knowledge of the C++ programming language. We do not spend time explaining object-oriented programming, C++ class design, or C++ language constructs. If you are not familiar with C, you should read *Al Stevens Teaches C*, by one of the authors of this book. (It should be obvious which author.) If you do not know C++, we suggest that you read *Teach Yourself C++, 4th Edition*, also by Al Stevens. We assume that you understand how to compile and link programs and what an object library is. You are expected to understand the implications of source code header files and C/C++ macros. You are also expected to have a minimal understanding of Visual C++, although readers new to Visual C++ should be able to catch on quickly. Beyond that, all you need is a desire to understand and build computer games.

It is a lucky coincidence that building a computer game requires the skills of a programmer. Programmers are the most inveterate of game players. We enjoy challenges, puzzles, and complex constructions. The very nature of programming involves building and solving the mysteries of the most intricate of mazes, the computer program. We are qualified games builders because we are inherent game players.

There are two possible reasons that you might be reading this book. Either you are fascinated with computer games—love them, fixate on them, can't live without them—and have a white-hot burning desire to build games of your own; or you are a programmer who sees all the money that the game builders are making, and you want a piece of that action. If you fit into the first category, you are the perfect candidate to read this book. If the second category describes you better, then you are in for a happy awakening. In addition to being rewarding, games development is pure fun. This subject matter is compelling. Unless you are a completely boring person, which we doubt very much, you will get into it, and we mean really into it.

What Do You Need?

To run the example games on the included CD-ROM, you need Windows 95. Windows 95 should be in a 256-color mode for the best performance. To use the GDKapp framework, you need the Microsoft Games SDK. You need Visual C++ 4.0 or later to modify the demos and write your own games. Visual C++ 4.0 includes language features that are part of draft ANSI standard C++ and are not currently available in all C++ compilers. If you are interested in using the frameworks with another compiler, make sure that the compiler supports RTTI (runtime type information). The GDKapp framework, because of its dependence on the Games SDK, works only with Visual C++.

Your Rights and Some Restrictions

The class framework source code is copyrighted by the authors. You may use it to your heart's content to build games, and you may distribute these games in any way that you like. We hope you build cool games (that we can play, too), and we hope that you make a million bucks doing it. We encourage you to give copies of the framework source code to anyone, but you may not sell it unless you are selling a copy of this book along with it, which, we presume, you acquired through legitimate channels. Under no circumstances may you publish any part of the source code and represent it as your own work.

The tools on the included CD-ROM come from many vendors and have different copyright and licensing restrictions. View the *readme* files for each tool to see what your rights and responsibilities are.

The songs in the MIDI files are copyrighted. You are encouraged to play them for your own entertainment, but please do not use them in programs that you intend to publish commercially.

The example games are just that: examples. With a little practice you can defeat any of them in short order. You may use them as launching pads for your own game programs. The sprites and backgrounds are not particularly exotic or original, so we do not mind if you use them. Your games, however, should be unique and unlike any others. You should build your own sprites. The POV-Ray source files (those that have the extensions **.POV** and **.INC**) that are part of the example games are hereby released to the public domain.

Getting Help

If you have questions about the software, you can E-mail us on CompuServe or the Internet. Stan Trujillo is on CompuServe as 75233,1506 and Al Stevens can be reached at astevens@ddj.com or on CompuServe as 71101,1262.

For help with a particular tool from another vendor, see the documentation file with that tool. Most of the vendors will help you with technical support if you have registered their product. Some of them maintain a presence on CompuServe or the Internet and offer to answer questions that way.

The Organization of This Book

The book is divided into three parts. The first part includes this chapter and deals with non-code issues, such as game theory, Windows 95 features, and Visual C++. The second part deals with developing games for the Win32 API. Sprite-based and ray-casting games are discussed. The final part deals exclusively with the Microsoft Games SDK. Each chapter (except this one) is outlined below.

Chapter 2 is about game theory. It uses the history and evolution of computer games to explain the components of games and the various kinds of games that run on computers.

Chapter 3 discusses the technical aspects of game-building strategies. This is where you learn to assemble the game components that are outside the program code. You learn to create scenery using techniques that depend on whether you want photographic realism or an arcade appearance. You learn to design and build animated sequences for the action in your game. This chapter describes how to build sound effects and the game's musical score.

Chapter 4 deals with issues specific to Windows 95. Windows 95 is examined and assessed from the game development perspective.

Chapter 5 describes the development environment. This chapter starts with a discussion of Visual C++. Then the framework projects and demos are dealt with. The chapter also addresses team development and final release issues.

Chapter 6 is an introduction to Theatrix. This chapter gives an overview of the class hierarchy and explains the theatrical production metaphor.

Chapter 7 covers the Theatrix utility programs.

Chapter 8 explains each of the Theatrix demo games. You learn how to use Theatrix; it teaches, by example, each of the features that the library supports. The discussion addresses the operation of the games and the code and data files that implement them.

Chapter 9 is the Theatrix reference manual, which documents the public interfaces of the C++ classes in the Theatrix class library.

Chapter 10 is the Theatrix technical discussion, which describes the implementation of the framework and the formats for the various data library files that game programs use.

Chapter 11 introduces Raycast. The ray-casting technique is discussed, along with the framework internals.

Chapter 12 covers the Tubas of Terror demo. The demo is explained, and instructions are given on how to write your Raycast game.

Chapter 13 introduces the Games SDK and gives an overview.

Chapter 14 is the GDKapp user's guide.

Chapter 15 is the GDKapp reference manual. The GDKapp interface is documented on a function-by-function basis.

Chapter 16 covers the GDKapp demo games, including the TankTop demo.

Appendix A describes the game developer's toolsett of shareware and freeware tools included on the CD-ROM.

GAME THEORY

This chapter is your introduction to computer games in general. We discuss some of the early computer games to provide an historical perspective on how they started and to illustrate how the evolution of games reflects advances in computing power. Then we address the factors that go into the design and development of a contemporary computer game.

You will read about these subjects:

- Early computer games
- Different kinds of games
- The components of a computer game
- The issues of violence and programming standards

Early Computer Games

In the early 1960s, one of the authors of this book played his first computer game. The computer was an IBM 1410, and it belonged to the U.S. government. I (Stevens) was a civilian programmer, and an Air Force sergeant named Guy Tibbets was the operator. The IBM 1410 was a character-based machine with 100,000 characters of memory and a Selectric-ball typewriter console device. The game was Tibbets's idea. We would fill memory with the NOP instruction (which consumed an instruction fetch and execute cycle but did nothing), press the **Reset** button to position the instruction pointer at address zero, and then press the **Start** and **Stop** buttons in rapid succession. The console displayed the instruction pointer address where the stop occurred. Our game was to see who could stop the computer faster, as measured by the lower stop address. I could never beat Tibbets. It was a simple and mindless exercise, but it passed the time on the night shift when we ran out of jokes to tell.

The point of this story is twofold. First, given the opportunity, most computer users will use a computer to have fun—when the General isn't around. Second, the manner in which a computer can entertain us is usually a function of its processing power. That 1410, which filled a room, was actually slow enough that a human being could move a hand from one button to another in less time than it took the computer to execute 100,000 NOP instructions. Thus the limitations of the 1410 computer permitted the game that Tibbets contrived.

Chess

Computer games predate that early experience with a 1410. In 1959, an MIT mathematics professor named John McCarthy wrote a chess-playing program on the school's IBM 704 computer. Chess programs are common today—you can buy small microprocessor-based chess machines at Radio Shack for a song—but at the time the program was a monumental achievement. It gave credibility to a new discipline called *artificial intelligence*, one that was generally regarded among the knowledgeable as showing little promise. Computer game construction continued for several years at MIT's Artificial Intelligence (AI) Laboratory, where students had relatively unrestricted and unmonitored access to government-funded computers.

Spacewar

In 1961, Steve Russell, one of McCarthy's students, was given access to the school's DEC PDP-1, which had an oscilloscope display device that you could control from a program—an early video terminal. Russell set about to create the first video game, an outer-space confrontation between two players. Each player controlled the movements and weaponry of a rocket ship by pressing switches on the computer's front panel console. The point of the game was to destroy the opponent's ship by firing a torpedo while at the same time avoiding the opponent's torpedoes.

The game survived for years, with improvements added by the programmers at the AI lab. One of those improvements was the invention of the first computer joystick, created from scrap parts by the programmers because computer console switches were difficult to use to fly spacecraft and fire torpedoes.

Life

The game of Life was invented by British mathematician John Conway and was published in *Scientific American* in 1970. Life simulates a universe of neighboring cells. Each cell, identified by its x/y address in a coordinate system, may have one of two possible states. The cell is either populated or unpopulated and is surrounded by eight neighboring cells. The game consists of a sequence of generations. Each generation examines each cell to see (1) whether it is populated and (2) how many populated neighbors it has. A neighbor is one of the eight adjacent cells in the 3 x 3 array of nine in which the target cell is the center cell. If an unpopulated cell has a certain number of populated neighbors, the cell becomes populated in the next generation. Conversely, if a populated cell has too few or too many neighbors, its population expires in the next generation. A cell is born if there are enough neighbors to spawn it and dies if there are either too few neighbors to support it or too many neighbors with which it must share resources. Some implementations of Life use screen character positions to represent cells, and the universe of cells is limited to the number of screen character positions. Others use dense graphical screens on which to display the simulation.

The game of Life simulates the evolution of generations. To play the game, you create the universe by specifying which cells are initially populated. Then you run the evolution and observe how each generation modifies the pattern of populated cells. The universe often takes on interesting symmetrical patterns as the generations pass. Some patterns result in a totally expired universe after a few generations. Other patterns result in a stable universe. Still other patterns endlessly repeat a cycle of births and deaths. A culture of Life players blossomed in the 1970s, and its members often published and shared interesting starting patterns.

As with Spacewar, Life was given its own life at the MIT AI lab in the early 1970s. For a time, Life dominated the concentration and lives of researchers and students, who programmed Life to run on the lab's PDP-6 and spent most of their time experimenting with Life patterns.

The executable and source code for a DOS text-mode version of Life is included on the CD-ROM that accompanies this book. See Michael Abrash's *The Zen of Code Optimization* (listed in the Bibliography) for a discussion of Life as a study in how to optimize computer simulations.

Adventure

Adventure was developed in the early 1970s at the Stanford AI Laboratory by Will Crowther and Donald Woods. Adventure uses keyboard input and console output to establish a dialogue with the human player. Adventure simulates a world of caves, dragons, dwarfs, and so on. The game tells you where you are and what the surroundings hold. For example, when you first begin to play, you see this message on the console:

```
Somewhere nearby is Colossal Cave, where others have found fortunes in
treasure and gold, though it is rumored that some who enter are never seen
again. Magic is said to work in the cave. I will be your eyes and hands.
Direct me with commands of 1 or 2 words. (Should you get stuck, type "help"
for some general hints. For information on how to end your adventure, etc.,
type "info".)

You are standing at the end of a road before a small brick building. Around
you is a forest. A small stream flows out of the building and down a gully.
>
```

From the prompt, you type terse commands and directions. Following each command, the program tells you where you are. For example, at the first prompt you can type **enter** or **go in** and the next message appears:

```
You're inside building.

There are some keys on the ground here.
There is a shiny brass lamp nearby.
There is tasty food here.
There is a bottle of water here.
>
```

Subsequent commands retrieve items and navigate you through the world of Adventure. It is a compelling and addictive game, particularly until you have mastered it and retrieved all the treasures in Colossal Cave.

Adventure is typical of the first generation of action games, using text displays and the player's keyboard commands. Joysticks were not widely available then, the mouse had not been invented, and computer graphics were too slow and too low in resolution to display the kind of images that Crowther and Woods described with words.

The CD-ROM with this book includes the executables and source code of Adventure as ported to C to run on a PC. The original program was written in FORTRAN and displayed all its messages in uppercase, another example of how the limits of computers influenced their games.

Contemporary Games

Early computer games had a certain charm and appeal that contemporary games lack. Because of the limitations of the hardware, early games used text mode or very primitive graphics. As a consequence, a principal ingredient in games was the player's imagination. The experience is akin to that of reading a book; the reader's mind provides the visual and audible details based on the writer's descriptions. Another analogy compares radio drama (for those of you who remember it) to that of movies and television. The radio listener supplied the scenery, the action, and faces for the actors. The medium provided only voices, sound effects, and background music to tell its story.

With vast improvements in display, controller, and sound technology, game development has advanced far beyond the simple interfaces from the early days, and the current crop of games reflects those improvements.

Typical of modern entertainment, today's games emphasize action represented by the visual and audible, leaving very little of those elements to the player's imagination. As a result, players concentrate more on honing motor skills or using deductive reasoning to unearth the clues and beat the game than they do on visualizing the scenery and characters.

Contemporary games come in many varieties; four common types are simulators, real-time 3-D mazes, static photo-realistic displays, and arcade-style animated sprite games.

Simulators

Not long after IBM introduced the PC in 1981, Microsoft began selling Flight Simulator, a program that it acquired from a company called SubLogic. Flight Simulator was a milestone program for two reasons. First, it was a realistic simulation of the cockpit of a small airplane in which the player-pilot could execute takeoffs, landings, and flight maneuvers. Second, the program became the benchmark for compatibility when the PC clone market was born. If a would-be PC-compatible computer could run Flight Simulator, chances were good that it would run anything that a true blue PC could run.

The first Flight Simulator was truly impressive. It ran in a 4.77-MHz 8088 machine with no hard disk and 512KB of internal memory. The Color Graphics Adapter display had a monochrome graphics resolution of 640 by 200 pixels. By today's standards, the original PC was tiny and underpowered. Yet Flight Simulator managed to display a full instrument panel with moving needles and changing digits; a pilot's view through the windshield that rendered the outside world in real time; a computer model of the terrain, a few buildings, and an airport in Chicago; and engine sounds through the PC's tiny speaker.

Flight Simulator has kept pace with advances in hardware. The latest version uses a photo-realistic instrument panel, fractal scenery, and enhanced visuals of some scenery that maps digitized aerial photography over the terrain renderings. It also requires a fast processor and many megabytes of hard disk space.

There are many other flight simulators for the PC. Most of them emphasize air combat missions, although a few, such as Chuck Yeager's Advanced Flight Trainer 2, teach the elements of flight rather than combat.

Others include simulators of bombers, fighters, helicopters, ultralights, gliders, biplanes, and even the space shuttle. An air traffic control simulator allows Flight Simulator pilots on networks to fly in controlled airspace. One player is the air traffic controller; the others are the pilots.

Simulators are now available for race cars, submarines, tanks, and every imaginable kind of spacecraft, including the *Starship Enterprise*. They all have one thing in common. They render their scenery in real time. The program maintains a computer model of the world in which the simulated object moves. That model describes the terrain and features such as buildings, bodies of water, towers, statues, trees, pylons, and so on. As the simulated object moves through this world, the program uses the model to render each frame of the player's view as the view changes.

This book is not about writing simulators, although you could use the Theatrix class library to implement one. Two books in the Bibliography address flight simulator technology and construction in detail. They are *Flights of Fantasy* and *Taking Flight*.

3-D Mazes: Doom

In the early 1990s, Apogee Software introduced a shareware game called Wolfenstein. In the game, the player is a hero of sorts who wanders through a 3-D maze of corridors and doors and does battle with Nazi types who appear at random from inside doorways and around corners and who shoot at the hero. The game and its display techniques launched a new generation of games culminating with Doom, the most successful shareware game ever produced. Doom was developed by the programmers who wrote Wolfenstein after they split off from Apogee. Doom originated as a DOS shareware game.

Wolfenstein, Doom, Blake Stone, Descent, and other 3-D maze games use a display software technology called *ray casting*, which is a way to rapidly compute successive frames of complex scenery in real time. These games are as close to virtual reality as the PC has gotten (so far). The Raycast framework included with this book supports this technique.

Static Displays: Myst

Myst is completely different from Doom. Although the two games represent different game development strategies, they are also the two most successful of contemporary computer games. Myst was originally a Macintosh game that was later ported to Windows. The Windows version is by far the more popular. A sequel to the original game is now under development, and it promises to be a runaway best seller.

Myst plays out its scenario beginning on an island where the player moves about and gathers information. From that information the player learns to travel to and return from other islands where the player gathers more clues. Gradually, the clues combine to reveal the purpose and eventual completion of the game. At first, players do not know the purpose—or even the premise—of the game. The magic of Myst is in the way the mystery unravels itself as players move around in the beautiful and mystical worlds that the game provides. In a sense, Myst is a modern version of Adventure. The text and typed command interface has been modernized with graphics and a point-and-click interface.

The scenery in Myst consists mostly of static displays. The player moves about by clicking the mouse on points on the screen. The program changes the player's view accordingly. These views are rendered in advance by a technique known as *ray tracing*, which provides photo-realistic images of scenes represented in a computer model.

Myst frequently uses small inserts of video clips superimposed over the static displays. Some of the video clips are actual video images created with a video camera. Others are constructed from animated sequences of scenes rendered in advance with ray tracing and compiled into video files that the computer can play back.

Sound effects and music are an integral part of Myst. Many of the clues depend on sound effects. The music provides no clues or information but greatly enhances the visual effects of the game by adding to the mood.

The Theatrix library supports the development of games such as Myst. The toolkit includes 3-D modeling and ray-tracing tools, and the library supports static displays, selective mouse control, coordinated sound effects, video clips, and music.

Sprites and Backgrounds

A *sprite* is a bitmap that moves across a complex background without disturbing the background. Sprite-based games frequently use scrolling backgrounds. The vast majority of games found in the coin arcades and on home game consoles use sprite animation. Classic games such as Pac-man, Defender, Centipede, Donkey Kong, and Galaga are sprite-based games. More recent hits including Mario Brothers, Sonic the Hedgehog, Donkey Kong Kountry, and the fighting games—are also sprite-based.

The PC has sprite-based games, too, such as Commander Keen and Duke-Nukem. However, PC sprite-based games have been weak compared to games that run on home game consoles and coin operated machines. The Microsoft Games SDK, covered in Part 3, changes this. The frameworks included with this book provide sprite support.

Your Game

All the discussions until now have been about games that other people have developed. Now it's time to consider your game, and that's what we'll concentrate on from this point forward. This chapter addresses the theory behind the components of a PC game and the options you have when you build one. Chapter 3 is about the technology and strategies that you apply in building your game.

After you have decided to write the next killer game and sweep the market, you have to build it. To do that, you start with the game's purpose (other than to make you a pile of money, of course). What is its point? What are the objectives? What is expected of the player? What does the game itself provide?

Develop a theme. Will your players kill or be killed? Or will they explore, collecting treasures and gathering clues? Must they manipulate a vehicle? How about weapons? Will there be one player at a time or more? Will the game support multiple players at a single PC session, or is a network involved?

Develop a scenario. Sketch out the scenes and the game's progress. Identify items that appear in each of the scenes and their consequence to the player.

Who are the players going to be? Small children? Teenagers? Adults? Senior citizens? Does the game make assumptions about the players' cultural or ethnic backgrounds?

Will music play a role? Sound effects? Video clips?

How will the player control the game? With the keyboard? With the mouse? With a joystick?

Will the scenery and characters be realistic? Surrealistic? Have an outer-space look? Be pastoral? Have an arcade look?

All these decisions help you select the technique for presenting the game and the tools that you need. The example games in this book have all the scenery and use all the features just mentioned—music, sound effects, video clips, mouse, joystick. You won't find all the elements in every game, but everything just discussed exists in one or more of the example games.

Scenery

Designing scenery is a major part of game design, but it's something that doesn't call on your programming skills at all. Whether you use the Windows 95 Paint program to construct a scene or render a 3-D model into a ray-traced, photo-realistic image, the result is a screen full of colored pixels that the program copies into video memory. When you use a class library such as Theatrix, all you do in the program is provide the name of the file. All the real work is done in the construction of the scene.

There might be parts of the scenery screen that are significant to the program. If a mouse click has meaning on a particular feature, you must record the pixel coordinates of the click boundaries. You will need to eventually plug these values into the program. If the scene includes a door that opens and closes, you need to record the coordinates that define the door's rectangle. If sprites move about in the scene, you need to map a path of screen coordinates that represent the movement.

Characters

The characters in a game—the sprites—are like the actors in a play. They move about among the scenery, speak lines, and make things happen. Through animation, sprites provide the action in the game.

Not all sprites represent living creatures. A door that opens and closes can be a sprite. So can a table that slides across the floor. Anything that moves against the static background scenery is a sprite.

Animation of a sprite involves rendering in advance all the frames necessary to represent motion. A walking sprite needs frames to display the character in each of the configurations of steps. If the character moves toward and away from the player's view of the scene, there must be frames of different sizes to suggest perspective. Sometimes you render these frames in advance. Other times you have one set of frames for each motion and compute and render the size at runtime.

Video Clips

Not all moving things in a game are implemented as sprites. Sometimes you use video clips. These clips can be animated sequences built from 3-D models or individually painted frames. They can also be real video sequences captured onto disk from a video input card connected to a video camera or VCR. There are standard formats for these video files, and Theatrix supports their display.

Myst uses many video clips. The scenes where the characters speak from behind books in the library are video clips. The porthole view of flying into the island of another world in a spaceship is a video sequence made by many renderings of a 3-D model of that flight.

Sound and Music

Sound effects and music add an extra dimension to a game. The PC has a programmable speaker, but its small bandwidth limits its use for effective sound generation. However, most game players have add-on sound boards in their PCs. These boards are capable of producing high-quality sound effects and synthesized or sampled music. By using these sound boards, even games that do not depend on sound to communicate with the player are more fun to play. If the game slams a door or fires a shotgun, the sound adds to the effect. Music, as played from MIDI files, adds mood and texture to a scene.

Menus

If there is more than one place for a player to start when playing a game or if the player can make choices at strategic points in the game, a menu is a good way to present the choices and get the selection. A *menu* shows a list of the possible selections and provides a way for the player to make a choice. Every computer user is accustomed to menus. Game programmers have the freedom to use any menu technique they like. Unlike other development environments, our frameworks do not impose a standard for menus on the game programmer. (See "What about Standards?" later in this chapter.) For that reason, there is no menu class in the library. You should design a menu to reflect the atmosphere that your game presents and use the Theatrix paradigm to display the menu and retrieve the player's choices. The menu should be simple and easy to use. Some of the example games on the included CD-ROM use menus, and you can use these examples as a guide.

Options

A game's options can be as simple as allowing the player to specify a skill level or as complex as letting the player modify the game itself. Most action games allow you to join in as a rookie or trainee and then raise your skill level as you become more experienced. This approach allows players to get into and enjoy the game well before they are proficient with it. If you do not provide such an option in a difficult action game, then either your game is not so difficult after all—it is too easy, in fact—or players will give up in frustration before they have discovered all that the game has to offer. This concept does not apply so much to passive games of discovery such as Myst, where players can take their time. It is more important in games— such as Doom—that require the player to apply refined motor skills and fast reflexes to survive.

As with menus, the way that you display options and get their values should look as if it belongs to the game. The example programs on the included CD-ROM show you ways to do this.

Saving Games in Progress

If a game is complex and takes a while to complete, you should provide the ability to save and restore the game's status. There's not much that a library can add to what Standard C++ already provides for reading and writing disk files, but you should understand the concept.

Saving a game's progress consists of recording a number of status indicators and values into a disk file that the game can read during the initialization of a subsequent session. You should identify each of these items when you design the game's scenario to facilitate designing the save and restore software logic. The current status of a game consists of the progress that the player has made and the options under which the game is running. If the game has successive levels, the current level is one item of progress. If there are foes that have been vanquished, that fact should be recorded for each one. If items have been moved or bodies are strewn about, the location and identity of each one is saved. Any persistent data value that influences how the computer plays the game or that affects the player's location, skill, or progress should be saved.

When the player shuts down without having won or lost, the game program should ask whether the player wants to save the game. If so, the game program writes the status data into a disk file.

When the game begins at another time, the player must have the option to restore a previous game, in which case the game loads the status data into memory and proceeds from the last point of departure.

Suppose more than one person plays the game at different times but on the same computer. The game program needs to tell them apart. There are two ways to do this. One way is to name each saved game data file. When saving the game, the player specifies the saved game's name. That name is used later to retrieve the game. Another way is to provide a sign-on log. When a player starts the game, the program displays a list of players and allows a player to select from the list or to sign on as a new player to be added to the list.

Multiple Players

There are two ways to support multiple players in a game. One way is to let both players have their own controllers and use the same computer. Such games usually use a joystick, because sharing a keyboard or mouse can be awkward. The other way is to connect two or more computers in a network. The computers all run the game in a multiple-player environment, and they communicate by exchanging packets across the network.

The network can be as simple as two computers connected with a serial cable or by modem across telephone lines. Although many multiple-player games run on local and wide area networks, the demands of a game are small. The programs exchange small packets about such things as where the sprites are and who is shooting in what direction.

Because Windows 95 has built in networking, the support for building network enabled games is better than ever. The Theatrix framework supports networking.

Keeping Score

If a game has scores or levels of achievement, then the game should offer the player an opportunity to record the results. A typical game displays a list of the highest scores and score makers, adding the latest score to the list if it ranks among the highest. This list gives new players an objective to aim for.

Simulators often maintain and record levels of player achievement. A pilot or driver can accumulate hours of experience and advanced ratings by successfully executing prescribed maneuvers, such as cross-country trips, instrument approaches, bombing raids, dogfights, and so on.

A game that records the progress of several players can use the same disk file to record the players' individual scores.

The Question of Sex and Violence

When people gather to discuss the issue of sex and violence in entertainment media, you have to watch for outside agendas. It seems that the only people whose opinions can be trusted are those who have no personal stake in the outcome, and no one seems to fit that description. Politicians posture for votes. The entertainment industry holds forth for profits. Parents worry about wrong influences on their children. Civil libertarians guard our rights to free speech and expression. It seems that everyone has a stake in sex and violence.

Leisure Suit Larry depicts a couple of cute sprites having sex—under the covers, to be sure, but there is no question about what they are doing. The game may have more sexually oriented action than that one scene, but we never got much further with it.

Doom is violent. It depicts death and carnage, complete with screams, blood, and bodies scattered all over the landscape. The player does most of the killing, selecting weapons from a deadly and varied arsenal.

Most flight simulators involve bombing or shooting down the enemy, who, it must be presumed, are human beings.

Myst has no active violence, but it tells the story of long-ago acts when beings did harm to one another. In one scene, a skeleton is seen hanging from a gallows, a remnant of earlier, unseen atrocities.

Descent takes a different approach to its violence. The player shoots down unmanned drones that are themselves programmed to mindlessly shoot down the player. The player never actually kills anything that is alive.

Some arcade games, such as Mortal Kombat, depict neo-gladiators tearing off one another's arms, legs, and heads. These games have come under public scrutiny, and a cry has gone up for some form of industry self-regulation and a ratings system.

Despite what you hear during political campaigns and on talk shows, no empirical evidence exists to support the position that children receive negative influences from seeing improper behavior in entertainment media. That is only emotional opinion. The absence of such evidence does not mean that the opinions are without merit, however, only that they are unproven by scientific means.

You must decide how you feel about this issue, because you have the opportunity to add to and influence this culture in one way or another. One thing is clear: There is a strong market for games that allow the player to fire weapons and vanquish the enemy. You may draw whatever conclusions you wish about a society that desires and seeks out such a release. If you think that you know what's right and acceptable, then you have found the answer for yourself, and that's what matters.

Until there are government regulations to control what people can publish in a computer game (which is inevitable, we fear), everyone has to exercise good taste and judgment. The market should guide us. If programmers make the right decisions and the games are good ones and are properly marketed, people will use and praise them. If, on the other hand, someone puts out an obvious piece of trash where evil nuns slaughter little fuzzy puppies (we hope we haven't given anyone an idea here) or something equally stupid and gratuitous, that work will be rejected and the programmer can move on to other pursuits.

What about Standards?

Every aspect of programming involves standards. There are standards for writing code, for documentation, and most particularly for the user interface.

When DOS reigned, applications prided themselves on their proprietary user interfaces. If you copied the menu and data entry screens of another application, the chances were good that you would find yourself the object of a *look-and-feel* lawsuit.[1] Now that Windows prevails, applications pride themselves on their common user interface, and they all look and feel alike. Go figure.

Should all games look and feel alike? We don't think so, not even if they are Windows games. Each of the example games on the included CD-ROM has its own unique interface. Some have menus, and others have options screens. Their screens are designed to consistently maintain the aura that the game supports. Some of the games use the mouse, others use the keyboard, and still others use both. They do not necessarily use those things in exactly the same ways.

The charm of games such as Doom and Myst is that their user interfaces reflect the underlying theme of the games and are unique. Their menus and options screens sustain the overall theme of the particular game. Command structures are designed to facilitate effective play based on how the game works rather than on a rigid definition of a standard way to do things.

Imagine playing Myst if you had to pop down menus and use dialog boxes to rotate the tower in the Library and view constellations in the Planetarium.

Imagine Doom with radio buttons to set the level of play and command buttons to fire a weapon.

It's a game, folks. It's supposed to be fun. It's for after hours. Leave the stuffy and constraining standards to those who wear ties and socks and who write and use commercial applications with databases, reports, and scheduled processing cycles. That description may fit you during your day gig, but when you are off the clock, you can forget the standards and have some fun.

---

[1]In a famous litigation, Lotus sued Borland because Quattro Pro's DOS user interface resembled that of Lotus 1-2-3 for DOS. It has been reported that during that period, Philippe Kahn, then Borland's CEO, greeted Mitch Kapur, CEO of Lotus, in a restaurant by saying, "Good morning, Mitch. How do you look and feel today?"

BUILDING GAME COMPONENTS

This chapter is about building game components. These components are separate from the game program; you can prepare and test them in isolation and add them to the game later. They fall into two categories: graphics and sound. The discussion starts with the theoretical and moves to the practical. We discuss the component's properties, and then we cover the methods with which each component can be created and manipulated. You will learn about the following subjects in this chapter:

- Graphics issues and techniques
- Bitmap manipulation
- Creating sprites for animation
- Sound and music

Graphics

An old cliché says that a picture is worth a thousand words. True enough, and unless you are writing a text-mode adventure game, your game will involve pictures. You need to understand the strengths and limitations of the PC's ability to display pictures from a technical as well as an artistic viewpoint.

Graphics for your game can come from many sources. You can even use a photograph, print, or painting that you scan into a **.BMP** file with a flatbed color scanner. Keep in mind, though, that paintings and photographs are artistic creations and are subject to the laws protecting intellectual property. If you are going to use the work of others, be sure that you have the right to do so.

Be careful, also, about what you yourself photograph. You might hold the copyright to pictures that you take, but if the picture includes people, make sure that you have their permission to use their images in your published work. Remember that people not in the public view have certain rights with respect to privacy, and you must observe these rights or bear the consequences. The same caution should be shown with pictures of the property of others, particularly if business icons or logos are involved. If you are going to use these things in your game, make sure that a lawyer has blessed the practice. Neither of the authors of this book is a lawyer, and the advice we give here should not be interpreted as authoritative legal opinion. When in doubt, get professional legal advice.

Bear in mind that you are building a game. It's supposed to look like a game. It's not necessarily supposed to look like a movie, although some contemporary interactive multimedia games are getting close to that kind of realism.

Choose an artistic genre in which to display scenery. Be consistent in that choice. A cartoon-like character wandering around a photo-realistic moonscape looks more like a cheap TV commercial than it does a game. Likewise, a shiny, ray-traced robot trekking through a Grandma Moses–like scene is unconvincing. We can believe in cartoon characters in cartoon worlds, and we can believe in photo-realistic characters in a photo-realistic world, but it is difficult to effectively mix the two.

Also be consistent in the appearance of different scenes in the same game. If you jump about from one style to another just because you happen to have the pictures and it is convenient to use them, your players will be, if not turned off, then at least confused about the story you are trying to depict.

Some games, such as flight simulators and 3-D maze games, render their scenery in real time at runtime. They have to, because the scene being viewed is a function of where the player has positioned the viewport, and the game permits a view from virtually anywhere in the three-dimensional universe. It would be impossible to compute every possible position and viewing angle and then render in advance every scene as viewed from every position.

Flight simulators typically use static graphics with animated inserts to represent the instrument panel. Then they render the outside scenery in real time by computing the view of each frame from a 3-D model of the scenery and features. They employ all the computer graphics tricks to provide solid geometric shapes with surface generation and hidden line removal. The technique is effective and impressive, but it limits the amount of texture and shading that the scenery can have. The incidence of buildings is sparse because the program can compute only so many features during the brief time it has to render each frame.

Three-dimensional maze games use techniques called *ray casting* and *texture mapping* to compute every frame of an indoor scene. They map the frames of animated characters over this scenery by choosing from a fixed number of views and sizing the view in real time to represent the distance of the character from the player's view. The result is a dazzling display of somewhat fuzzy scenes that suggest, rather than accurately depict, the walls and doors of the maze as they slide by. Players do not mind, because the action is so fast that the passing scenery would be a blur anyway. And, if you hold still long enough to regard the scenery, something ugly will kill you.

Video Modes and Video RAM

So how does a picture come to appear on a computer screen? A computer program displays pictures on the screen by writing data values into video memory. The video controller translates these data values into pixels that light up dots of phosphor on the face of the cathode ray tube. This translation is a function of the video memory contents, the current video mode, and the video palette.

The standard PC video configuration is the Video Graphics Array (VGA). Most computers today have super VGA cards, which have more memory and can display higher-resolution modes. By default, Windows uses a 640 by 480 standard VGA mode with 16 colors. This mode has 640 columns of pixels and 480 rows. Each pixel is capable of displaying one of 16 colors at any given time.

Each pixel is mapped to RAM on the video card. The amount of memory it takes to represent each pixel depends on the number of colors the mode is capable of displaying. Four bits are needed to store a 16-color pixel, and 8 bits for a 256-color pixel. There are 32-bit color modes, which use four bytes to represent each pixel and can display 4,294,967,296 colors simultaneously. The more colors a mode has, the more memory is required. Also, as the resolution of the mode increases, so does the number of pixels, so again more RAM is needed. Most games, including the demos in this book, operate with 256 colors.

Bitmapped Graphics Files

A bitmapped graphics file records the pixel values for a picture in a raster graphics representation. For a 256-color bitmap, each pixel is represented by an eight-bit byte, and the value, from 0 to 255, represents the pixel's color taken from the picture's palette. The file has header information that identifies the picture's resolution, number of colors, color palette, and so on.

Table 3.1 lists the most common bitmapped graphics file formats.

Table 3.1 Bitmapped Graphics File Formats

BMP	Microsoft Windows Bitmap Format
GIF	CompuServe Graphics Interchange Format
PCX	ZSoft PC Paintbrush Format
TGA	AT&T Targa Format
TIFF	Aldus Tagged Image File Format

Most of the time we will be dealing with **.BMP** files, because the framework utilities use **.BMPs** exclusively. There are, however, some impressive and useful tools and utilities on the CD-ROM that use other formats. This difference causes no trouble; we've included tools that can convert between these bitmap formats. Later in this chapter, you'll learn how to convert bitmaps.

For a complete discussion of bitmapped graphics file formats, see *Bitmapped Graphics Programming in C++*, listed in the Bibliography.

The Palette

Each 256-color bitmap file consists of two parts: the image and a *palette* of colors. The image is represented by an array of bytes. Each eight-bit value in this array is an index into the palette. The palette contains 256 or fewer entries, and each entry represents a different color.

Image construction utility programs, such as paint programs and ray-tracers, determine the palette for the image being constructed. You can easily wind up with bitmaps that have different and incompatible palettes, and, because the VGA card can work with only one palette at a time, some of the bitmaps will appear with random colors. If you superimpose a sprite on a background and the palettes of the sprite and the background are incompatible, the sprite's colors will be wrong. If you use a system-generated mouse cursor and the cursor's palette conflicts with the current image, the cursor's color will not be what you expect. It is even possible for frames of a video clip to have different palettes.

Ray-tracers, which are discussed in more detail in later in this chapter, cause the biggest problem. They generate images from subtle combinations of colors to achieve their photo-realistic effects of lighting, shading, reflection, refraction, and diffusion. Two renderings of the same 3-D model with a slight change of camera angles will surely result in two different palettes. This is not a problem if you are simply changing from one image to the next, because each bitmap can use its own palette information. But if you are using a common sprite or cursor in the two scenes, the palettes of these images will conflict with at least one of the palettes of the scenery.

With all these palette problems to worry about, you might wonder how you can coordinate everything. The framework utilities include utility programs that process sets of images and *normalize* all the palettes so that the pictures display the way you want them to. You will learn more about palette correction later in this chapter.

Scenery

Scenery is the background of a scene in a game. You create scenery by building a bitmapped graphics file. There are three strategies: You can scan in a scene from an existing picture, manually design the scenery by using a paint program, or render the scenery by ray-tracing a 3-D model of the scene. We discuss each method next. Regardless of which method you use, the scenery will have to be converted to the **.BMP** format to be used by the frameworks. Also, a background need not be a single bitmap that covers the screen. It might be a group of tiles that are used to assemble a background. This technique is typical in games with scrolling backgrounds.

Scanning

We've never seen a game in which the background scenery was scanned in from a photograph or a print of a painting, but there is no reason you could not do it. Imagine a game that uses photos of Mount Rushmore, the Grand Canyon, or the Eiffel Tower as its background.

> Color flatbed scanners are expensive (about $1000 at this time). They are also as difficult to install properly as any other nonstandard PC extension (IRQs, DMA, ports, and so on). But when you need one, there is no substitute. If you will be scanning rarely, you might be able to find a local business that offers the service. Be aware, though, that once you scan your first color photo, you will be hooked. Greeting cards and invitations take on a new dimension when they include color snaps of the kids. Of course, then you need a color printer...

As an alternative to scanning, you can use the services of companies that develop your film as diskette images to display on your computer. The local photo shop should be able to refer you to the right companies. If you can get a picture to display in a Windows application, for example, you can use the Clipboard to import it into Windows Paint or another image program to convert it to 256-color **.BMP** format.

Paint Programs

There are many different types of paint programs, ranging from simple freeware utilities to expensive commercial packages. Windows 95 comes with a good one. Which one you use depends on what you have access to and what your personal preferences are. Most paint programs have features that can be useful for drawing graphics for your games. Some have fancy shading abilities. Some can distort, stretch, blur, and even sharpen images.

It doesn't matter which paint program you use. Virtually any format that the program writes is convertible to the **.BMP** format and, therefore, can be used for your game.

3-D Modeling

Another option for creating scenery is to use a *modeler* and a *renderer*. The scenes don't always look like actual photographs (although they could), but they have realistic features based on perspective, textures, shadows, reflections, refraction, diffusion, and so on.

First you build a 3-D model of the scene, and then you render ray-traced images of the scene taken from various views. We'll discuss the first step, creating the model, first.

A 3-D model is a computer representation of planes and objects organized to resemble something real. You build the model using a 3-D modeling tool that produces files in the source code format of a ray tracing tool. The Appendix describes several modeling and ray tracing tools that you can use for these purposes. They are included on the CD-ROM that accompanies this book. Figure 3.1 shows a 3-D model of a Jeep that we built for the town game.

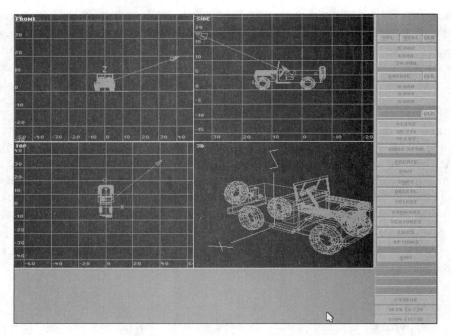

Figure 3.1 3-D model of a Jeep

The Jeep model is complex, but it is only one element in a scene. The Town example game on the CD-ROM has scenery that includes several buildings, and each building is a separate model created from common component models. For example, we built one house frame, one door, one window, one dormer, and so on, and then built several house models from these components. Figure 3.2 shows one of the house models.

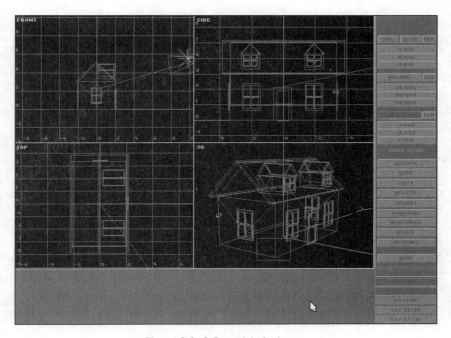

Figure 3.2 3-D model of a house

To complete the scene, we built a town model with the three houses, a church, two streets, some trees, and two copies of the Jeep. Figure 3.3 shows the town model.

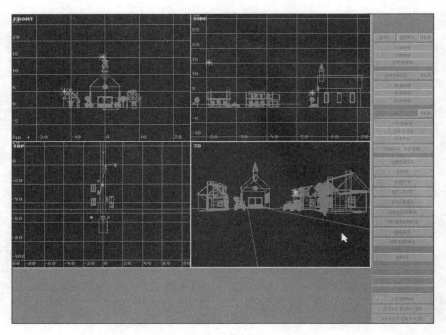

Figure 3.3 3-D model of a town

Ray-Tracing

The second step in producing scenery from a 3-D model is to render the various scenes with a ray-tracer which reads files of ASCII source code and translates the statements in the source code into an image.

Ray tracer source code statements specify shapes, textures, planes, lighting, camera position, and so on, and a ray tracer uses these data to compute every pixel of the rendered image.

The ray tracing source code includes the camera positions and lighting that you established with the modeler; these values define only one scene. Even though the game will have several scenes, only one source code file is needed. Each scene's source code file differs only with respect to its camera position. Everything else is the same.

First, decide how many background scenes the game will use from the model you're working with. The Town game, for example, uses 11 different scenes built from the same model. To build these scenes, we used a 3-D modeler to determine the ideal camera locations, directions, and apertures for each scene. This procedure involved moving the camera until the scene looked right in the isometric view. Then we wrote down the camera position for each scene. Next, we used a text editor to create alternative camera positions in the source code file, but we commented out all the settings except one. Listing 3.1 shows part of the *camera* statement in the **TOWN.POV** file. This example assumes that only three scenes are used instead of the actual 11, but it illustrates the point.

Listing 3.1 TOWN.POV, Camera Statement

```
camera {  //  Camera Camera01
    location  < 0.000, -10.000, 1.600>  // TOWN01
//  location  < 0.000, -24.500, 1.600>  // TOWN02
//  location  < 0.000, -24.500, 1.600>  // TOWN03
    direction <0.0,     0.0,  1.0>       // All scenes use these values
    sky       <0.0,     0.0,  1.0>       // "    "    "    "    "
    up        <0.0,     0.0,  1.0>       // "    "    "    "    "
    right     <1.3333,  0.0,  0.0>       // "    "    "    "    "
    look_at   <  0.000, -55.000, 1.600>  // TOWN01
//  look_at   <  0.000, -55.000, 1.600>  // TOWN02
//  look_at   <-10.000, -24.500, 1.600>  // TOWN03
}
```

The *camera* statement declares the camera parameters for the scene. The *location* statement specifies coordinates in the model where the camera is positioned. The *look_at* statement specifies the point in the model where the camera is focused. These are the statements you will change for each rendering. In this example, all the statements except TOWN01 are commented out. After TOWN01 was rendered, we commented out its statements, uncommented the statements for TOWN02, and rendered the scene for TOWN02. We repeated this procedure until all 11 scenes for the Town game were rendered into **.TGA** bitmapped graphics files.

Ray tracing source code looks a lot like C++ source code, so programmers are comfortable with it. Some programmers and modelers work directly with the source code rather than use a modeler. Most people, however, prefer to work in a visual medium rather than use the abstract expression of source code.

An advantage of this approach is that you do not need to be concerned with perspective when you design scenery the way you would if you hand-painted every scene. If you build a set that has objects whose relative sizes are consistent with one another, then the ray-tracer will properly render the scene with correct perspective. All you have to do is position the camera.

Converting Graphics File Formats with Alchemy

Ray tracing output is often in the **.TGA** (Targa) bitmapped graphics format. To use the pictures as scenery with one of the frameworks, you must convert them to **.BMP** format. For that purpose we use shareware graphics conversion programs.

Figure 3.4 shows **TOWN01.BMP** as the ray tracer rendered the scene and as the conversion utility converted the **.TGA** file into the **.BMP** format.

Figure 3.4 TOWN01.BMP, a rendered scene

Before the **.BMP** files are used in the Town demo, they are normalized so that they all use the same palette. This step isn't absolutely necessary, because only one image is displayed at a time, but it reduces the "flash" that can occur when the video palette is changed. The flash occurs either because the new palette is installed before the new image is displayed or because the new image is displayed before its palette has been installed. Another solution is to clear the display to a color that both palettes have in common. Usually, color zero is black, so the display can be filled with zeros before a new palette is installed. This technique causes a little flicker between scenes but allows each scene to use its own palette.

Sprites

Sprites are the characters in your game. As with scenery, you build sprites in one of three ways depending on the look you want. You can use a paint program to build sprites, you can build a 3-D model and render sprite images, or you can use photographs of actual models. Like scenery, sprites must be converted to **.BMP** files before they can be used by the frameworks.

Painting Sprites

Figure 3.5 is the skating figure from the Skater game

Figure 3.5 A skating sprite

Sprites such as the skater have an arcade, cartoon look. In the enlarged figure, you can see all the jags and increments. With more work, we could have made this sprite look better. By using different color tones, you can suggest form, shading, and texture. This sprite is small, though, and its movement is fast. Much of the detailed work would be lost in the motion.

3-D Modeled Sprites

When the sprite in Figure 3.5 is displayed in its actual size and moving on the screen, the effect is more realistic, although not as realistic as ray-traced sprites (see Figure 3.6).

Figure 3.6 Ray-traced sprites

The sprites in Figure 3.6 were built from 3-D models and rendered with a ray tracer. The only difference between the sprite in Figure 3.5 and those in Figure 3.6 is the method of creation.

Using Real Models

For this approach, you need more equipment: a good camera with lenses and filters, a tripod, and good color-corrected lighting. You also need a studio environment where you can photograph the model in various poses against a solid background with minimal ambient light interference.

You make a snapshot of every pose of the sprite in its animated role. (See the "Animation" section.) Then, as with photographed scenery, you translate those photographs into **.BMP** files using a scanner or by using a diskette medium developing service.

What can you use for models? Toys are good. You may use anything that isn't copyrighted. This could be a problem. A game featuring Ken and Barbie is bound to get the attention of a lawyer or two at the Mattel Corporation. Almost every toy is protected by copyright law, and yet toys provide the best source for game models.

You might be able to alter a toy in such a way that it no longer resembles the original. For example, costumes and makeup could help you turn GI Joe into a drag Dracula. For vehicle sprites, you could build and drastically customize plastic models that you buy at the hobby shop, perhaps using components from several models to create a hybrid. There should be no problem using models of military aircraft and commercial automobiles, but models of the *Starship Enterprise* or Han Solo's space junker are off limits— unless you get written permission from the copyright holders, of course (fat chance).

The best approach is to create something original. If you can sculpt or sew creatively, you can make models of anything you like. A pleasant afternoon spent watching *The Nightmare before Christmas* on your VCR will give you ideas of what can be done with original models.

Whatever you use for a model, it must be able to maintain a rigid pose long enough for you to photograph it. To support animated sequences, it should permit small changes in its appendages. You might have to suspend it from a wire or mount it on a black shaft to get the pose you want. Figure 3.7 is a photographed sprite.

Figure 3.7 A photographed sprite

Animation

Animation is where the action is. To add action to a game, you make a sprite move around the screen and do interesting things. Whether the sprite is a spaceship or a cowboy, a street fighter or an ice skater, the underlying principle is the same: Animation is the product of showing a sequence of frames, with each frame representing the next increment of motion in the sequence. The motion is an illusion. Nothing really moves. Every picture that we see is a still frame. But when the frames are shown in rapid succession, our brains are tricked into thinking that we are seeing motion.

Motion: One Frame at a Time

Figure 3.8 shows five successive frames that, when shown in rapid succession, make the sheriff in the Shootout game seem to be walking. The sequence of five frames repeats until the game program wants the sheriff to do something other than walk to the right, at which point the program changes to a different sequence of frames. Each repetition of the five frames reverses the order in which the frames are shown so that the complete walk sequence is an eight-frame sequence as follows: 1-2-3-4-5-4-3-2. Then the sequence repeats itself.

Figure 3.8 The sheriff's animated frames

Prove it to yourself. Make several copies of Figure 3.8 on a copier. Cut the images into uniform rectangles, stack them up in the sequence we just described, and staple them together at one of the edges. Now you have one of those flip comic books from the 1950s. Flip through the pages and watch the sheriff take a walk.

We drew the five pictures of the sheriff using a paint program. We started by drawing the first picture. Then, to build the second frame, we copied the first and modified it so that the swinging left arm was closer to the body and the two legs came closer together. In the third frame, we made the arm and legs straight down. The legs of frames four and five are duplicates of those in frames two and one, except that we changed the line that defines which leg is closer to the front of the scene.

There are several other sequences in the game. One sequence has the sheriff walking in the opposite direction. To build that sequence, we just reversed each frame. Because the sheriff carries only one gun, we erased the gun and holster from each of the frames in the right-walking sequence, and we put a badge on the left side of his chest.

Other sequences depict the sheriff drawing and shooting in four directions, reloading his gun, and getting shot from both directions.

Each sprite has its own frames and its own update frequency. The sheriff gets updated every two clock ticks, or approximately nine times per second, so it takes about one second for the sheriff to start out with his left foot forward and take two steps ending with his left foot forward.

Plotting the Two-Dimensional Coordinates

The screen is a two-dimensional plane with an X coordinate and a Y coordinate. The coordinate ranges are the same as the resolution of the video mode. The standard 640x480 VGA mode has X coordinates of 0 to 639 horizontally and Y coordinates of 0 to 479 vertically.

As a game program displays the frames of an animated sprite, the program must also provide the screen coordinates where the frame is to be displayed. Sprite frame positions on the screen are assigned according to where the upper left corner of the sprite image is positioned, *even though that point might be transparent*. (See "The Transparent Regions of a Sprite" later in this chapter.) Therefore, if the sprite moves around the screen, the game program computes the path and provides the correct coordinates for the upper-left corner of each frame.

A game may compute frames and frame positions for many sprites for each full-screen display, so the action on the screen can be complex and the demands on the CPU can be considerable.

Smooth Animation

The sheriff in Figure 3.8 walks along the street in the Shootout demo. The scenery remains static and the sheriff walks. Animating a sprite consists of telling the video system where in the two-dimensional coordinate system to paint each frame. The sheriff moves from left to right during this sequence. To make the walk believable, we plot each position in the first five frames of the eight-frame sequence so that the toe of the sheriff's left boot is always in the same x/y coordinate on the screen. For frames six, seven, and eight and frame one of the next sequence, the toe of the right boot is held in the same x/y coordinate. This procedure gives the sheriff's walk a smooth, natural appearance.

Z-Order

When a game has more than one sprite and the sprites' paths cross, the game must display the intersecting sprites so that the one closer to the player passes in front of the one closer to the background. This relationship between sprite positions is called their *Z-order*, because it reflects each sprite's location in the Z axis of a pseudo three-dimensional coordinate system. However, instead of being a scalar as in a true three-dimensional graphical system, the Z axis is represented by the positional relationship of the game's components. The background is at the lowest (most distant from the player) position in the Z-order, and the sprites are at various Z-order positions toward the front.

Figure 3.9 is a screen shot of the Skater game, which uses Z-ordering to control sprite placement.

Figure 3.9 Z-order

The skater in Figure 3.9 skates a figure eight around the two stationary sprites. At first the skater is foremost in the Z-order because he is in front of the other two sprites. When he makes his first turn to go between the other two, his Z-order changes to put him in front of the rearward sprite and behind the forward sprite. When he goes behind the rearward sprite, his Z-order changes to put him behind both of the other sprites. The skater demo is written with Theatrix. The source code provides a good example of how to change the Z-order of sprites during the execution of a game.

Perspective

The Raycast framework takes care of perspective for you. As a sprite approaches, it gets bigger, and as it retreats, it gets smaller. Because Theatrix and GDKapp are not true 3-D graphical systems, you might have to manage certain aspects of the 3-D effect yourself. For example, as the skater moves around the figure eight in Figure 3.9, the program computes the coordinates where the skater displays. To suggest a third dimension, the game moves the skater up the Y axis when the skater is skating away from the player and down the Y axis when the skater is skating toward the player.

As objects get farther into the distance they appear to get smaller. That illusion is due to *perspective*. Observe that the rearmost stationary sprite is smaller than the forward one, which is smaller than the skater. When the skater is between the two sprites, then, he should be bigger than the one at the rear but smaller than the one at the front.

Raycast uses algorithms to shrink and expand graphical images in real time. The other two frameworks don't support perspective so elaborately. Proper perspective in sprite-based systems is a matter of painting or rendering enough frames to display the sprite at whatever Z-order locations the game allows it to occupy. If you are rendering or photographing sprites, you must position the real or virtual camera far enough away to capture each frame. If you are painting the sprites with a paint program, you should paint the first set of frames in their largest configuration. Then, using the Scale command, you can make smaller and smaller copies of the frames for the more distant Z-order images. Scaling pictures down sometimes loses critical pixels from the details, so you should keep an eye on the results and touch them up when necessary. Figure 3.10 shows the skater at his farthest location away from the player.

Figure 3.10 Sprite perspective

The Transparent Regions of a Sprite

Sprite images are 256-color rectangular **.BMP** files of a size appropriate to the sprite's role and position on the screen. No matter which technique you use to build sprites, you must deal with the issue of *transparency* the same way. Every sprite image has regions that must be transparent to let the background show through. For example, all the space around the outer edges of the sprite and to the borders of its image rectangle must be transparent. If the sprite has holes, you have to let the background show through them, too.

Transparent regions are marked by color zero—that is, each pixel in a transparent region must have a palette offset value equal to zero. It does not matter which actual color is assigned to color zero in the palette—color zero is the transparent color when the framework displays the sprite. Color zero is usually solid black.

Black backgrounds are easy to make when you use a paint program or POV-Ray to build sprite images. With paint programs, you start with a white background, because that way it's easier to see what you're painting. When you are finished, you use the Fill tool to replace the white background with black. You can have black elements in the sprite's image by assigning black to a nonzero palette offset.

When rendering sprites, don't provide any background objects such as the sky, walls, and floors. The background will be rendered all black.

Creating transparent regions from photographed and scanned sprites is more difficult but still possible. Even though you use a solid black background in the photo session, chances are that some stray ambient light source will create subtle textures that are not completely black. To do some touchup, load the file into a paint program and use the Eraser tool to change rough areas to all black. Then zoom in and touch up the remaining pixels.

Sometimes there are points of solid black in the image that you do not want to be transparent. They show up as dots of background bleeding through when you run the game. This effect can happen with rendered and photographed sprites. You have better control over colors when you manually paint the sprite, but this bleed-through can still happen if you make a mistake. To correct for these unintended holes, load the offending frame into a paint program and manually change the holes from color zero to another color in the palette that is black.

Animation Buffers

The frameworks all use off-screen buffers to prepare elements of the next scene. These buffers are then copied to video RAM. Figure 3.11 illustrates the use of buffers during a screen update.

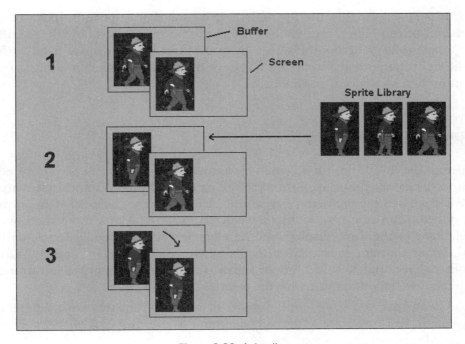

Figure 3.11 Animation

The figure shows three states of animation. Each state involves what is actually on the screen (the foremost image) and what is in the off-screen buffer (the image behind the screen image). In the first frame, the buffer and the screen have identical images. This is the case most of the time. In step 2, a new image is loaded into the off-screen buffer. This step may involve copying multiple sprites to the buffer. The order in which they are copied depends on each sprite's Z-order. In our example, we are using only one sprite. Once the buffer is prepared, its contents are copied into video RAM and become visible (step 3). It is important that this step occur quickly. Slow video updates result in an effect known as *tearing*. Windows performs this step for you in both Win32 and the Games SDK, so there is little that can be done if this step is too slow. Once the full screen has been updated, the off-screen buffer can be prepared for the next scene.

It isn't indicated in the figure, but each time that a sprite is drawn into the off-screen buffer, it can be at different locations. This is how the sheriff is made to walk across the screen. A sprite's freedom to display itself with different frames and at different places in the buffer means that almost any animation sequence is possible.

Palette Correction

Before the **.BMP** files for a game's background and sprites can be integrated into the game, you must normalize the palettes of each graphical element. We discussed the problem early in this chapter. Every graphical element in a video game can have a different palette. When you mix more than one element in the same display and the elements use different palettes, only the ones that are consistent with the active palette display properly. The others have strange colors. In our games, flesh tones seem prone to turning green if we forget to normalize the palettes.

Given that you have some number of graphical entities with different palettes, you first have to derive a common palette from all of them. This procedure involves three steps.

First, extract palette files from all the graphical elements. Palette files contain the palette information taken from a **.BMP** file.

Second, use all these extracted palette files to compute a common palette file. This procedure finds all the colors in all the palettes and tries to squeeze them into one. For example, if seven **.BMP** files have the color green in seven different color slots in their respective palettes, the common palette chooses one slot for green. The object is to get each of the colors in use in all the palette files assigned to only one slot. The hope is that, altogether, the images don't use more than 256 different colors. When they do, the utility program finds the closest possible match for the excess colors.

Finally, use the new palette file to modify all the original **.BMP** files. This modification changes the palette index value for each of the **.BMP** file's pixels so that the index value points to the correct color in the new palette.

When this procedure is complete, all the **.BMP** files in your game operate with the same palette. The utilities for normalizing palettes are discussed in Chapter 7.

Sound

Sound effects dramatically enhance a game's operation. The Shootout example on the accompanying CD-ROM illustrates this principle. The game works as well without the sound effects, but it is much more fun when you can hear them. Doors open and close, guns fire shots, bodies thump when they hit the ground, the sheriff's gun clicks instead of fires when it is empty, and the citizens applaud when you win the game.

What Is Sound?

Sound occurs when something disturbs the air. The movement of the air vibrates our eardrums, which send signals to our brains. If a tree falls in the forest and no one is there to hear it, the air still gets moved around whether or not anyone or anything is there with ears to interpret it.

Sound can be viewed as a *waveform*. Push the air one way and the waveform rises. Pull the air the other way and the waveform drops. Increase the frequency and the pitch rises. Increase the amplitude and the volume rises. Mix two different signals and you combine sounds.

Anything sensitive enough to move with the air vibrates in a pattern that resembles the waveform. If you turn it around and cause the air to vibrate in the same pattern by duplicating the waveform mechanically or electrically, you can reproduce the sound.

Recording Sound

Edison recorded and played back sound mechanically. He simulated an eardrum with a diaphragm at the base of an amplifying horn. At the center of the diaphragm he positioned a needle. Edison spoke the words of "Mary Had a Little Lamb" into the horn. His voice moved the air, which vibrated the horn, which vibrated the diaphragm, which vibrated the needle, which etched a groove pattern across a wax cylinder that Edison rotated with a crank as he spoke. Thus the waveform of Edison's voice was recorded. Then he tracked the needle back through the etched pattern's groove to vibrate the needle, which vibrated the diaphragm. The horn amplified the vibrations, and Edison's recorded poem was reproduced—played back.

You can demonstrate this principle for yourself in the kitchen. Get a tin can and a sewing needle. Remove the lid from one end of the can. Dump out the string beans. Punch a tiny hole in the other end and wedge the blunt end of the needle into the hole. Connect a piece of tableware to the can with tape to act as a tone arm. Now get out an old phonograph record that you don't particularly treasure, maybe something by Barry Manilow. Put the record on a salad spinner and get it turning. Lower the needle into the track and listen to the sound being amplified by the tin can. Throw away the Barry Manilow record. Eat the string beans.

Records and audio tapes are *analog* devices. They store their information as analog signals that represent, as accurately as possible, the waveform of the original sound. The recording equipment starts with air moving a microphone's sensitive diaphragm the same way that Edison did. But from that point the process is quite different. Instead of mechanically transferring the vibrations to an etched track, the electronics convert the vibrations into an analog, amplitude-modulated electrical signal and store the signal as charged particles of emulsion on magnetic tape. If a vinyl record is to be made (rare today because of the popularity of compact disks), the master pressing is made in fundamentally the same way that Edison made his first recording except that an electrical signal played back from the master tape vibrates the etching needle.

Digital Recording

The recordings just described are analog recordings. Computers reproduce sound as *digital* recordings. They store sound signals as binary strings. Except for synthesized sound, which uses algorithms to approximate sound waveforms, computer sound originates as real sound that is recorded digitally. If Edison had owned a PC with a Sound Blaster, he would have recorded "Mary Had a Little Lamb" onto a hard disk file as a digital bit stream.

Sampling

The digital bit stream that records sound in a computer is a *sample* of the original analog sound signal waveform. The computer samples the amplitude of the waveform at fixed intervals. The interval frequency is called the *sampling rate*. At each of these intervals, the computer stores a binary value that represents the amplitude (the height on the waveform) as a signed integer. The higher the sampling rate, the more accurately the digital bit stream represents the original audio sound.

Another variable in a bit stream sample is its *resolution*, which is the number of bits available for each sample. The more bits you use, the wider the dynamic range of the signal when it is played back. Eight to 16 bits are typical. Professional recording equipment uses 16 bits of resolution. Sixteen-bit sound cards are not unusual on PCs now, but eight-bit cards are far more common.

The combination of signal length, sampling rate, and resolution determines how much storage space is needed to record the signal. This value is an important concern. The game program needs to store the sound clips in a disk file to distribute with the game, and it needs to load them into RAM to play them back.

Most game sound effects play back well with a sampling rate of 5,000 to 11,000 and with eight bits of resolution. One thing is certain: You must play back a sound clip with the same sampling rate and resolution with which it was recorded. Otherwise the sound is garbled and its duration is wrong.

WAV Files

The frameworks use the standard Windows **.WAV** file format for sound effects. Windows 95 has built-in support for WAV playback, so the framework's task is simple. Once you have a WAV file, it is easy to play in your game. Getting an original WAV file for your game is the challenging part.

Recording Sound Effects

The best choice is to make your own noises and voices. You'll need a sound card that supports recording. For voices you need a decent microphone. Radio Shack has several that work well.

You can also go out into the wilderness and record the birds and bees and make **.WAV** files by patching your tape player into the line input jacks on your sound card.

Beyond that, all you need is your imagination. The Myst guys tell about how they made clock chimes by banging two wrenches together, adding echo effects, and changing the playback rate of the sound. They got water gurgling sound effects by flushing the company commode.

Music

Every game programming book that we have read either ignores the subject of music or addresses only the technical issues of how to play back a MIDI file. The authors defer the creation of their music to contributors to their book, make no effort to explain the process, and suggest that you do the same. Yet many programmers are musicians, too, and can understand the creative side of the musical aspects of game construction. We discuss some of that here, assuming that you have some understanding of musical theory or, at least, an appreciation of the implications of music in any kind of entertainment medium.

How important is music to a game? Many arcade games do not use music. The creators of Myst considered leaving music out of their production. Fortunately, they reconsidered and applied the additional effort to include background music in each scene. As you move from place to place in the five Myst islands, mood music dramatically enhances the visual effect at every change of scenery. The game would not be nearly as effective without background music.

Adding background music requires several steps. First, you identify where in the game the music occurs and what kind of music you want at each scene. Next, you compose or acquire the music. Then you translate the music into a format the computer can read and play back. Finally, you integrate the musical score into the game.

Setting the Mood

Background music sets a mood. Imagine the Lone Ranger without the *William Tell Overture*. Ta da dum. Ta da dum, ta da dum dum dum. The two go together. Rick's without Sam playing "As Time Goes By" wouldn't be Rick's. When, in *Psycho*, the corpse of Mrs. Bates spins around in the chair to face the audience, the effect would not be nearly as scary without the pulsating, piercing, screaming music.

As in the movies, each scene in a game has a theme, and music can dramatically reinforce that theme. If the player is deep in the bowels of a dark cave, the cave music could have an ominous, dank feeling. Eerie, scary music could accompany a trip through a haunted house. A child's game might use a happy tune that the child recognizes.

We learn through experience to associate different kinds of music with certain moods, and thus our mood changes when we hear the music. A funeral dirge elicits sadness. The Charleston is a happy dance. The blues make us feel sorry for ourselves. Old-time rock and roll is uplifting. Heavy metal is mind-numbing. A march evokes rousing feelings of patriotism. Some music is scary. Some music is romantic.

Some music is foreboding. Music prepares the player for coming events by foreshadowing a mood. You look at a closed door. Without music, the door is nothing more than that—a door. Add a low, sustained diminished chord played on an organ, and you know that something bad will happen if you open that door. The mood created by the music compels you to either run away or open the door and accept the worst.

Watch contemporary TV commercials to see how music sets a mood. Sad music plays quietly. A woman speaks. "I didn't realize that Sam's funeral would set us back six thousand dollars." The message: Don't be sad. Buy our life insurance. Whitney Houston sings, "Your true voice," bending her notes around in a way to suggest a caring, soulful mother. The message: We care for you deeply. Come back to our long distance service.

Try not to use music inappropriately. An urban scene of cars, noise, and street people does not fit with excerpts from the *Grand Canyon Suite*. Ragtime would be out of place in a funeral parlor. The *1812 Overture* would not work with a scene of fluffy clouds, flowers, songbirds, and butterflies. A polka would not particularly enhance a scene set in the House of Parliament.

MIDI

Even though music is sustained sound, game programs do not usually use **.WAV** sound files for music clips. The storage requirements would be too restrictive. Music clips are usually longer than sound effects, and they require a higher sampling rate to prevent the distortion that people don't notice with voice and sound effects. Fortunately, you have an alternative, something called the musical instrument digital interface (MIDI).

Several years ago, the electronic music industry did something that the computer industry is rarely able to do: It established standard protocols and formats for data streams of packets that represent musical sounds. All the industry members uniformly adopted and implemented the MIDI standard in their products. The effort was collaborative, cooperative, and friendly, and was undertaken without rivalries or market pressures. The computer industry could learn a lot from the music industry.

The MIDI protocol was designed to allow various electronic synthesizers to be connected in a standard way. A *synthesizer* is a device that produces musical sounds electronically. Electric pianos, organs, drum machines, and so on are synthesizers. The synthesizer produces the sound of each note electronically either with an algorithmic synthesis of the desired instrument sound or by playing the note from a library of samples.

A sample is a recording of one note made with a musical instrument. The note is digitized and stored in a sample library. Sample libraries usually have several versions of each note for each instrument, reflecting various attacks, dynamics, and so on.

The MIDI protocol specifies digital packets that tell synthesizers which notes to play, how long to sustain them, and other variables such as the level of attack to apply when the note is first sounded, the pressure to apply while the note sustains, and so on.

A stream of MIDI packets tells one or more synthesizers how to play a song. A MIDI stream is the electronic equivalent of a player piano roll but with much more potential.

You can create MIDI packet streams in real time by playing music on a synthesizer (typically a keyboard). The synthesizer translates the notes you play into MIDI packets and transmits a stream of packets through the synthesizer's MIDI output port.

Synthesizers and sequencers (discussed soon) read MIDI streams into their MIDI input ports and play the notes from the stream. MIDI synthesizers can be connected in series so that you have several synthesizers interpreting and playing from the same stream.

Each MIDI note packet specifies one of 16 channels. Each of the synthesizers in the series typically processes the packets addressed to only one of the channels.

A *sequencer* is a device that can read files of MIDI data and transmit the packets to the instruments. A sequencer can also record MIDI files by reading the notes being played on a MIDI synthesizer. You can record the notes from each synthesizer independently, adding each new channel to the channels already laid down. In this way one person can independently record all the instruments of an entire orchestral arrangement. Each of the 16 channels in a sequencer is assigned a unique instrument voice selected from a standard table of 128 instruments. The sound assigned to an instrument is called its *patch*.

With a sequencer you can make corrections and modifications to the notes in a MIDI file. This permits a sequencer programmer to touch up a performance after it has been originally laid down. You can also change the patches that have been assigned to selected instruments and change the instrument voices assigned to selected channels.

Contemporary PC sound cards have all the hardware necessary to support sequencing. They have MIDI input and output ports, and they can produce the sounds of all 128 of the standard patches. This means that you need only a PC, a good sound card, speakers, a MIDI keyboard, and a sequencer program to record and play back MIDI files. Furthermore, all that the game player needs is a PC with a sound card and speakers to play your game and hear the background music.

Composing Music

Several of the example games on the included CD-ROM have original songs composed for this project or adapted from other original compositions from the author's portfolio. Three of them were composed extemporaneously at the keyboard by using a sequencer program to capture the MIDI data. You can listen to them in the Town demonstration game on the CD-ROM.

Two of the extemporaneous songs have no structure and are meant to imply a mood. When you get close to the church door in the game, you hear what sounds like a funeral processional played on a church organ. This song consists of random chords played in slow succession with an occasional but mostly unintentional harmonic resolution. We dubbed another track with a constantly repeated chime to suggest the church bell ringing mournfully in the background.

The second formless song plays at the front of the brick house. It uses a Hammond organ voice and is meant to suggest something ominous. The song consists mainly of a progression of minor and diminished chords, although anyone could get the same effect with a random pattern of chords of three and four unrelated notes each.

The third extemporaneous song is a ragtime improvisation on a common eight-bar chord progression (A7-D7-G7-C) repeated twice. This song plays during the video clip sequence of the Town game and is the background music for the street scene in the Shootout game. One of the benefits of MIDI is that musicians can produce music beyond their own technical abilities. By using a sequencer program, you can record the stride style of the ragtime piece in two passes at a slower tempo. One pass provides the octave-chord pattern of the left hand, which you can play with two hands in the first pass. Then you can overdub the right hand patterns in the second pass. This technique is how intricate player piano rolls of long ago were often made.

Even if you do not play the piano, you can transcribe music manually into a sequencer program by reading the score and using the manual note entry features of the program. Most of the songs that you download from on-line services were built that way. The result is usually a mechanical effect with no emotion or human interpretation built into the performance.

Acquiring Music

Not every programmer possesses the musical ear or skills to build an effective musical score for a game program. Likewise, not every skilled musician knows how to get the best effect from a MIDI system. Sometimes you have to look elsewhere for what you need. Locating someone who can get the job done might not be as difficult as you think.

To start with, you can probably find professional MIDI composers and scorers in your home town. Look in the Yellow Pages for recording studios and audio technicians. Call around. You will find someone who has the skill and equipment to build effective MIDI files. Be prepared to pay dearly for this service, particularly if you want original compositions.

Amateur musicians are plentiful, too, and you might be able to find someone who is willing to help you in exchange for a royalty arrangement or perhaps even for the exposure of an acknowledgment in your credits.

Be careful about downloading and using MIDI files from on-line services and the Internet. There are plenty of such files, but the issues about who owns the intellectual rights to the compositions, the arrangements, and the files themselves are rarely clear. The CompuServe Information Service recently removed many of the MIDI files from its libraries and suspended accepting any more uploads of MIDI files because of complaints that distribution of the files might violate copyright law.

Public domain songs are usually a safe way to go if you cannot compose original music yourself or if you cannot afford the services of a composer. Most classical compositions, hymns, and old traditional folk songs are in the public domain.

Use extreme caution with respect to public domain material. Make sure that you know the status of anything you use. You wouldn't want to wind up in court. Make no assumptions about anything, and do your research. Not everything that is old is necessarily in the public domain. For example, in the early 1950s the copyright was about to expire on Debussy's "Claire de Lune." To retain the copyright for an additional period, the beneficiaries of Debussy's estate had lyrics added to the melody. The result was an abomination called "Moonlight Love." The popular crooner Perry Como, in an uncharacteristic lapse of taste, recorded the song.

Once again, we are not lawyers. Ask one if you are not sure.

Recording Music

If you know how to use a MIDI keyboard, you can use a sequencer program to enter musical tracks into your computer and create a MIDI file. Once everything is connected and the program is running, you can begin to construct your song one channel at a time. You choose a channel and assign an instrument to the channel from the standard instrument table. By convention, channel 10 is assigned to the drum sounds, and specific drum sounds—cymbals, snares, bass drums, wood blocks, and so on—are assigned to the notes of the scale.

Some sequencer programs allow you to select from a collection of musical styles. The sequencer adds drum machine patterns to the song in keeping with the style—bossa nova, swing, rock, and so on—that you have chosen.

While you record a new channel, the sequencer plays back the existing channels so that you can stay synchronized with the song.

Most sequencers allow you to *quantize* a channel after you have entered the notes. It is impossible for human beings to accurately play precise sixteenth, eighth, quarter, half, and whole notes, no matter how well they read music. The sequencer captures exactly what you play, and the musical score, if you were to print it, would be unreadable due to the many thirty-second and sixty-fourth notes that represented what you really played. The quantizer normalizes those notes to the resolution that you specify.

A sequencer can *transpose* a song, which changes the key signature in which the song is played. Perhaps you can play only in the keys of C, F, and G—not uncommon among amateur pianists—but the song sounds better or better conveys the mood in a different key. You can transpose the song into any key at all after you have it programmed.

Playing Back Music

Once you have your MIDI file (**.MID**), the hard work is behind you. In all three frameworks, playing it is as simple as specifying the file name. See the frameworks' specific chapters for the details.

WINDOWS 95 AS A GAMES PLATFORM

Windows 3.x enjoyed tremendous success. Many different kinds of applications were ported to Windows, taking advantage of features such as the graphical interface and robust device support. Few games, however, were successfully ported to Windows. Although Windows had attractive features, game developers stayed with DOS. Part of the problem was that Windows was slow and too restrictive. Windows 95 has some of the same drawbacks as Windows 3.0, but because of some new features and APIs, Windows 95 is a strong games platform. In this chapter, we'll look at Windows 95 from the perspective of game development. We'll discuss the following topics:

- Graphics
- 32-bit computing
- Digital sound and music
- Game timing
- The event-driven programming model
- Disk caching and virtual memory
- Device independence
- Network support
- Interface standards

61

High-Performance Graphics

Good graphics are essential to any computer game. A video game looks better when care is taken with the design and construction of the bitmaps. Graphics performance—the rate and regularity with which the screen is updated—is vital for action-based games.

The Microsoft Games SDK

One of the most exciting tools for Windows 95 is the Microsoft Games SDK. The SDK consists of four independent APIs, each designed to support games development. The graphics portion of the SDK, which we will discuss now, is called *DirectDraw*. The DirectDraw API gives developers device-independent access to high-performance accelerated graphics hardware.

Video Hardware Acceleration

Video hardware acceleration is not a new technology for games; it has been used in coin-operated video game machines for years. Inasmuch as these machines are dedicated to playing games, they use special hardware that exists solely to update the graphics display. This acceleration provides smooth animation and leaves the main processor free to do other tasks.

PCs have had graphics hardware acceleration in the form of video accelerators. Soon after the success of Windows 3.0, Windows video accelerator cards began appearing. With the proper software drivers, these cards allowed Windows to relegate screen updates to the video card. The hardware improved the performance of Windows applications and has become standard issue for multimedia computers. Until recently, this hardware could not be controlled directly by applications. DirectDraw gives the programmer access to the hardware acceleration features of the video card.

Programming with DirectDraw is similar to programming VGA games in DOS. You are given access to a *linear memory buffer*, which is a buffer that can be filled with graphical data and copied to the screen. DirectDraw allows you to write games with refresh speeds of up to 72 frames per second, even in a high-resolution video mode such as 640 by 480. Traditional DOS games, even the most successful ones, rarely achieved half that rate at one fourth that resolution. Better still, the processor does far less work than before because much of the video work is off-loaded onto the video card.

Hardware acceleration for PC games has one major drawback. If the game is developed to use acceleration but runs on a machine without an accelerated video card or the correct video driver, performance degrades significantly.

Mode Switching

In Windows 3.x, applications cannot change the mode of the video card. Games are forced to use the video mode that Windows is running in. Games such as Myst compensated for this with a window the size of the video mode's current resolution, a black border, and the game window displayed at 640 by 480. This arrangement is convincing if you have Windows running at 640 by 480, but at 1024 by 768, the graphics appear in a little window in the middle of the screen.

DirectDraw allows games to change the video mode on the fly (without re-booting). This support also allows you to change the *pixel depth*, or number of simultaneous colors of the video mode. So, for example, if a game player is running Windows 95 in a 16-color mode, DirectDraw can change to a 256-color mode for the game play and restore the original mode when the game is over.

Win32 Graphics

The Games SDK allows for hardware-accelerated graphics and mode switching, but the regular Win32 graphics have also been improved. The Win32 bitmap functions in Windows 95 are as fast as or faster than those in WinG. The key feature of Win32 bitmaps is the DIB (device independent bitmap). The DIB drawing routines are fast, and the DIB itself is an addressable bitmap, which means that you can obtain a pointer to the bitmap memory and manipulate the bitmap directly. Previous to DIB support in Win32 you had to use API functions to operate on bitmaps.

32-Bit Operating System

Windows 95 is a 32-bit operating system. This helps games programmers by providing a flat address space and improved performance.

Flat Address Space

A flat, linear address space is provided by 32-bit programming. Pointers do not have segment and offset values. There is no 64KB limit for contiguous buffers. You can declare buffers to contain bitmaps at virtually any resolution. A flat address space eliminates memory models.

Performance

Performance of a 32-bit program is better than its 16-bit counterpart because newer microprocessors are designed to execute 32-bit code better and more reliably. Windows 95 is a 32-bit program.

Intrinsic Types

There are a few code differences between 16- and 32-bit programming. Keywords **near** and **far** have no meaning because all pointers are the same size (32-bit). In addition, some intrinsic types have different sizes. For example, in 16-bit programming, an **int** is a 16-bit value and can store a number from 0 to 65,535 (for an **unsigned int**). In 32-bit programming, an **int** is a 32-bit value and has a range of 0 to 4,294,967,295. Care must be taken with binary file data. A data file containing 16-bit **int**s will not load properly into a 32-bit application's **int** data type because the 32-bit application assumes that an **int** is 32 bits. The solution is to use the type qualifiers **short** and **long**.

Digital Sound and Music

Readers familiar with games programming in DOS remember the hassle of programming sound and music support because DOS by itself doesn't support digital sound and music. To write DOS games, you must either write your own sound card code or aqcuire a function library. Windows 95 has built-in digital sound and music support.

Multimedia

Windows supports digital sound and music so that it can support multimedia applications. Digital sound and music are supported though the Media Control Interface (MCI). MCI offers a high-level interface for media devices such as CD-ROM players, laser-disk players, and video playback devices. Games need MCI's waveform audio support for digital sound and its MIDI-sequencer support for music.

Mixing Sounds

Most sound devices can play only one digital sample at a time. Games that need to play two or more sounds at the same time have to mix the sounds in memory and play the result on the sound device at runtime. DirectSound, the audio component of the Games SDK, can mix sounds at run time and uses sound card mixing hardware if it is available.

High-Performance Timing

Timing is critical in games. Most games have an opponent or opponents that move or act periodically to oppose the player. The speed of this opponent should be consistent from one machine to another regardless of processor speed. The actions of the user should be read and translated at regular intervals to prevent the controls from getting too touchy on fast machines or too sluggish on slow machines. Because the DirectDraw component of the Games SDK can produce high frame rates, high-resolution timers are more important than ever.

Under DOS, the system clock runs at 18.2 *hertz* (cycles per second), which means that unless you reprogram the PC's clock chip, the smallest regular timer interval is roughly 1/18th of a second. Windows 3.1 introduced timers for multimedia, that had millisecond resolution (1/1000th of a second). In practice, the API allows you to specify millisecond resolutions, but the actual performance of the timer is not accurate to the millisecond. Windows 95 supports timer resolutions accurate to the millisecond (1000 timer ticks per second).

The Event-Driven Programming Model

Windows programming uses an event-driven model. Windows applications are written as a set of event handlers that respond to messages sent from the system and between windows. This model is ideal for game programming. Windows sends messages to your game program indicating external events: a key has been pressed; a timer has run down; the mouse has been moved or clicked, and so on; and your code responds.

Disk Caching and Virtual Memory

Disk caching allows frequently read disk files to reside in memory so that when they are needed, it isn't necessary to access the disk drive. This caching occurs outside the application's control. Virtual memory allows programs to allocate memory even when there is no main memory to allocate. By swapping portions of memory to disk, Windows allows all allocated buffers to be processed. Disk caching and virtual memory use disk space and memory interchangeably in a way that is invisible to applications.

Disk caching and virtual memory allow operations that would otherwise be inefficient or impossible. The impact of these features on games is not as positive. Because these two features allow memory and disk space to be interchanged, the performance of an operation can vary. If a bitmap is displayed from memory, the update is instantaneous. If an image is read from disk, there is a perceptible delay before the image appears on the screen. Bitmaps and sounds must be read directly from memory for optimum performance.

One way to deal with these features is to exploit them. In Theatrix, sound files are not read into memory by the framework. Only the names of the files are stored. When it is time to play a sound, the **PlaySound** function is called with the file name as parameter. The first time the file is played, there is a perceptible delay, but after the file has been played once, the delay goes away.

Not all the data files used by Theatrix are handled this way. Graphics are read into memory at startup so that there is no delay when a bitmap is first displayed.

Device Independence

Device independence has been an attractive feature of Windows from the start. Windows provides a programming interface for a generic device and uses specific device drivers to communicate with the devices. Games programmers are finally free from having to program at the device level. You can forget everything you ever knew about a particular sound card or how to program for the joystick. Windows 95 takes care of it all.

Network Support

For years, multiplayer games have been popular among university students using Unix workstations. This is in part because UNIX is a networked environment, and universities usually have direct Internet access. PC users have been slower to adopt network games. Given that Windows 95 has built-in network support and that more and more PCs are hooked up to networks and BBSes, network games are bound to be popular in the future.

Win32 Networking

The Win32 API allows general-purpose network communication between computers connected via a network. The Marble Fighter demo on the CD-ROM takes advantage of this support, allowing two players to play against each other. The Win32 network support is built into the Theatrix class library, so adding network support to games written with Theatrix is simple.

Games SDK: DirectPlay

Network support in the Games SDK is provided via the DirectPlay component. The network support provided by DirectPlay is automatic. If a game is DirectPlay-enabled, it will automatically detect the presence of other DirectPlay-enabled games on the network. DirectPlay also allows the game to inquire about previous and existing game sessions. DirectPlay is not supported by the frameworks in this book.

Autoplay

The Windows 95 autoplay feature allows applications that are distributed via CD-ROM to launch automatically. Software can be installed by simply putting the disk into the drive. The idea is that game installation on PCs should be as simple as it is on game consoles such as Sega and Nintendo. What this means to you as a game developer is that if you take the proper steps, your CD-ROM game will have a foolproof installation. To make matters even better, it is easy to add autoplay support to your game. The autoplay feature means that for the first time, users of PC games need not have any special knowledge of computers or installation procedures. See the Microsoft Games SDK to learn how to enable Autoplay for your CD-ROM game.

Built in Video Clip Support

Previous versions of Windows did not support playback of *video clips* (moving pictures) without additional software. This became a nuisance for game developers who wanted to include video support, because the only way to guarantee that the game would run was to include a copy of the video playback software, which the user would then have to install in addition to the game.

Video playback clips can add a new dimension to a game. Many games available today use embedded video to inform the game player of his or her status. Video support is well suited for CD-ROM applications because the video clips tend to be large.

Interface Standards

Standardized interfaces are not new to Windows 95. One of the primary goals of Windows 3.0 was to encourage and facilitate interfaces that were intuitive and consistent from one application to the next. Because so few games were written for Windows 3.0, it was difficult to measure the impact that interface standards might have on games.

One positive aspect of interface standards is that they assure you as a game developer that, if you adhere to the standards, there is a large population of Windows users who will understand the layout of your software and will be less likely to be confused and frustrated by your interface. On the other hand, the Windows 95 interface guidelines were not written with games in mind. Games are supposed to be innovative and challenging. The new and exciting games of the future will bring with them new concepts and interfaces. As a game developer, you must walk the fine line between challenging and frustrating your user. As a rule of thumb, use new and innovative interfaces for the game itself, but use the interface guidelines to develop help and installation components.

DEVELOPMENT ENVIRONMENT

Games come in a wide variety of forms. Some, such as Tetris, are simple. The implementation is straightforward and the plot is easy to explain. Other games, such as strategy games, are complex and can take weeks for a game player to fully understand. Regardless of the complexity of a game, you can be sure that it was not written overnight. Someone put in the time to figure out the idea, draw or render the graphics, write and test the code, and so on. It is fitting, then, that we talk about the development environment, where you will be spending most of your time. You will learn about these subjects:

- Working with Visual C++ 4.0
- Special project settings
- Using the examples on the CD-ROM
- Data-file generation

Visual C++ 4.0

The frameworks and the demos in this book were written with Visual C++ 4.0. Visual C++ is a large application and certainly cannot be covered in one chapter, so we'll discuss only the issues and features that are sure to affect you. The Visual C++ on-line help is pretty good and getting better. It is integrated directly into the Visual C++ environment, so it is always handy.

Workspaces (Projects) and Project Types

A *workspace*, or *project*, is a collection of source code modules and settings that, when compiled, produce an application or application component. The Visual C++ environment and documentation use the terms *project* and *workspace* interchangeably. The Visual C++ environment allows only one workspace to be open at a time, although it is possible to run two copies of the environment and load one project into each copy. Workspaces consist of file components and project settings and are saved with a **.MDP** extension. The project settings specify how the file modules are to be used. There are several different kind of projects built into Visual C++. In addition, custom projects can be added. When creating a new project, you are given a choice of which kind of project you would like. Figure 5.1 is the New Project Workspace window.

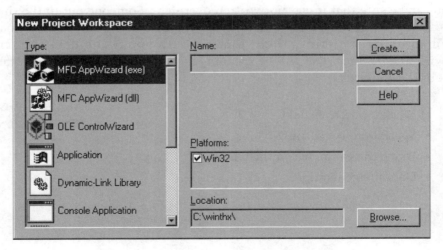

Figure 5.1 The New Project Workspace dialog box

MFC AppWizard Projects

The most common is the MFC AppWizard project, which is an MFC application that is generated to your specifications when you request a new project. Application Wizard projects are a great way to start a new application if you are writing an MFC application.

Console Applications

The Console Application project type creates programs that look like DOS programs, because they do not use any of the Windows GUI features. Some of the utility programs on the CD-ROM are written as console applications because they are designed to be called from batch files or scripting utilities. Despite their appearance, console applications are not DOS applications. They are full-fledged 32-bit Windows applications, minus the windowing ability.

Static Libraries

Static library projects do not produce executable programs directly. Instead, the code is compiled and a LIB file is produced, which can then be used as a component in other applications. The framework projects in this book are static library projects. The LIB files that they produce are used by the demo projects. The framework projects do not require compilation unless the framework code is modified.

Applications

Application projects are projects that produce Windows applications but do not generate any code automatically. The demo projects are all of this type.

Configurations

Each project (or workspace) has two configurations: **Debug** and **Release**. Both configurations use the same code and resources, but they have different project settings. In essence, the difference is that the **Debug** configuration produces output that includes information necessary for use in the debugger. The **Release** configuration produces smaller, more optimized output but cannot be executed in the debugger. Figure 5.2 is the Visual C++ development environment. The current configuration is displayed in the pick box on the lower toolbar. Most of the time you should have the debug configuration active (as in the example).

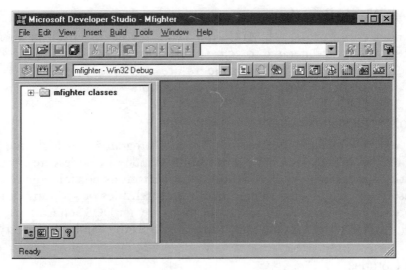

Figure 5.2 The Visual C++ development environment

Adding Files to a Project

Regardless of which project type you are working with, it is likely that at some point you will want to add existing or new files to the project. Before we discuss adding files, however, we should look at the way files are displayed after they have become part of a project.

The ClassView Tree Control

Visual C++ 4.0 introduces the *ClassView dialog* to the Project Workspace window. Previous versions of Visual C++ used a similar workspace window, but it was limited to displaying the project files. A *FileView dialog* is still available in the workspace window, but the window defaults to ClassView. The *ClassView dialog* displays the project in term of classes. Class definitions can be viewed by double-clicking on the class name. The *ClassView dialog* is a tree control, so each entry can be opened or expanded. Opening a class entry causes the class's members to be displayed. Again, double-clicking on an item causes Visual C++ to display the member function or data definition. Figure 5.3 shows the ClassView tree control in action.

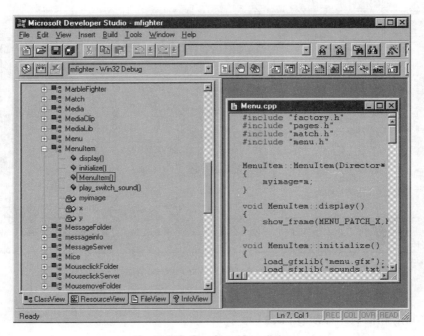

Figure 5.3 The *ClassView dialog*

In the figure, the *MenuItem* class has been opened and the constructor has been double-clicked, causing Visual C++ to display the definition for the constructor. The new ClassView window means more than just quick access to your code. By using the ClassView window to navigate your projects, you begin to think of the project more in terms of objects than of files.

The FileView Tree Control

The *FileView dialog box* can be used for file access as well, but it also serves to display which files are part of the project. Figure 5.4 is the Visual C++ environment with the *FileView dialog box* displayed.

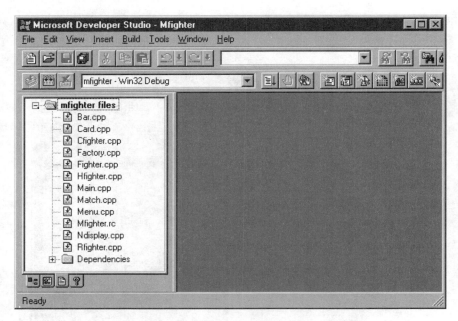

Figure 5.4 The FileView tree control

Inserting and Removing Files

New and existing code files can be added to a project by using the **Files into Project** option on the Insert menu. You can add multiple files at a time by holding down the **Ctrl** key while clicking on the desired files. To delete a file from a project, click on the file (in the *FileView tree control)*, and press the **Del** key.

File Dependencies

The last entry in the FileView dialog in Figure 5.4 is a folder labeled Dependencies. For the most part, dependencies are the **.H** files that are named in **.CPP** files using the **#include** directive. Dependency means that the **.C** or **.CPP** file must be recompiled if the **.H** file which it is dependent on is modified.

It is good practice to use the **Update All Dependencies...** command in the Build menu after any **.CPP** files have been added to a project. Keeping the dependencies updated means that Visual C++ will always compile the right files. If too few files get compiled, the resulting executable can be unstable. If too many files get compiled, the compilation process will take longer than necessary.

Project Settings

There are scores of different project settings, and we won't try to cover them all. Most of the settings are best left with their default values. It does no harm to experiment with the settings, but it is also wise to do experimentation on a test project, because it is easy to lose track of what you have changed. The Settings dialog box is displayed by choosing the **Settings...** option on the Build menu. Figure 5.5 is the Project Settings dialog box.

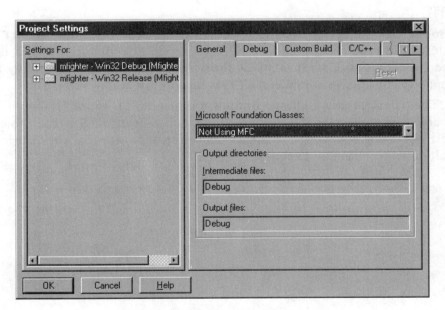

Figure 5.5 The Project Settings dialog box

The Project Settings dialog box has eight tabs. Some of the tabs are attached to complicated dialog boxes. What makes the Project Settings dialog box even more complicated is that each configuration has its own settings. For example, the dialog box in Figure 5.5 has a field called **Intermediate Files,** and the field is set to **Debug.** The **Debug** entry applies only to the **Debug** configuration. Notice that the **Debug** configuration is selected. If you select the **Release** configuration instead, a different value will appear in the field.

If you select both the **Debug** and **Release** configurations (by holding down the **Ctrl** key, and clicking on the configuration not highlighted), only the fields having exactly the same values for each configuration will be displayed. This selection can be convenient when you want both configurations to have the same values. It can also lead to problems, because even though the fields look empty, entering data overwrites the values for both configurations. It pays to play close attention to which project configuration is active when you use this dialog box.

RTTI

Among the project options is RTTI (runtime type information). RTTI allows the type of an object to be determined at runtime. RTTI is not specific to Visual C++; it is a new feature for C++ and will eventually be supported by all C++ compilers. RTTI is new to Visual C++ version 4.0.

The Theatrix and GDKapp frameworks use RTTI, so RTTI should be enabled in projects that use these frameworks. Figure 5.6 is the Project Settings dialog box, with the **C/C++** tab selected. Notice that the Category pull-down box has **C++ Language** selected.

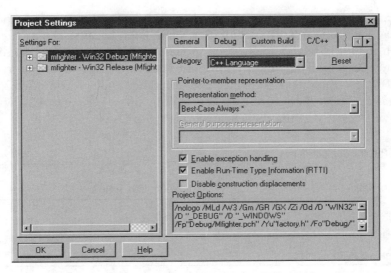

Figure 5.6 The Project Settings dialog box with the RTTI checkbox displayed

By default, RTTI is disabled. Code containing RTTI features in a non-RTTI–enabled project will produce compiler errors.

Precompiled Headers

Microsoft has long been criticized for the sluggishness of its compilers, and, in that sense, Visual C++ 4.0 is a typical Microsoft compiler. Even with a fast processor, lots of memory, and a fast hard drive, compiling can be slow. You can decrease compilation time by using precompiled headers.

Precompiled headers is a feature that allows **.H** files to be compiled in advance. Subsequent **.CPP** compilations are faster, because the **.H** files used by each **.CPP** file have already been processed. This can make a significant difference, especially in an environment such as Windows, which requires large **.H** files. Table 5.1 illustrates the difference that precompiled headers can make. These benchmarks were taken on a Pentium 100 with 32 megabytes of RAM using the Theatrix framework.

Table 1: Theatrix Compile Times

Project Settings	Compilation Time
No precompiled headers	5 minutes
Automatic precompiled headers	2 minutes
Manual precompiled headers	48 seconds

It pays to use this feature. It is easy to configure projects to use automatic headers. Manual precompiled headers require extra steps. Figure 5.7 is the Project Settings dialog box. The **C/C++** tab has been selected, and **Precompiled Headers** has been selected in the **Category** field.

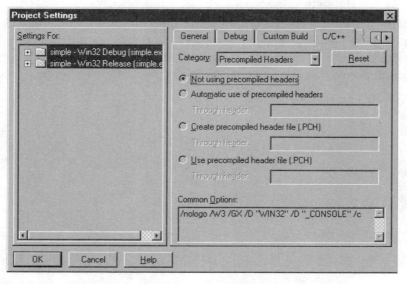

Figure 5.7 The Project Settings dialog with the precompiled headers settings displayed

There are four radio buttons for precompiled headers. In the figure, the first is selected, indicating that precompiled headers should not be used. The second radio button is for automatic use of precompiled headers. Using this option is as simple as selecting the button. An optional **.H** file can be entered in the **Through header** field. The last two buttons are used to configure a **.PCH** file that will store the precompiled data.

To use a **.PCH** file and get the best performance, you must first decide which header files should be precompiled. Good candidates are files such as **windows.h** and **fstream.h**, because they are big and they do not change from build to build. Organize the header files in your project so that all the header files to be precompiled are used in one (and only one) **.H** file. The projects in this book usually use a file named **factory.h** for this purpose. We will use the **factory.h** file name in this example, but the name is arbitrary. In the case of the demos, the **factory.h** file usually contains only one line. Figure 5.8 is a **factory.h** file from a Theatrix demo.

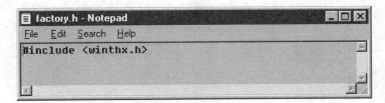

Figure 5.8 factory.h

It isn't necessary to include **.H** files such as **windows.h**, because **winthx.h** includes them. You also need a **factory.cpp** file that includes **factory.h**. Figure 5.9 is **factory.cpp**.

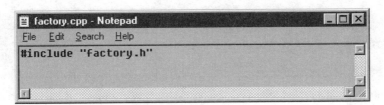

Figure 5.9 factory.cpp

The next step is to ensure that every **.CPP** file in the project includes the **factory.h** file. The file must be included before any other **.H** files. Figure 5.10 is a **.CPP** file from the *Marble Fighter* demo.

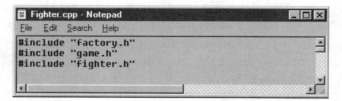

Figure 5.10 fighter.cpp—from the Marble Fighter demo

From the Build|Project Settings dialog box, select both project configurations in the **Settings For** tree control on the left, as shown in Figure 5.11. This ensures that the project settings we are about to change apply to both configurations. Next, select the last radio button, labeled **Use precompiled header**, and enter **factory.h** in the **Through header** field, as shown in Figure 5.11.

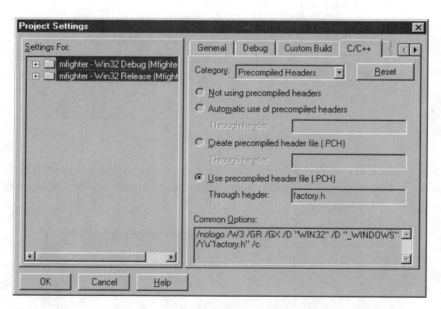

Figure 5.11 The Project Settings dialog box with factory.h specified as the PCH source.

Next, expand the **Debug** and **Release** configurations by clicking on the small boxes to the left of each configuration. This action displays each file in the project. Click on the **factory.cpp** file for the **Debug** configuration, and then hold down the **Ctrl** key while you click the **factory.cpp** file in the Release configuration. Then select the third radio button, labeled **Create precompiled header**, and enter **factory.h** in the **Through header** field. Figure 5.12 shows the final settings.

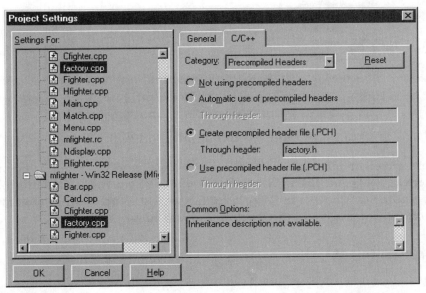

Figure 5.12 The Project Settings dialog box with factory.cpp specified for PCH creation

Now select **Build|Update all dependencies**. The project is now ready to compile.

Visual C++ Environment Settings

Environment settings apply to the Visual C++ environment, so they apply to all projects. These settings can be modified by choosing **Tools|Options**. Figure 5.13 is the Options dialog box.

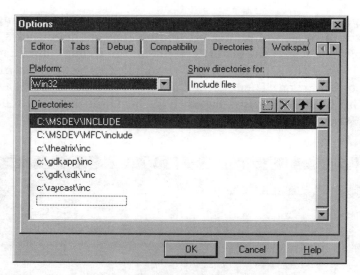

Figure 5.13 The Options dialog box

There are eight tabs on the Options dialog box, and we won't attempt to cover each of them. The only tab that is sure to affect you is the Directories tab. Figure 5.13 shows the Directories tab with the **Include files directories** displayed. You must specify directories for the library files, too.

Linker Warnings

Visual C++ sometimes produces the following linker warning:

```
LINK : warning LNK4098: defaultlib "libcd.lib" conflicts with use of other libs;
```

There is probably a way to get this warning to go away, but warnings do no harm, so you can ignore it.

The Framework Projects

There are three framework projects on the CD-ROM. These project's won't concern you unless you decide to modify the framework code. If you do plan to modify the frameworks, the informarion found here will be of interest.

The Framework Directory Structure

Each framework is located in a directory bearing its name. This directory contains subdirectories that contain the source code, header files, utilities, and demo programs for the framework. Figure 5.14 is the directory structure for the Theatrix framework.

Figure 5.14 The Theatrix directory structure

The figure shows the Theatrix directory, but the same structure is used for all the frameworks. The **bin** directory is where framework utilities are kept.

The **demos** directory holds the framework examples and demos. The projects in this directory depend on the presence of the framework, but the framework does not depend on any of the projects or files in this directory. This directory can be deleted, and the framework will still be intact.

The **inc** directory is where the framework **.H** files are stored. Projects using the frameworks require that the **inc** directory be specified as an include file path in the environment. The **lib** directory stores the LIB files that the framework project produces. Two LIB files are produced by each framework project: one for **Release** and one for **Debug** configurations.

Finally, the **src** directory contains the source code for the framework and the utilities.

Project Settings

The framework projects are all static library projects. The LIB file that they produce is required by the game projects that use the framework. The project settings for the frameworks require that RTTI be enabled, as discussed earlier in this chapter.

Modification Concerns

Care should be taken with modifications made to the framework code, because framework modifications affect all of the projects that use the framework. You should test any significant changes with as many demos as possible.

Demo Game Projects

The best way to learn a class framework is to study examples of its use. The demo games provide ample instruction, whether you study them in detail or use them as a reference. Some of the demos are intricate and are good examples of the benefits of keeping a project organized.

Directory Structure

All the demos use similar directory structures. We will discuss one of the demos, focusing on the subdirectories that are common to all the projects. Figure 5.15 is the directory structure for the Marble Fighter demo.

Figure 5.15 The Marble Fighter directory structure

The **Debug**, **Release**, and **Exec** subdirectories are common to all the demos. The **Debug** and **Release** directories contain intermediate files such as **.OBJ** files, and the game executable, or **.EXE**, file. The **Exec** directory contains the data files that are needed by the game. Data files contain resources such as bitmaps and sound clips and are discussed in detail next. Because all the data files are kept in the **Exec** directory, it is easy to prepare a version of the game for distribution. The contents of the **Exec** directory, along with the executable in the **Release** directory, are the only files that are necessary for distribution. (Some documentation files might be nice, too.)

Generating Data Files

Visual C++ is a powerful tool for developing code. A game, however, is more than an executable. The game executable must have input, or data, to manipulate. Bitmaps, sound clips, and music files must be loaded when the game program starts. The construction of these data files can be as complicated and time-consuming as the code is. Regardless of how your data files are created, they must be converted to a form that is recognized by the framework you are using. In addition, the process of conversion should be automated as much as possible. The objective is to make maintenance as easy as possible. You should be able to run your game, see that a resource needs editing, edit the resource, and then rebuild the game easily. If it is easy to incorporate changes into your game, you are more likely to make improvements.

The data files needed for the demo games are generated outside the Visual C++ environment. Visual C++ supports custom build steps and can be made to generate data files, but the custom build steps can be cumbersome and difficult to modify. Instead, the *nmake* utility is used.

Given a list of rules, the nmake utility executes commands that assemble a *target*. The rules, given in a text file, specify target dependencies and the commands required in order to construct the target. This file is called a *makefile*. Each demo that requires data file generation has its own makefile. All these makefiles are named **data.mak**, and they depend on a file called **make.cfg**.

MAKE.CFG

The **SRC** subdirectory in each framework directory contains a file named **make.cfg** that you must modify in order to use the makefiles with the demo games. The makefiles include **make.cfg**, which establishes some global macros. You change these macros to reflect where you have installed the library and tools. Pay careful attention to these macros and double-check to ensure that you set them correctly. They permit the game makefiles to locate tools and directories.

Listing 5.1 shows the Theatrix **make.cfg** file with typical settings.

Listing 5.1 MAKE.CFG

```
#=================================================================
# MAKE.CFG - common make configuration (!included in makefiles)
#=================================================================
#         --->    User-configurable macros    <---
#-----------------------------------------------------------------
# Set DRIVE to where you installed everything
# Example: DRIVE=c:
# (you can override individual DRIVE usages if you install on
# multiple drives>)
#-----------------------------------------------------------------
DRIVE=c:
#-----------------------------------------------------------------
# Set THEATRIX to where you installed Theatrix
# Example: THEATRIX=$(DRIVE)\thx
#-----------------------------------------------------------------
THEATRIX=$(DRIVE)\theatrix
#-----------------------------------------------------------------
# Set POVRAY to where you installed POV-Ray
# Example: POVRAY=$(DRIVE)\povray2
#-----------------------------------------------------------------
POVRAY=$(DRIVE)\povray
#-----------------------------------------------------------------
#        --->    End of user-configurable macros    <---
```

```
#===============================================================

!ifndef DRIVE
!error DRIVE isn't defined
!ENDIF

!ifndef THEATRIX
!error THEATRIX isn't defined
!endif

!ifndef POVRAY
!error POVRAY isn't defined
!endif

THXBIN=$(THEATRIX)\bin
EXEC=..\exec

POVFILES=$*.def -i$*.pov -o$*.tga
POVSW=+v +x
POVDIRS=-l$(POVRAY)\include
POV=$(POVRAY)\povray $(POVDIRS)
```

A Typical data.mak File

The makefile in a game pulls together the graphical and sound elements to
build the game's data files. Listing 5.2 is a makefile from the Theatrix
Plane*t* demo.

Listing 5.2 The Planet data.mak file

```
!include ..\..\make.cfg

all :   Exec\planet.bmp   \
        Exec\demo.gfx     \
        Exec\sounds.txt
```

```
Exec\planet.bmp : planet.pov demo.pal
    povray -l$(POVRAY)\include -iplanet.pov -oplanet.tga -w320 -h240 +V +A
    alchemy -o -w -8 planet.tga
    cvtpal planet.bmp demo.pal
    move planet.bmp Exec

Exec\demo.gfx : sphere.pov demo.pal
    $(POV) -isphere.pov -osphere.tga -w32 -h32 +V +A
    alchemy -o -w -8 sphere.tga
    cvtpal sphere.bmp demo.pal
    gfxmake demo.gfx sphere.bmp
    move demo.gfx Exec

Exec\sounds.txt : sounds.txt bounce.wav
    copy bounce.wav Exec
    copy sounds.txt Exec
```

The nmake utility is invoked from the command line. The **/f** command is required to use a makefile that is not named "makefile."

Network Rendering

Ray tracing is a time- and processor-intensive procedure. Some of our games have many scenes and sprites that we render with POV-Ray. Each time we change a model, POV-Ray has to render a new image of the scene or sprite frame. POV-Ray is slow.

In managing our project, we found many uses for a network. One of the most productive ones off-loads the rendering task onto a server on the network. We wrote a program named POVNET that runs on a server, waits for **.POV** model files to render and launches POV-Ray to render the models into image files.

The POVNET program, described in more detail in Appendix A, runs in a DOS box in the server (we used a Windows 95 site for the server). Whenever one of us has a new model to render, we copy the **.POV** model file into a designated subdirectory on the server. POVNET observes the new model and launches POV-Ray. We can monitor its progress from our workstations and retrieve the newly rendered image file to add to our game when POV-Ray has completed rendering it.

Configuration Management

Every software development project has this problem: how do you keep up with all the components of a program or system when more than one programmers are working independently on common or dependent elements of the system? With a one-person project, it is easy to lose control when there are many elements in a complex system. As you add people, the potential for error rises exponentially. A game project might involve many people—programmers, artists, sound effects specialists, musicians, script designers, and so on. Each of them can be building and adding pieces to the game as development proceeds. Coordination and synchronization of the various pieces and parts can be an arduous task. There are steps you can take to get it under control.

Formal development projects use computer assisted software engineering (CASE) and version-control tools. We think that these tools not only are overkill for a game project, but they also tend to formalize, institutionalize, and bureaucratize an activity that starts out mainly to be fun.

We'll discuss guidelines that you can use to implement procedures to help you control your project. They work if everyone is easy to get along with and can adjust to inconvenience from time to time. If, however, there are prima donnas on your team who are disagreeable and uncooperative, then these guidelines will not work. Neither will anything else.

The Objective

Your objective in software configuration management is to make sure that everyone works from a common baseline of software components and that when someone changes a part of the system, the following things happen:

- The change is tested with the baseline and works as intended.
- The change is tested to ensure that it does not interfere with, conflict with, or otherwise compromise the work that others are doing.
- When approved, the change is integrated into the baseline and everyone gets the new stuff.

These objectives seem reasonable and attainable. But anyone who has worked on a software development project of any size knows how elusive these goals can be. Game projects are more fun than other jobs, but they are as susceptible to the vagaries of a disparate staff as any other kind of cooperative enterprise is.

The Network

The network is a valuable tool in keeping a grip on the software configuration, especially if the network supports primitive groupware actions such as broadcast messages and protected read or write access at the subdirectory level. Netware, Windows NT, Windows for Workgroups, and Windows 95 all support mail and password-protected read-only access to remote subdirectories.

The Configuration Manager

In a big software development project, configuration management is a full-time job, perhaps even involving a staff of several people who watch over the configuration and keep it under control.

A game project will not usually be that big unless you are building one of those extravaganzas that involve Hollywood actors and who knows what. Nonetheless, on any multiperson software development project, the responsibilities of configuration manager must be assigned. One person should assume these duties, and the other team members must acknowledge and respect that person's authority.

This delegation of authority introduces an anomaly. The boss never wants the mundane duties of configuration manager. Yet the boss is usually writing code. All programmers view configuration management as a pain in the hindquarters—an impediment to getting things done—because it places a wall between them and the current baseline. They have to go through a bothersome procedure to implement a change. The boss, being a programmer, runs into that wall just like everyone else and sometimes uses his or her position to overrule the configuration manager's authority. If you are the boss, don't let that happen.

Nobody likes the configuration manager, so don't take the job if you need to be liked.

The Baseline

The *baseline* is a read-only repository of source code and raw graphics and sound files. Team members can retrieve files from the baseline, but only the configuration manager can change files in it or add files to it. The baseline represents the currently approved version of the system.

Making Changes

When team members work on parts of the system, they work with local copies of the baseline. The configuration manager maintains a record of which files are likely to change. Therefore, the configuration manager always knows—or should know—which files are being modified by whom and, in rare cases, which files are concurrently and independently being modified by more than one team member.

When a change is completed, the team member submits it to the configuration manager and the other team members for review. You can use a public subdirectory on the file server for these submissions. The configuration manager then does whatever is necessary to achieve the three objectives listed above, sometimes merging the work of more than one team member to install their respective changes.

If you do all these things, you will maintain control of the configuration of your software. It is, however, a fact of software development that people throw out the time-consuming and bothersome control mechanisms when the deadlines loom near. You will, too. So did we.

The Final Product

As much fun as game programming is, the best part is being finished. Here are some issues to consider before you present your creation to the world.

Hackability

Before you release or upload the final version, you should consider the game's *hackability*, or the ease with which it can be modified. For instance, if your game uses data files with a common extension, such as **.BMP**, it will be easy for users to load your backgrounds into paint programs, modify them, and put them back into your game. Part of Doom's success was that the game was easily modified. Doom has an open architecture, and fans wrote tools and editors that allowed players to design their own levels. Releasing an open architecture game does not guarantee success, but it has some advantages.

Testing

Before a game is released it should be tested thoroughly. Once you upload a game or distribute the CD-ROM, the game has a life of its own. If it has a bug or a virus, all you can do is release a fixed version and apologize. There is no way to take back what you've released.

In particular, final testing should include tests on new machines. Take the game to a friend's house and try it on his or her computer.

Another test is to remove important data files from the game, one at a time, and run your game to make sure that it detects the problem and displays a message box that explains what the problem is and how to fix it. No one is impressed by a game that brings up an empty window and then crashes, and no one needs a message box that says "Fatal error, quitting." Tell users what is wrong if there is any chance that they can fix it. If the problem is as simple as a missing or damaged file, chances are good that the user can replace it.

THEATRIX: A C++ CLASS LIBRARY

This chapter describes Theatrix, a C++ class library from which you build game applications. You will learn about:

- The Theatrix metaphor
- Class hierarchies
- Hands
- Cues
- Directors

The Theatrix Metaphor

Theatrix uses a theatrical production metaphor to provide an easy and intuitive way for us to think about our task of building games. The paradigm also provides terminology that we can use to communicate.

Games written with Theatrix use a theatrical production as a model. In a play, the director coordinates a cast of actors as well as stagehands and technicians to present a performance. Each member of the crew has specific tasks to perform for the play to be a success. Some members, such as actors, are visible to the audience, whereas others, such as stagehands, are not.

Timing is important in a play. The director cues members of the crew when it is time for a member to perform a task. Sometimes, a cast or crew member takes cues from the actions of others instead of directly from the director.

This concept has stood the test of centuries and works well for plays. What about games? Is it possible to describe a game using these ideas? Sure it is. The games and demos in this book that are written with the Theatrix framework use a theatre model. Remember, however, that the metaphor is only a model and not a strict set of rules. The metaphor makes it easier to think about a game; use it to an extent that you find comfortable.

Theatrix Class Hierarchies

Theatrix consists of two class hierarchies: one that encapsulates your game and another that encapsulates all the graphical, musical, and vocal components of your game.

The Theatrix Class

Figure 6.1 shows the class hierarchy within which you encapsulate the components of a game.

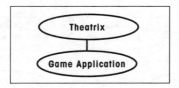

Figure 6.1 Encapsulating the game

The *Theatrix* class in Figure 6.1 encapsulates the controls needed to run a game. The class manages events and message queues, and it initializes and shuts down system components such as timers, sound and music generators, the joystick, the mouse, and so on.

The Game Application bubble in Figure 6.1 represents your game program. It is a class named by you and derived from the *Theatrix* class. This class contains data members that are objects and references to objects of classes derived from the Theatrix class library (discussed next) that you need to run your game. The class can also contain anything else specific to the game. We will show you soon what this class looks like in a real program.

The Theatrix Class Library

Figure 6.2 is the Theatrix class library. To build a game, you derive specialized classes from these classes, and, in some cases, you instantiate objects of these classes. These classes implement the Theatrix metaphor.

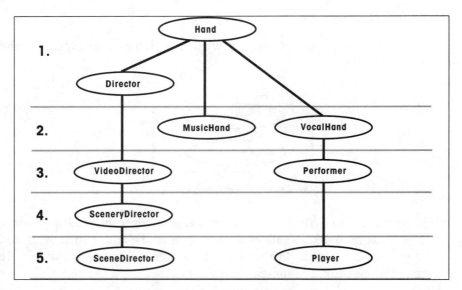

Figure 6.2 The Theatrix class hierarchy

The five levels in Figure 6.2 represent the five levels of abstraction at which you can design your game. The highest level of abstraction is shown at the bottom of the hierarchy, and the lowest is shown at the top.

Most of the classes in Figure 6.2 are designed to be base classes. You build your games by deriving from them. The *MusicHand* class, however, is designed to have an object of the class instantiated. Any game that plays music does so through one instance of the *MusicHand* class.

As you work at lower levels of abstraction, you must understand and use—and in some cases, provide—more of the details of implementation. The higher levels of abstraction encapsulate these details. When you work at higher levels you can ignore the details of the lower levels.

The example games on the included CD-ROM work at different levels of abstraction. Table 6.1 lists the games and shows where they fit on the chart.

Table 6.1 Levels of abstraction of example games

Example Game	Level of Abstraction
Textmode	1
Planet	3
Theatris	3
Marble Fighter	3
SkyScrap	3
TicTacToe	4
Mouse	4
Town	4
Skater	5
Shootout	5

A game can use the details from several levels of abstraction. For example, the Shootout game, implemented at level 5, uses level 4's *SceneryDirector* to implement introductory screens and level 2's *MusicHand* class to play music selections from a musical score.

The Hand Class

Usually, you do not directly derive anything from the *Hand* class, although it is possible. This class hosts and manages the events and messages that game program components use to communicate with the system. Usually, your program derives classes from the classes that derive from *Hand*.

The *Hand* class allows its derived objects to request *cues*, which are messages that the system sends to *Hand* objects. Messages are usually associated with system events such as keystrokes, but messages may also be posted by game components to be received by *Hand* objects that register for the messages.

The CUELIST Table

A derived *Hand* class requests cues for its objects by defining a CUELIST table, which specifies the cues to be received and the class's member functions to receive them.

The class declaration includes a DECLARE_CUELIST statement that declares the existence of a CUELIST table for the class:

```
class MyHand : public Hand  {
    // ...
    DECLARE_CUELIST
};
```

Then the class definition includes the CUELIST table:

```
CUELIST(MyHand)
     KEYSTROKE('A',on_key_a)
     TIMER(1,on_timer)
ENDLIST
```

The CUELIST statement specifies that a table of cues follows. The ENDLIST statement terminates the table. The CUELIST statement's parameter identifies the class for which the cues in the list are being registered, which means that the CUELIST statement must be within the scope of the class declaration. A CUELIST declaration generates a memory-resident table, so you should put CUELIST declarations in the **.CPP** source code file of your program rather than in the header file that declares the class.

The CUELIST table just shown includes a KEYSTROKE entry that registers objects of the class to receive a keystroke cue. The table also includes a TIMER entry that registers a cue based on the system clock.

The *on_key_a* and *on_timer* parameters to the KEYSTROKE and TIMER statements are member functions. They are called *callback* functions because the table entries pass to the system the addresses of functions to be called. Whenever the user presses the *a* key, for example, the system calls the registered class's *on_key_a* member function once for each instantiated object of the class. The *on_key_a* function defines the object's behavior when the *a* key is pressed. The callback function might be defined like this:

```
void MyHand::on_key_a(int)
{
    print_string("the 'A' key has been pressed!");
}
```

Notice that the **int** parameter that is passed to *on_key_a* is not given a name. Because this callback is used in only one KEYSTROKE statement, there is no point in testing the value of the parameter; this callback will be called only when the A key is pressed. There are nine types of cues. Table 6.2 lists the cues and gives examples of their entries in the CUELIST table.

Table 6.2 CUELIST events

Event	CUELIST Entry
Keystroke	KEYSTROKE(`a',on_key_a)
Hotkey pressed	HOTKEY(SCAN_CTRL, on_ctrlkey)
Clock tick	TIMER(1, on_timer)
Message posted	MESSAGE(on_message)
Mouse click	MOUSECLICK(LEFTMOUSEBUTTON, on_mousebutton)
Mouse movement	MOUSEMOVE(on_mousemove)
Joystick moved	JOYSTICKMOVE(on_joystickmove)
Joystick button	JOYSTICKBUTTON(on_joystickbutton)
Network packet	NETPACK(`X', on_netpack)

Callback Function Signatures

The callback function for each cue type has its own function signature depending on what the system passes as arguments. The class and callback identifiers are up to you, but callbacks should have return types of *void* and, if you are expecting to use the arguments, parameter lists that match the signatures. The discussions that follow identify the signatures for the callback functions.

Callback Functions

A callback function must be a member function of a *Hand* class or of a class derived from *Hand*. When the system calls a *Hand* callback function, it passes data arguments depending on which cue is being sent. Table 6.3 lists the cues and the prototypes for their associated callback functions.

Table 6.3 Callback function prototypes

Event	Callback Prototype	Arguments
Keystroke	void cb(int key)	Virtual key code
Hotkey pressed	void cb(int key)	Virtual key code
Clock tick	void cb()	
Message posted	void cb(int p1, int data1, int data2)	App-dependent values
Mouse click	void cb(int x, int y, int b)	Coordinates, button
Mouse movement	void cb(int x, int y, int b)	Coordinates, button
Joystick moved	void cb(int x, int y)	Coordinates off center
Joystick button	void cb(int x, int y)	Coordinates off center
Network packet	void cb(int pkt)	Packet byte value

The callbacks in your game must match the signatures shown here.[1]

KEYSTROKE

A keystroke cue is sent each time the key associated with the cue is pressed.

The keystroke cue callback function has this signature:

```
void ClassName::callbackname( int vk );
```

The parameter's argument is the key that was pressed. This value is a Windows virtual key code. If this callback is registered to be cued for only one key, then the parameter's argument will always have that one value. If, however, you use one callback to handle multiple keys, you will need to test the value of 'k'.

---

[1]The DOS version of Theatrix allowed you to use any signature at all for callbacks. This was convenient for situations where the parameter was to be ignored, because the callback could be written to take no parameters at all, even if a parameter was being sent. This was also a bit dangerous, because it was possible to use a signature that didn't match the data being sent.

HOTKEY

Hotkey cues occur whenever a key is down. Hotkey cues are different from keystroke cues because hotkey cues occur for the duration of the key press, and keystroke cues occur only once per key press unless the key is held down long enough to activate the type-matic mechanism. Also, hotkey cues occur for each key that is pressed at a given time. Keystroke cues occur only for the last key that was pressed. Hotkeys are great for intense arcade action, but it is difficult to write a menu using hotkeys because they often report multiple cues even if the user pressed the key once. The hotkey cue delivery rate is not dependent on the type-matic rate set by Windows.

The hotkey cue callback function has this signature:

```
void ClassName::callbackname( int vk );
```

Like keystrokes, hotkey callbacks take a single, integer parameter, which is the Windows virtual key code for the key in question.

TIMER

Timer cues are a vital part of any arcade game. The first argument in the TIMER entry specifies the number of cues sent each second. Because Theatrix is a port from the DOS framework, the maximum number of timers available per second is 18.

The system sends timer cues at a regular rate regardless of the processor's speed. Games use timer cues to float objects across the screen or to maintain a constant speed for bullets, rockets, and so on. The timer cue also paces the frame refresh rate of animated sequences.

The timer cue callback function has this signature:

```
void ClassName::callbackname();
```

Timer callbacks take no parameters.

MESSAGE

Message cues are different from the other types of cues because they are sent by a component of the game rather than in response to an event. Messages allow the *Hand* objects in your game to communicate. When a *Hand* object posts a message, other *Hand* objects that have registered for the message are cued. Messages may have data values associated with them.

The message cue callback function has this signature:

```
void ClassName::callbackname( int msg, int data1, int data2 );
```

Message callbacks have two parameters. The first parameter is the message that was posted. The second parameter is the optional data value that can be sent along with the message.

MOUSECLICK

Mouse click cues are sent whenever either button on the mouse is pressed. The mouse click cue callback function has this signature:

```
void ClassName::callbackname( int x, int y, int b );
```

Mouse click callbacks are sent three integer parameters. The first two parameters are the x/y location of the mouse on the screen at the time of the click. The third parameter is set to either LEFTMOUSEBUTTON or RIGHTMOUSEBUTTON depending on which button was pressed.

MOUSEMOVE

Mouse movement cues are sent whenever the player moves the mouse. The mouse movement cue callback function has this signature:

```
void ClassName::callbackname( int x, int y, int b );
```

Mouse movement callbacks are sent three integer parameters. The first two parameters are the x/y location of the mouse on the screen at the time of the click. The third parameter is set to zero if no button is being held down or is set to LEFTMOUSEBUTTON or RIGHTMOUSEBUTTON if a button is being held down. Programs can use the button parameter to implement mouse drag operations.

JOYSTICKMOVE

Joystick movement cues are sent whenever the joystick is positioned away from the center position. The joystick movement cue callback function has this signature:

```
void ClassName::callbackname( int x, int y );
```

Joystick movement callbacks are sent two integer parameters indicating the distance from the center position. A negative x value indicates left of center; positive x indicates right of center; negative y indicates below center, and positive y indicates above center.

JOYSTICKBUTTON

Joystick button cues are sent when a joystick button is pressed. The joystick button cue callback function has this signature:

```
void ClassName::callbackname( int x, int y );
```

Joystick button callbacks are sent the same two integer parameters that joystick movement callbacks receive.

NETPACK

Network packet cues are sent when Theatrix reads a packet from the network. Network packets are present only in games that use network communications. The network packet cue callback function has this signature:

```
void ClassName::callbackname( int p );
```

The single parameter is simply the value that was sent across the network.

Requesting and Stopping Cues During the Game

A *Hand* requests cues either with the CUELIST table or by calling member functions that make the requests at runtime during the course of the game. The CUELIST table establishes an initial list of registered cues when the game begins.

If your game has a *Hand* that requests and stops cues during the course of the game, you can use *Hand* member functions that perform these operations. Table 6.4 lists the *Hand* member functions that request and stop cue callbacks during the game's execution.

Table 6.4 Cue request and stop functions

```
void request_keystroke_cue( int key, callback );

void stop_keystroke_cue( int key, callback );

void request_hotkey_cue( int scancode, callback );

void stop_hotkey_cue( int scancode, callback );

void request_timer_cue( int rate, callback );

void stop_timer_cue( int rate, callback );

void request_message_cue( int msg, callback );

void stop_message_cue( int msg, callback );

void post_message( int msg, long data );

void request_mouseclick_cue( int b, callback );

void stop_mouseclick_cue( int b, callback );

void request_mousemove_cue( callback );

void stop_mousemove_cue( callback );

void request_joystickbutton_cue( int b, callback );

void stop_joystickbutton_cue( int b, callback );

void request_joystickmove_cue( callback );

void stop_joystickmove_cue( callback );

void request_netpack_cue( int ,callback );

void stop_netpack_cue( int, callback );
```

Level 1: Directors and Hands

Level 1 in Figure 6.2 is the lowest level of abstraction for a Theatrix game program. Game-dependent classes at this level derive from the *Director* and *Hand* classes. Nothing at this level supports graphics, sound effects, or music. Level 1 serves to launch a game program and manage events and cues.

The Director Class

The *Director* class implements objects that control the running of the game. A game may declare many *Director* objects, usually of classes derived from *Director*, but only one *Director* object is in control of the game at any given time.

Stopping the Director

A game cannot go on forever, so there must be a way to stop it. A *Hand* object calls *stop_director* to terminate the *Director* object that directs the *Hand's* activities. If the *Hand* is itself a *Director*, it terminates itself by calling the *stop_director* function.

When the terminated *Director* object is the only *Director* in a game, a call to *stop_director* terminates the game as well. You learn later how games with multiple directors pass control among one another.

Level 2: MusicHand and VocalHand

Abstraction level 2 derives classes from *Hand*. *VocalHand* provides sound support, and *MusicHand* supports playing selections from a musical score. A game written at this level would have full music and sound support, but no graphics. We opted not to do any demos at this level, but there is no reason that a game, perhaps for the visually impaired, couldn't be written at this level.

The MusicHand Class

Theatrix uses the *MusicHand* class to provide support for music in games. *MusicHand* reads a text file that contains the names of one or more MIDI files, one on each line. The text file represents the game's musical score. *MusicHand* takes the name of the file as a parameter to the constructor:

```
musichandptr=new MusicHand("tunes.txt");
```

When the time comes to play a selection from the score, a call to the *MusicHand* object can be made:

```
musichandptr->play_music_clip(clip);
```

The *clip* argument in the *play_music_clip* function call is an integer that specifies which entry in the text file should be played. The value must be greater than zero and less than or equal to the number of clips in the file that was specified as an argument to the *MusicHand* constructor. If a previous selection is playing, this function stops that one and starts the new one.

To ask the *MusicHand* object whether it is still playing a selection from the score, call the *music_clip_is_playing* member function:

```
while (musichandptr->music_clip_is_playing()) {
    // do something while music is playing
}
```

To tell the *MusicHand* object to stop playing a selection, call *stop_music_clip*:

```
musichandptr->stop_music_clip();  // current selection stops
```

The VocalHand Class

VocalHand also uses text files to store the name and order of the files to be played.[2] In this case, the entries are the names of .**WAV** files. Figure 6.3 is the text file for the Marble Fighter demo.

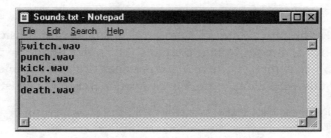

Figure 6.3 The Marble Fighter sound list

---

[2]Both *MusicHand* and *VocalHand* use regular text files to specify the names and order of the files to be played. This means that both the text file and the audio files can be modified easily. Chapter 5 addresses "hackability."

A game program can derive from *VocalHand* or instantiate a *VocalHand* object, although many games will use the *Performer* class (discussed soon), which is derived from *VocalHand*.

The *VocalHand* constructor accepts a pointer to the *Director* for which the object is running. If you omit that argument, the constructor builds the object with no associated *Director*, and the class may not have a CUELIST entry or request and stop cues with function calls.

Following is a small class that derives from *VocalHand* to implement sound effects for a game.

```
class SoundTech : public VocalHand  {
    char *sfxfile;
    void initialize()
        { load_list( "sounds.txt" ); }
public:
    SoundTech(char *sfx)
        { sfxfile = sfx; }
};
```

The call to *VocalHand::load_sfxlib* tells the object the name of the **.SFX** library to load. All the sound clips that can be played by the *VocalHand* object are in that library. A game can instantiate an object of such a class, as the following example shows:

```
static SoundTech *soundtech;

soundtech = new SoundTech("sounds.txt");
```

The game that uses such a class can then call *VocalHand* member functions through objects of the derived class, as shown here:

```
soundtech->play_sound_clip(clip);      // play a sound clip
// ...
soundtech->stop_sound_clip();          // stop the sound clip
// ...
if (soundtech->sound_clip_is_playing()) // test if clip is playing
    // sound clip is playing
```

The clip number argument in the *play_sound_clip* function call is an integer that specifies which entry in the text file to play. The argument must be greater than zero and less than or equal to the number of clips in the file that was loaded for the *VocalHand* object.

Level 3: Performers and VideoDirectors

Abstraction level 3 derives classes from *VocalHand* and *Director*. *Performer* provides basic graphics support, and *VideoDirector* provides the screen update mechanisms that make the graphics visible.

The Performer Class

Performer, which supports graphics, is derived from *VocalHand*, which is derived from *Hand*. In addition to being able to request cues, *Performer* loads **.GFX** libraries, which are files that contain images that you provide in the form of **.BMP** files. Once *Performer* loads a **.GFX** library, it can display the images inside the library at any time.

.**GFX** libraries are created using the Theatrix utility programs, which are explained in Chapter 7.

The VideoDirector Class

VideoDirector is derived from *Director*. *VideoDirector* is responsible for all the graphical elements in a game, including animation. *VideoDirector* is designed for use as a base class and is not usually derived from directly. The *SceneryDirector* and *SceneDirector* classes both use *VideoDirector* as a base class.

Level 4: SceneryDirectors

Until now, our discussion has related mostly to the action part of the game. Few games, however, jump immediately into the action. Most of them have an introductory screen, and many have a trailer screen that comes up after the game is over. Most games also have a menu that allows players to choose from selections such as whether to play another session, get help, change options, exit the game, and so on.

At its fourth level of abstraction, Theatrix implements the *SceneryDirector* class, which implements scenery without animation.

The SceneryDirector Class

SceneryDirector takes the name of a **.BMP** file as a parameter to its constructor. In the game, when the *SceneryDirector* takes over, the **.BMP** file is displayed. If the **.BMP** file is a different size than the game window, the window is resized automatically. *SceneryDirector* is designed to be used as a base class.

```
class IntroPage : public SceneryDirector
{
public:
    IntroPage() : SceneryDirector("intro.bmp")  { }
}
```

By creating an instance of *IntroPage* before any other *Director* objects, you've added an intro page to your game. *SceneryDirector* can be used to display intro screens, help screens, and trailer screens. The demos on the CD-ROM—such as Marble Fighter, Theatris, and Shootout—all use *SceneryDirector*. *SceneryDirector* waits for the **Enter**, **Space Bar**, or **Esc** key to be pressed before it releases control.

Level 5: Players and SceneDirectors

At level 5, Theatrix provides two classes that encapsulate the operations of video pages and bitmaps. *Player* is derived from *Performer*, and *SceneDirector* is derived from *SceneryDirector*.

These two classes make it easy to animate multiple sprites simultaneously. At first glance, animating two sprites doesn't seem any more complicated than animating one sprite—but it is. With single sprite animation, a scene can be updated simply by erasing the old image (with a portion of the background image) and drawing the new one. This technique doesn't work with two sprites, because the sprite that is moving might overlap the sprite that is not moving, thereby erasing part or all of the second sprite. In short, to animate two or more sprites, the updating must be coordinated.

Another facet of multiple sprite animation involves Z-order, or the ability of one sprite to consistently appear above or in front of another sprite. This requires the sprites to be updated in a specific order. Both of these issues are taken care of by the *SceneDirector* and *Player* combination.

THEATRIX UTILITIES

This chapter describes the utility programs that accompany and support the Theatrix C++ class library. You will learn about these subjects:

- Graphics file libraries
- Sound effects
- Palette utilities
- Miscellaneous utilities

Managing Graphics File Libraries

GFX libraries are files that contain one or more bitmaps. Except for the background images, every image in a game must be part of a GFX library. Memory permitting, Theatrix games can load as many as 30 GFX libraries, and each library can contain as many as 100 bitmaps.

GFXMAKE

Graphics bitmaps are supplied to GFXMAKE in the form of **.BMP** files. There are two ways to use GFXMAKE: The file names can be included on the command line, or a *list file* can be supplied that contains a list of the **.BMP** files to be included.

Let's say that we are going to write a game in which a character moves around the screen in four directions. We'll need four bitmaps of our character: one with the character moving up, one moving down, one moving left, and one moving right. The construction of the images is up to you. Whatever your source is, you need to produce each image in the **.BMP** format. Almost any format can be converted to the **.BMP** format using Image Alchemy. See Appendix A for more information on Image Alchemy.

Once you have the four **.BMP** files of the character moving in four directions, place the four images in the same directory. Then, in that same directory, execute this command:

```
GFXMAKE test.gfx up.bmp down.bmp left.bmp right.bmp
```

Make sure that GFXMAKE is in the command path. If all goes well (and you've named your **.BMP** files **up.bmp**, **down.bmp**, and so on), GFXMAKE will create a **.GFX** file called **TEST.GFX**, which contains four images. Then, in your game, in a *Performer*-derived *initialize* member, include this line:

```
MyPerformer::initialize()
{
    // ...
    load_gfxlib( "test.gfx" );
    // ...
}
```

Now your *Performer* will be able to use the *show_image* member:

```
show_image( x, y, 1 );
```

This line will display the first image (**up.bmp**) of the **test.gfx** file with its upper-left corner located at x/y. Likewise, using *2* as the last parameter will display the second image, and so on.

Managing Sound Effects

Theatrix uses sound effects in the Windows **.WAV** format. The name and order of the **.WAV** files are given to Theatrix in a text file. The text file and the **.WAV** files should be in the directory where the game will be launched. In the program, the list can be loaded by *VocalHand*-derived classes using the *load_list* member function.

```
void MyVocalHand::initialize()
{
    // ...
    load_list( "sounds.txt" );
    // ...
}
```

In a callback in that same class, you can play any of the sounds in the list by using this command:

```
play_sound_clip( clip_number );
```

The parameter is an integer that specifies which sound clip to play. The sound clips are numbered starting at 1.

Palette Management Utilities

Theatrix provides a suite of palette management utilities that allow you to display any number of images simultaneously even if the images use different palettes. Because these utilities allow the process of palette management to be virtually automated, it isn't necessary to understand every detail of palette theory or of the Windows palette manager. We will go over the basics.

Every **.BMP** file includes a palette, which is a list of colors. There are usually 256 colors in the palette (for 256-color **.BMP** files, which are the only type the utilities handle). The **.BMP** file also includes an array of bytes that represents the actual image. Each byte is an index into the palette. The color indicated by this index is used in the image at that particular location.

Each **.BMP** file often has a different palette. This is especially true with ray-traced images. In order for multiple **.BMP** files to be displayed in the same window, each must use exactly the same palette.

To further complicate matters, Windows does not allow applications to install palettes directly. The Windows palette manager oversees each palette request and often compromises a palette to reduce the number of installed colors. The palette manager also reserves 20 system colors, so only 236 colors of any given palette are likely to get installed.

Briefly, the Theatrix palette utilities are as follows:

- GETPAL extracts the palette portion of a **.BMP** file.
- GENPAL creates new palettes by merging old ones.
- CVTPAL installs new palettes into **.BMP** files.

Each of these utilities deals with palette files, which have a **.PAL** extension.[1] These utilities are described in detail shortly, but first let's outline the procedure for preparing a set of **.BMP** files for use in Theatrix:

1. Produce all the **.BMP** images that will appear on the same screen. Usually, this means a background and several sprites. If the sprites have multiple frames, or poses, those files must also be included.

2. Extract the palette from each **.BMP** file using GETPAL. If there are more than 10 files or so, select samples from the total collection. The samples should include the background and at least one pose from each sprite. Large images and images with unusual or striking color make good choices.

3. Create a master palette with GENPAL, using the extracted palettes as input. It may take several tries using different settings to produce a palette of the right size. Any output from GENPAL can be used, but, if the output palette contains more than 236 colors, the remaining colors are ignored. It is better to produce a palette with slightly fewer than 236 colors. The master palette is saved as **NEW.PAL**.

4. Using CVTPAL, convert all the files (including those that were not used as samples) to use **NEW.PAL**.

---

[1]The .PAL files are regular ASCII files and can be viewed and edited with any text editor, such as Windows Notepad.

Now all that remains to be done is to produce **.GFX** files with your new sprite images. When the background image is displayed, its palette is installed automatically by Theatrix. Because the background and the sprites now share the same palette, all of them will appear correctly.

The palette utilities are discussed in more detail next.

GETPAL

GETPAL extracts palettes from **.BMP** files. The resulting **.PAL** file can be used with GENPAL and CVTPAL. GETPAL is used this way:

```
GETPAL picture1.bmp
```

This command causes GETPAL to create a palette file called **picture1.pal**. By default, GETPAL names the output file after the input file. A name can be supplied for the output file:

```
GETPAL picture1.bmp pal1.pal
```

If file extensions are not supplied, GETPAL assumes the typical extensions.

GENPAL

GENPAL merges multiple palettes and produces a master palette. The command looks like this:

```
GENPAL 0 first.pal second.pal third.pal ...
```

The first parameter (zero in the example) is the tolerance level. Zero means that GENPAL will omit only exact color matches. Increasing this number means that more colors will be omitted and that a smaller palette will be produced. This setting should be used to create palettes with as close to 236 colors as possible.

Each specified palette is used to create the new palette. The palettes should be named in order of priority, the most important ones appearing first. The new palette is saved as **new.pal**.

CVTPAL

CVTPAL installs palettes into **.BMP** files. CVTPAL performs two steps: It replaces the existing palette, and it adjusts the image to match the new palette. CVTPAL adjusts the image as much as possible, but if the new and old palettes are radically different, the image quality will decay. CVTPAL is used like this:

```
CVTPAL picture1.bmp pal1.pal
```

This command causes CVTPAL to replace the existing palette in **picture1.bmp** with the palette in **pal1.pal**.

Miscellaneous Utilities

There are two remaining Theatrix utilities. These tools are useful but are not necessary to use Theatrix.

PASTE

PASTE creates images by pasting or merging two images together. PASTE is useful for laying text or lettering over a complex background. PASTE allows you to prepare a separate image, containing only the text, and paste the text over the background image. If you decide to change the text color or move the text, you make the change in the text image and rerun PASTE. PASTE copies anything that is not color 0 (usually black). The two input images must have the same dimensions. The command looks like this:

```
PASTE scene.bmp text.bmp
```

The first file is treated as the background, and the second file is pasted onto the first. This command produces a file named **OUT.BMP** unless a third parameter is supplied. The output image uses the palette from the background image.

REGION

REGION extracts image portions. For example:

```
REGION big.bmp small.bmp 100 100 199 199
```

This command extracts a region of **big.bmp** and saves it as **small.bmp**. The upper-left corner of the extracted region is located at 100/100, and the lower-right region is at 199/199.

EXAMPLE GAME PROGRAMS

Chapter 6 discusses the levels of abstraction at which you can work and explains the Theatrix class library hierarchy. This chapter completes that discussion by describing the demo game programs at each level of abstraction. You'll also learn how to implement different game features and styles.

Each program covered here teaches a lesson, and our discussions concentrate on what is unique about the lessons and the concepts the lessons introduce. You will learn about:

- Instantiating and running games
- Using the mouse
- Sound effect
- Video clips
- Sprite animation
- Skeleton
- Music
- Menus and help screens
- Multiple-player games
- Games with many sprites
- Background scrolling

Skeleton

We start with the simple Skeleton demo because it is an ideal starting place for a Theatrix game. The Skeleton demo includes essential game components such as an application class, a *Director* class, and a *Hand* class. The Skeleton demo is written at the first, and lowest level of abstraction. It does not include animation, sound, or music.

The SkeletonApp Class

The *Theatrix* class represents the whole game. Each game has one and only one *Theatrix*-derived class, and it contains all the Directors in the game. Here is the *SkeletonApp* class:

```
class SkeletonApp : public Theatrix
{
public:
      SkeletonApp(HINSTANCE h,int s) : Theatrix("Skeleton",h,s)
      {
            demo=new SkeletonDirector;
      }
      ~SkeletonApp()
      {
            delete demo;
      }
private:
      SkeletonDirector* demo;
};
```

When a *SkeletonApp* object is instantiated, it passes a string to the *Theatrix* constructor. This string appears on the window border. The other two parameters are passed to *WinMain* by Windows, are used to construct the *Theatrix* class. The *SkeletonApp* constructor creates an instance of *SkeletonDirector*. The destructor deletes the *SkeletonDirector* object.

The SkeletonDirector Class

The *SkeletonDirector* class is derived from *VideoDirector*, which means that *SkeletonDirector* inherits the abilitiy to perform screen updates and coordinate animation sequences. The following code shows the *SkeletonDirector* class:

```
class SkeletonDirector : public VideoDirector
{
public:
    SkeletonDirector()
    {
        myhand=new SkeletonHand(this);
    }
    ~SkeletonDirector()
    {
        delete myhand;
    }
    void display();
    void on_timer();
    DECLARE_CUELIST
private:
    SkeletonHand* myhand;
};
```

The *SkeletonDirector* constructor creates a *SkeletonHand* object, and the destructor deletes the object. We'll discuss the *SkeletonHand* class soon. The *SkeletonDirector* class has two member functions. The *display* function overrides the virtual *Director::display* member function, and is called by Theatrix whenever the *Director* becomes active. The *on_timer* member function is a callback that is called periodically. The DECLARE_CUELIST statement tells the compiler that a CUELIST table accompanies this class.

The *display* member is defined like this:

```
void SkeletonDirector::display()
{
    init_video();
    show_bmp("plain.bmp");
    blt_window();
    fill_background_buffer();
}
```

All four of the functions called are inherited from *VideoDirector*. The *init_video* function resets the window contents. The *show_bmp* function loads **plain.bmp** into the display buffer but does not display the image. The image becomes visible after *blt_window* is called. The *fill_background_buffer* function copies the contents of the display buffer to a background buffer.

The *on_timer* callback function looks like this:

```
void SkeletonDirector::on_timer()
{
        TRACE("timer tick...\n");
}
```

The callback displays a message indicating that the callback has been executed. Theatrix is instructed to call the *on_timer* function with the CUELIST macro:

```
CUELIST(SkeletonDirector)
        TIMER(1,on_timer)
ENDCUELIST
```

The first parameter is the number of times per second that the callback will be called. The second parameter is the name of the callback that will handle the cue.

The SkeletonHand Class

The *SkeletonHand* class is derived from *Hand*. *SkeletonHand* looks like this:

```
class SkeletonHand : public Hand
{
public:
        SkeletonHand(Director* p) : Hand(p)  { }
        void on_key(int k)
        {
                if (k==VK_ESCAPE)
```

```
                stop_director();
        else
                TRACE("space bar was pressed...\n");
        }
        DECLARE_CUELIST
    };
```

The class constructor takes a *Director* pointer as a parameter. This parameter is passed to *Hand*. *SkeletonHand* contains one callback, the *on_key* member function. The *on_key* function is responsible for handling two cases because of the way that *SkeletonHand's* CUELIST macros are written:

```
CUELIST(SkeletonHand)
        KEYSTROKE(VK_ESCAPE, on_key)
        KEYSTROKE(VK_SPACE, on_key)
ENDCUELIST
```

Because the *on_key* function is named for both the **Esc** key and the **Spacebar**, a test must be performed when the function is called. Another approach is to use separate callbacks for each key.

The main Function

The Skeleton program's *WinMain* function looks like this:

```
int PASCAL WinMain(HINSTANCE hInstance,HINSTANCE,LPSTR,int show)
{
        SkeletonApp* demo=new SkeletonApp(hInstance,show);
        demo->go();
        delete demo;
        return 0;
}
```

The *main* function creates an instance of the *SkeletonApp* class. Then the program calls the *Theatrix::go* member function and starts the game. When *go* returns, the game is over, and the *SkeletonApp* object is deleted.

Running the Skeleton Demo

The Skeleton game's only actions are to display a background and print some messages in the debug window. Figure 8.1 shows the Skeleton demo running.

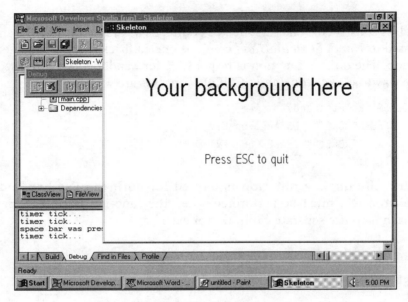

Figure 8.1 The Skeleton demo

When Skeleton is executed in the Visual C++ debugger, you see the "timer tick..." message displayed in the output window once every second. The message is displayed as the result of the timer cue that is delivered once per second. Now press the **Spacebar**. A new message appears, indicating that the **Spacebar** was pressed. To exit the program, press **Esc** at any time.

Planet

The Planet demo displays a small moon bouncing around in front of a large planet. The file **planet.bmp** contains an image of the background scene, which depicts the planet. The file **sphere.bmp** contains an image of the sprite.

The game achieves this bouncing effect by doing the following:

1. It draws the moon on top of the image in the display buffer.
2. It copies the display buffer to the window so that the newly constructed image becomes visible.
3. It erases the sprite in the display buffer by restoring the original portion of the image.
4. It repeats these steps until the **Esc** key is pressed.

The DemoDirector Class

The *DemoDirector* class displays the background, creates and updates the moon, and ends the demo when the user presses **Esc**:

```
class DemoDirector : public VideoDirector
{
public:
        DemoDirector();
        ~DemoDirector();
private:
        void display();
        void on_timer();
        void on_esc(int);
private:
        Sprite* moon;
        int x,y;
        int xinc,yinc;
        DECLARE_CUELIST
};
```

DemoDirector has two callback functions: *on_timer* and *on_esc*. The *display* member is not a callback; it overrides a *virtual* member function of the base *Director* class. Theatrix calls *display* each time when the *Director* object takes control of the game, so this is where we write our code to display the background.

The *DemoDirector* constructor is shown next:

```
DemoDirector::DemoDirector()
{
        moon=new Sprite("demo.gfx","sounds.txt");
        x=y=20;
        xinc=yinc=INC;
}
```

The first line creates an object of a class called *Sprite*, which we will look at soon. The *Sprite* object is the moon that moves over the background. Note that the *Sprite* constructor takes two parameters. One is the **.GFX** library that contains the moon's bitmap image to display on the screen, and the other parameter is the sound list, which contains one sound clip. (The moon makes a noise when it changes direction.)

The next two lines in the *DemoDirector* constructor initialize some integer data members. The moon's location starts at screen position 20,20. The *xinc* and *yinc* members are initialized with the constant INC, which the program defines as the value 4. These variables are used to increment the moon's position on each update.

DemoDirector first displays the background on the screen from its overridden *display* member function. *DemoDirector::display* is shown here:

```
void DemoDirector::display()
{
        init_video();
        show_bmp("planet.bmp");
        blt_window();
        fill_background_buffer();
}
```

This seems like a lot of code just to display a background, so let's consider what has happened. The *init_video* member function clears the window and resets VideoDirector's buffers. The *show_bmp* function loads **planet.bmp** into the display buffer. The *blt_window* function copies the display buffer to the client area of the window, which makes the image visible. The *fill_background_buffer* copies the contents of the display buffer to the background buffer.

The *DemoDirector* class needs a CUELIST table:

```
CUELIST(DemoDirector)
     TIMER(18,on_timer)
     KEYSTROKE(ESC,on_esc)
ENDCUELIST
```

The TIMER statement in the CUELIST table tells Theatrix to call our *on_timer* callback 18 times a second. The KEYSTROKE macro causes Theatrix to call our *on_esc* function whenever the user presses **Esc**. Here is the *on_esc* function:

```
void DemoDirector::on_esc(int)
{
     stop_director();
}
```

The *stop_director* function instructs the *Director* to give up control.

The *on_timer* function looks like this:

```
void DemoDirector::on_timer()
{
     moon->move_to(x,y);
     blt_window();

     x+=xinc;
     y+=yinc;
     if (x<0 || x>320-moon->getw())
     {
          xinc=-xinc;
          x+=xinc;
          moon->bounce();
     }
     if (y<0 || y>240-moon->geth())
     {
          yinc=-yinc;
          y+=yinc;
          moon->bounce();
     }
}
```

The first line tells the moon to move to a new location. Once the moon has displayed itself, the display buffer contents are copied to the window with the *blt_window* function.

The *if* statements after *blt_window* reverse the moon's direction when it gets too close to the edge of the screen. When the moon's direction changes, the *Sprite::bounce* member is called to play a sound effect.

The Sprite Class

The *Sprite* class declaration looks like this:

```
class Sprite : public Performer
{
public:
      Sprite(char* gfxlib,char* soundlist);
      void initialize();
      void move_to(int x,int y);
      void bounce();
      int getw()  { return w; }
      int geth()  { return h; }
private:
      char gfxlib[13];
      char soundlist[13];
      int image;
      int w,h;
      int x,y;
};
```

The *Sprite* constructor initializes the object's data members:

```
Sprite::Sprite(char* gfxlibname,char* soundlistname)
{
      strcpy(gfxlib,gfxlibname);
      strcpy(soundlist,soundlistname);
      image=IMAGENO;
}
```

When the game starts, the sprite must load resources such as **.GFX** libraries, sound lists, and music lists. Each *Hand* has a virtual member function called *initialize* that is called when the game program is starting. The *initialize* function is where resources are loaded. The *Sprite::initialize* member is shown next:

```
void Sprite::initialize()
{
        load_gfxlib(gfxlib);
        load_sounds(soundlist);
        w=get_image_width(image);
        h=get_image_height(image);
        x=y=0;
}
```

The *initialize* function loads its libraries and calls two *VideoDirector* member functions to get the height and width of the image. It sets its initial screen position to 0/0.

The *Sprite::move_to* function changes the moon's position at each tick of the timer. The function is defined this way:

```
void Sprite::move_to(int newx,int newy)
{
        VideoDirector::restore_patch(x,y,x+w-1,y+h-1);
        show_image(newx,newy,image);
        x=newx;
        y=newy;
}
```

The first line of *Sprite::move_to* erases its old image. The *VideoDirector::restore_patch* function copies rectangular patches from the background buffer to the display buffer. (Remember that we filled the background buffer with a copy of the background image.) After the old image is erased, the new image is drawn at the new location with a call to *Performer::show_image*. Before the function returns, the *x* and *y* data members are updated.

The PlanetDemo Class

The *PlanetDemo* class is derived from the *Theatrix* class to implement and run the game:

```
class PlanetDemo : public Theatrix
{
public:
        PlanetDemo(HINSTANCE h,int s) : Theatrix("Planet",h,s)
        {
                demo=new DemoDirector;
        }
        ~PlanetDemo()
        {
                delete demo;
        }
private:
        DemoDirector* demo;
};
```

The *PlanetDemo* constructor instantiates a *DemoDirector* object from the free store. The destructor deletes that object.

The WinMain Function

The *WinMain* function instantiates an object of type *PlanetDemo* and calls its *Theatrix::go* function. When the *go* function returns, the *PlanetDemo* object is deleted and the application terminates.

```
int PASCAL WinMain(HINSTANCE hInstance,HINSTANCE,LPSTR,int show)
{
        PlanetDemo* demo=new PlanetDemo(hInstance,show);
        demo->go();
        delete demo;
        return 0;
}
```

Figure 8.2 is a screen shot taken from the Planet demo game. The graphics were rendered with POV-Ray, and the data files are in the **\Theatrix\demos\planet** directory along with the code.

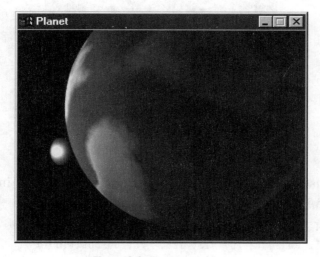

Figure 8.2 The Planet demo

Tic-Tac-Toe

The Tic-Tac-Toe demo game is a typical board game. It demonstrates the use of the *Performer* class as a base from which to derive non-animated sprites. The game also adds sound effects. Each move is punctuated by a silly spoken message from the game to the player. Figure 8.3 shows the board with a game under way.

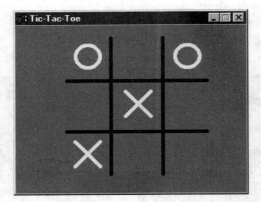

Figure 8.3 The Tic-Tac-Toe board

The game uses a CURSORLIST table to divide the board into its nine segments, as shown here:

```
CURSORLIST(TicTacToe)
    MOUSE_CURSOR(  70,  18, 128,  75, 0, position1)
    MOUSE_CURSOR( 136,  18, 200,  75, 0, position2)
    MOUSE_CURSOR( 208,  18, 266,  75, 0, position3)
    MOUSE_CURSOR(  70,  82, 128, 146, 0, position4)
    MOUSE_CURSOR( 136,  82, 200, 146, 0, position5)
    MOUSE_CURSOR( 208,  82, 266, 146, 0, position6)
    MOUSE_CURSOR(  70, 154, 128, 210, 0, position7)
    MOUSE_CURSOR( 136, 154, 200, 210, 0, position8)
    MOUSE_CURSOR( 208, 154, 266, 210, 0, position9)
ENDCURSORLIST
```

The game player makes the first move by clicking on one of the segments. Each time the player makes a move, the game posts that move and calculates its own next move.

Sound Clips

Before making a move, the game speaks a phrase. The contents of the phrase depend on whether the game is making a winning move, blocking the player's winning move, or simply getting the next available space. Here is how the game identifies the different phrases:

```
enum soundclip
{
        iwin = 1,
        youwin,
        tie,
        notthere,
        hmm,
        ohno,
        nowwhat
};
```

A Voice Class

The game uses a *Voice* class to encapsulate the sound effects:

```
class Voice : public VocalHand
{
        void initialize()
                { load_sounds("sounds.txt"); }
public:
        Voice(Director *dir) : VocalHand(dir)
                { }
};
```

The **sounds.txt** file contains a lists of **.WAV** files:

```
iwin.wav
youwin.wav
tie.wav
notthere.wav
hmm.wav
ohno.wav
nowwhat.wav
```

Playing Sound Clips

The game instantiates an object of this class and uses the object to speak the phrases in **sounds.txt**, as shown here:

```
void TicTacToe::say(soundclip clip)
{
        voice->play_sound_clip(clip);
        while (voice->sound_clip_is_playing())
                ;
}
```

Skater

The Skater demo program illustrates sprite animation at the fifth and highest level of abstraction. The Skater demo also uses music and sound effects. You learned from the discussion of Tic-Tac-Toe how to add sound effects to a game. Now we'll discuss how to add music.

The Skater demo is found on the included CD-ROM in the **\THEATRIX\DEMOS\SKATER** directory. The demo involves a skating pond with three skaters. Actually, only one of the skaters is skating; the other two remain standing. The skater is doing a figure eight around both of the standers. The demo illustrates the use of *Player* and *SceneDirector* and is also an example of how to manage the Z-order of sprites. The skater, in the course of his figure eight, skates at one point behind the far stander, then, at the center of the eight, between the two standers, and, finally, in front of the near stander. This pattern is made possible by changing the skater's Z-order relative to the two standing sprites.

The Pond Class

First, a class named *Pond* is derived from *SceneDirector*:

```
class Pond : public SceneDirector
{
        Stander *stander1;
        Stander *stander2;
        Skater *skater;
        MusicHand *conductor;
        void on_timer();
        void on_enter(int);
        void display();
        void hide();
public:
        Pond();
        ~Pond();
};
```

Let's look first at the constructor:

```
Pond::Pond() : SceneDirector("pond.bmp")
{
        // --- most distant stationary sprite
        stander1 = new Stander;
        stander1->set_imageno(10);
        stander1->setxy(180,100);
        stander1->appear();
        // --- closest stationary sprite
        stander2 = new Stander;
        stander2->set_imageno(9);
        stander2->setxy(140,130);
        stander2->appear();
        // --- moving sprite
        skater = new Skater;
        conductor = new MusicHand("music.txt");
}
```

In addition to creating two *Stander* objects and one *Skater* object, the constructor gives instructions to the *Stander* objects. The *set_imageno* member function tells the *Stander* which image to use to draw itself. The *setxy* member tells the *Stander* where to stand. Finally, the *appear* member tells the *Stander* that it is visible. *Stander* is derived from *Player*; these member functions are defined in *Player*.

The *Pond* destructor (which is not shown) deletes the three objects created in the constructor. The *on_timer* callback function implements most of the *Pond* class's functionality:

```
void Pond::on_timer()
{
    if (skater->mode < 9 && conductor->isconducting() &&
            !conductor->music_clip_is_playing())   {
        skater->on_enter(ENTER);
        return;
    }
    SceneDirector::on_timer();
    if (skater->steps == 0)      {
        switch (skater->mode) {
            case 1:
                // -- front lateral segment
                //    set moving sprite in front of others
                MoveZToFront(skater);
                break;
            case 3:
            case 7:
                // -- center lateral segment
                //    set moving sprite between other two
                ChangeZOrder(skater,stander2);
                break;
            case 5:
                // -- rear lateral segment
                //    set moving sprite behind others
                ChangeZOrder(skater,stander1);
```

```
                                  break;
                                  default:
                                  break;
                          }
                  }
          }
```

Here is how the Z-order is maintained during the figure eight. Each mode of *Skater* represents a segment of the figure eight. Each section in the *switch* statement handles a different segment. For some segments (mode 2, for example), no change in Z-order is needed, but others require that the skater's Z-order change, and this is done with calls to the *SceneDirector::changeZOrder* member function.

The first thing that the *Pond::on_timer* callback does is to call *SceneDirector::on_timer*. This *Pond::on_timer* member function overrides *SceneDirector::on_timer*, which needs to execute, so the overriding function calls the overridden function. Because *SceneDirector::on_timer* is responsible for updating the *Player* objects, forgetting to call it produces unwanted results.

The Skater Class

Now let's examine the *Skater* class:

```
class Skater : public Player
{
        short int steps;      // number of steps taken current segment
        short int mode;       // 1-8 = skating pattern #; 11-13 = splash
        friend class Pond;
        void on_enter(int);
protected:
        DECLARE_CUELIST
public:
        Skater();
        virtual ~Skater() { }
        void update_position();
};
```

A callback function named *on_enter* is defined, and because the callback is to be connected to the **Enter** key cue via the CUELIST macros, the DECLARE_CUELIST statement is required. A member function called *update_position* overrides *Player::update_position*, which is called by *SceneDirector* for each frame interval. *Player::update_position* gives the *Player* an opportunity to change its location and image.

The *steps* data member keeps track of how far along in a segment the skater is. It is incremented by *update_position* at each frame interval until it has reached the length of the segment the skater is currently on, whereupon a new segment starts. The *mode* member indicates which segment the skater is on.

The Skater constructor looks like this:

```
Skater::Skater() : Player("skater.gfx", "sounds.txt")
{
    setxy(90,145);  // initial position on pond
    set_imageno(1); // first skater frame
    appear();
    steps = 0;
    mode = 1;
}
```

The *Skater* constructor passes two file names to the *Player* constructor. This is because *Player* loads the **.GFX** libraries and sound lists for you.

Player updates the screen automatically. The *Skater* class decides where its sprite should be and what it should look like, and the *Player* class takes care of displaying it.

The *setxy* member function tells *Player* where to draw itself (when the time comes). We saw this member when *Pond* was creating the *Stander* objects. The *set_imageno* function tells *Player* which bitmap image in the **.GFX** library to use to draw the skater. The *appear* function tells the *Skater* that it is visible. Finally, the *steps* and *mode* data members are initialized.

The *update_position* member function, shown in Listing 10.1, is where all the action occurs. The skater's location is calculated here, depending on the values of *mode* and *steps*.

Listing 10.1 The update_position Member Function

```
void Skater::update_position()
{
    switch (mode)
    {
        case 1:
        case 3:
        case 5:
        case 7:
            // --- side to side movement
            if (++steps == sidesteps) {
                steps = 0;
                set_imageno(++mode);
                break;
            }
            if (mode & 2) // modes 3 and 7: to the left
                setx(getx() - sstepincr);
            else          // modes 1 and 5: to the right
                setx(getx() + sstepincr);
            break;
        case 2:
        case 4:
        case 6:
        case 8:
            // --- front or back movement
            if (++steps == fwdsteps)
            {
                steps = 0;
                if (mode == 8)
                    mode = 0;
                set_imageno(++mode);
                break;
```

```
            }
            if (mode < 6)  // modes 2 and 4: away from the screen
                    sety(gety() - fstepincr);
            else               // modes 6 and 8: toward the screen
                    sety(gety() + fstepincr);
            break;
        case 9:
            setinterval(3);  // slow down refresh rate
            set_imageno(13); // 1st frame of ice-breaking splash
            mode++;
            play_sound_clip(1);
            break;
        case 10:
            set_imageno(12); // 2nd frame of ice-breaking splash
            mode++;
            break;
        case 11:
            set_imageno(13); // 3rd frame of ice-breaking splash
            mode++;
            break;
        case 12:
            set_imageno(11); // hole in ice
            mode++;
            steps = 0;
            break;
        default:
            if (steps++ == 30)
                    stop_director();
            break;
        }
    }
```

The figure eight is broken into eight modes. The odd-numbered modes represent the left/right segments of the squared figure eight, and the even-numbered modes represent the far/near segments. When the user presses **Enter** (we'll look at that callback next), the mode is set to 9, which initiates a sequence in which the skater falls through the ice. The cases near the end of the function handle this sequence.

Now let's look at the *OnEnter* callback function:

```
void Skater::on_enter(int)
{
    if (mode < 9)        {
        int yp = 35;
        if (mode == 3 || mode == 7)
            yp = 25;
        else if (mode > 3 && mode < 7)
            yp = 15;
        setxy(getx()-10, gety() + yp);
        mode = 9;
    }
}
```

First, the mode is checked. If it is less than 9, we know that the figure eight is still in progress. If it is, a test determines where the splash sequence should be drawn. Finally, the mode is set to 9, which initiates the splash sequence.

The SkaterDemo Class

The *SkaterDemo* class derives from the base *Theatrix* class and is the vehicle with which the program initializes and runs the game:

```
class SkaterDemo : public Theatrix  {
    Pond* pond;
public:
    SkaterDemo(HINSTANCE h,int s) : Theatrix("Skater",h,s)
        { pond=new Pond; }
    ~SkaterDemo()
        { delete pond; }
};
```

The WinMain Function

The *WinMain* function looks like this:

```
int PASCAL WinMain(HINSTANCE hInstance,HINSTANCE,LPSTR,int show)
{
        SkaterDemo demo(hInstance,show);
        demo.go();
        return 0;
}
```

Unlike many of the other demo games, this one's graphical elements—the *Player* objects—deal only with what should be drawn and where. The previous demo (the Planet demo) had to deal with not only what should be drawn and where but also how large the image was and where on the last video page the sprite appeared. Although Performers and VideoDirectors are powerful, you will probably use Players and SceneDirectors more often because they encapsulate more of the details of animation than do the classes at the lower levels of abstraction.

The MusicHand Object

The Skater program's *Pond* class has a pointer to a *MusicHand* object. The constructor initializes that pointer:

```
class Pond : public SceneDirector
{
        Stander *stander1;
        Stander *stander2;
        Skater *skater;
        MusicHand *conductor;
        void on_timer();
        void on_enter(int);
        void display();
        void hide();
public:
        Pond();
        ~Pond();
};
```

```
Pond::Pond() : SceneDirector("pond.bmp")
{
    // ...
    conductor = new MusicHand("music.txt");
}
```

Building the Music List

The file named **music.txt** is a text file that contains a list of the MIDI (.MID) files you wish to play during your game. The music.txt file for the Skater demo has only one entry, but each music list can have as many as 20 entries.

```
skater.mid
```

Playing a Music Clip

The Skater game plays one music clip from the beginning of the game until the player ends the game or until the music clip completes. The game starts playing the music clip by overloading the *Director::display* function:

```
void Pond::display()
{
    SceneDirector::display();
    conductor->play_music_clip(1);
}
```

Stopping a Music Clip

If the music is still playing when the player stops the program (by pressing **Enter** or **Esc**), the overloaded *hide* function stops the music clip:

```
void Pond::hide()
{
    conductor->stop_music_clip();
    SceneDirector::hide();
}
```

You can stop a music clip at any time in a game by calling the *stop_music_clip* function. If no music clip is playing, there is no effect.

Testing for Music Playing

At every timer interval, the *on_timer* function tests to see whether the skater sprite is still skating and whether the music clip was started and has now completed. If all these conditions are true, the program calls the *on_enter* function to stop the program.

The *on_enter* function is the callback that runs when the user presses **Enter**. This function causes the skater sprite to crash through the ice and then terminates the program. By calling this function when the music stops playing, the program crashes the sprite through the ice at that time:

```
void Pond::on_timer()
{
    if (skater->mode < 9 && conductor->isconducting() &&
            !conductor->music_clip_is_playing())
    {
        skater->on_enter(ENTER);
        return;
    }
    SceneDirector::on_timer();
    // ...
}
```

The *isconducting* function returns true if the game program was able to load and initialize the music driver at the start of the program. The *music_clip_is_playing* function returns true if a music clip is currently being played.

Terminating the Music Driver

When the game is over, the *Pond* destructor deletes the *MusicHand* object, which frees the memory where the object loaded the **.XMI** library:

```
Pond::~Pond()
{
    delete conductor;
    // ...
}
```

You can instantiate and delete *MusicHand* objects during the course of the game. Only one such object should be instantiated at any one time.

Marble Fighter

The Marble Fighter game pits two players in a kick-boxing match. Both players can be humans playing at different PCs, or one player can play against the computer. Marble Fighter is the first of our games that uses an intro screen, a help screen, and a menu in addition to the action part of the game.

Intro and Help Screens

An intro screen is a static, full-screen image that the game displays when the program starts. A help screen is a static, full-screen image that the game displays when the player requests help, usually from the menu. Theatrix games implement these screens by assigning them to directors.

Marble Fighter implements its help and intro screens by using identical constructs. We'll discuss the intro screen here, and you can apply the same principles to the help screen. This code shows the game's *IntroPage* class, which implements an intro screen by deriving from *SceneryDirector*:

```
class IntroPage : public SceneryDirector
{
public:
    IntroPage() : SceneryDirector("intro.bmp") { }
    const type_info& get_next_director() { return typeid(Menu); }
};
```

The game instantiates an object of type *IntroPage* and, by instantiating it as the first director, arranges for that object to be the first director to get control.

Figure 8.4 shows Marble Fighter's intro screen.

Figure 8.4 Marble Fighter's intro screen

Figure 8.5 shows Marble Fighter's help screen.

Figure 8.5 Marble Fighter's help screen

Later you will see how *SceneryDirector* is used as a base class for an animation class called *SceneDirector*.

Menus

Most games have menus, but seldom does a game have a menu that looks like the menus of other games. This is the way it should be. Marble Fighter uses a tombstone for a menu. Other games, discussed soon, use other kinds of menus. Theatris uses spinning cubes. Shootout uses a bullet as a menu pointer.

Marble Fighter's *Menu* class is derived from *VideoDirector*. A **.BMP** file of the tombstone is displayed in the *Menu::display* routine. The *Menu* class has callbacks for the **Up**, **Down**, and **Enter** keys. The **Up** and **Down** keys change the image being displayed and make a sound. The **Enter** key stops the director, because a menu selection has been made and the menu no longer needs to be in control. The *Menu* class is shown here:

```
class Menu : public VideoDirector
{
public:
      Menu();
      ~Menu();
      const type_info& get_next_director();
      void initialize();
      void display();
      void on_up(int);
      void on_down(int);
      void on_enter(int);
      void on_escape(int);
      void on_fight(int);
      void on_help(int);
      void on_quit(int);
protected:
      DECLARE_CUELIST
private:
      int cur;
      MenuItem* item[ITEMS+1];
};
```

The *Menu* constructor assigns the *item* array with *MenuItem* objects:

```
Menu::Menu() : VideoDirector()
{
        item[1]=new MenuItem(this,PLAY);
        item[2]=new MenuItem(this,HELP);
        item[3]=new MenuItem(this,QUIT);
}
```

The *item* array is declared with a size of ITEMS+1 because we are not using the element item[0]. The *Menu::display* member function looks like this:

```
void Menu::display()
{
        init_video();
        show_bmp("menu.bmp");
        if (cur!=PLAY)
                item[cur]->display();
        blt_window();
}
```

In addition to displaying the actual background, the menu displays a specific item if the current item is not equal to the value PLAY. The **.BMP** file has been prepared with PLAY selected, so, if *cur* is equal to PLAY, then the menu is already correct. Otherwise, the correct menu option is displayed on top of the background scene.

Most of the member functions in the *Menu* class are callbacks. Here is *on_up*, the callback for the **Up** arrow keystroke:

```
void Menu::on_up(int)
{
        if (cur>PLAY)
                cur--;
        else
                cur=ITEMS;
        item[cur]->display();
        item[cur]->play_switch_sound();
        blt_window();
}
```

The function decrements the *cur* integer, making sure that if *cur* is as high as it can go, the lowest selection is chosen. The *display* call tells the new current selection to display itself. Then a sound is played. In this menu, each selection makes the same sound, but you could have each selection make a different sound. The call to *blt_window* displays the newly constructed image.

Most of the other callbacks in the *Menu* class look just like the *on_up* callback. Notice that callbacks such as *on_help* are used when the user presses a shortcut key. In the case of *on_help*, if the user presses the **H** key, the menu jumps directly to the help option. Here is the *on_help* function:

```
void Menu::on_help(int)
{
      if (cur!=HELP)
      {
            cur=HELP;
            item[cur]->display();
            item[cur]->play_switch_sound();
            blt_window();
      }
}
```

The callback forces the option to the HELP setting, unless it is already there. Now let's examine how the menu communicates with the rest of the program. First, if the user presses **Enter**, the current item is selected. The *on_enter* callback function is shown next:

```
void Menu::on_enter(int)
{
      stop_director();
}
```

Pressing the **Enter** key stops the *Menu* director object.

Whenever a director gives up control (when its *stop_director* member is called), Theatrix determines which director to put in charge next. If no director can be found to take over, the application exits. Theatrix determines which director is next by calling the current director's *get_next_director* member. The *Menu* class's *get_next_director* function looks like this:

```
const type_info& Menu::get_next_director()
{
    if (cur==PLAY)
            return typeid(Match);
    if (cur==HELP)
            return typeid(HelpPage);
    return typeid(TrailerPage);
}
```

The *cur* variable was set as the user made selections while viewing the menu screen. If *cur* is equal to PLAY, the *Match* director is next, and its *typeid* is returned. (In Marble Fighter, the game object is of type *Match*.) Likewise, if HELP is the current option, the *HelpPage* director takes over. If neither is true (if QUIT was selected), then *get_next_director* returns the typeid of the final scene (TrailerPage).

Figure 8.6 shows the Marble Fighter menu display.

Figure 8.6 The Marble Fighter menu

The Fight

The action of the Marble Fighter game is controlled by the *Match* class, which is derived from *VideoDirector*. The class instantiates two fighter objects of classes derived from the base *Fighter* class and lets them fight. *Fighter* is derived from *Performer*. In the single-player mode, one of the fighters is the computer itself. The fighter objects can kick, punch, and block. A fighter knows when it has hit its opponent. The fighters use sound effects for hits, groans, and shrieks. Each hit or kick is a score, and the first player to reach the highest possible score is the winner. The game records the scoring in video slider bars that are displayed above the fighters. Figure 8.7 shows a fight in progress.

Figure 8.7 A Marble fight

When you start the Marble Fighter game in single-player mode, You can choose to be the left or right player by including the word "left" or "right" on the command line.

Network Play

Marble Fighter makes use of the Theatrix network support. Include the word "net" as a command line argument to activate network sessions. The Marble Fighter network support code is in the rfighter.cpp file.

Town

Town is a Myst-like game. Town consists of static full-screen displays, mouse navigation, music clips, sound effects, and one video clip. You can use the *SceneryDirector* class to build games with images that consist primarily of static scenes. The Town demo game uses *SceneryDirector* objects to display its scenery. Town is implemented at the fourth level of abstraction. There is no animation, so there are no *Performer* objects. The Town demo is found on the included CD-ROM in the **\THEATRIX\DEMOS\TOWN** subdirectory.

The Town Class

The Town game consists of 12 scenes, each rendered from a single 3-D model. There is a *Town* class from which 12 subclasses are derived. Each subclass represents one scene in the game. The *Town* class is shown here:

```
class Town : public SceneryDirector
{
        static int townct;
        int tune;
        int clip;
        virtual void look_forward(int)         { }
        virtual void look_right(int)           { }
        virtual void look_left(int)            { }
        virtual void look_back(int)            { }
        void on_escape(int);
        DECLARE_CUELIST
        DECLARE_MOUSECURSORS
protected:
        static MusicHand *conductor;
        static SoundTech *soundtech;
        Town(char *bmp, int tn = 0, int cl = 0);
        ~Town();
        virtual void display();
        virtual void hide();
        void on_timer();
};
```

The *Town* class includes data members that point to objects of *MusicHand* and *VocalHand* classes. These objects play the music and sound effects for the game. The *Town* constructor builds them as shown here:

```
Town::Town(char *bmp, int tn, int cl) :
                SceneryDirector(bmp, NoTransition)
{
    if (townct == 0)       {
        conductor = new MusicHand("music.txt");
        soundtech = new SoundTech("sounds.txt");
    }
    tune = tn;
    clip = cl;
    townct++;
}
```

The *townct* data member is a static reference-counting variable. It ensures that the *MusicHand* and *VocalHand* objects are instantiated and deleted only once. Because *Town* is a base class to 12 subclasses of which there is one object each, this measure is necessary. The *Town* destructor waits until *townct* is zero before deleting the two objects, as shown here:

```
Town::~Town()
{
    if (--townct == 0)
    {
        delete soundtech;
        delete conductor;
    }
}
```

CUELIST and CURSORLIST Tables

The *Town* class's CUELIST table captures keystrokes and timer ticks:

```
CUELIST(Town)
        KEYSTROKE(LF,  look_left)
        KEYSTROKE(UP,  look_forward)
        KEYSTROKE(DN,  look_back)
        KEYSTROKE(RT,  look_right)
        KEYSTROKE(ESC, on_escape)
        TIMER(18, on_timer)
ENDCUELIST
```

The *Town* class has a CURSORLIST table, which controls how the game handles mouse cursors. Here is the CURSORLIST table:

```
CURSORLIST(Town)
        MOUSE_CURSOR(  0,   0, 105, 239, IDC_CURSOR_LT, look_left)
        MOUSE_CURSOR(106,   0, 211, 199, IDC_CURSOR_UP, look_forward)
        MOUSE_CURSOR(106, 200, 211, 239, IDC_CURSOR_DN, look_back)
        MOUSE_CURSOR(212,   0, 319, 239, IDC_CURSOR_RT, look_right)
ENDCURSORLIST
```

Each MOUSE_CURSOR entry in the CURSORLIST table specifies a region on the screen with the X and Y coordinates of the region's upper-left and lower-right corners. The MOUSE_CURSOR entries name cursor shapes for the mouse to assume when its pointer is in the entry's region. The entries also specify callback functions to call when the user clicks the mouse in the regions.

The cursor shapes used by the Town were drawn in the Visual C++ cursor editor. Visual C++ automatically generates constants for resources and places them in a file called **resource.h**. The file will not appear in the FileView window until you **#include** it in your program and select **Build|Update All Dependencies**.

Callback Functions

The callback functions in the CURSORLIST table are the same as the callback functions associated with arrow keystrokes in the CUELIST table.

This approach allows the user to play the game without a mouse by pressing arrow keys.

Playing Music and Sound Effects

The *Town* class overrides its base class's *display* function to start any music clips or sound effects associated with the derived *Town* subclass scene. The overridden *hide* function turns off the mouse, music clips, and sound effects.

The *Town::on_timer* callback function keeps a sound effect playing. If the scene has a sound effect and if the sound effect has played to completion, the function starts the sound effect again.

The three functions that manage music clips and sound effects are shown here:

```
void Town::display()
{
     SceneryDirector::display();
     if (tune)
          conductor->play_music_clip(tune);
     if (clip)
          soundtech->play_sound_clip(clip);
}


void Town::hide()
{
     if (tune)
          conductor->stop_music_clip();
     if (clip)
          soundtech->stop_sound_clip();
     SceneryDirector::hide();
}
void Town::on_timer()
{
     if (clip && !soundtech->sound_clip_is_playing())
          soundtech->play_sound_clip(clip);
}
```

Stopping the Game

The *Town::on_escape* callback function executes when the user presses **Esc**:

```
void Town::on_escape(int)
{
        set_next_director(&typeid(StopDirector));
        stop_director();
}
```

The call to *set_next_director* tells the *SceneryDirector* class to shut down when *stop_director* is called. Ordinarily, a *SceneryDirector* object always switches to the next director in the list of instantiated directors when *stop_director* is called.

The Derived Town Subclasses

There are 12 derived *Town* subclasses, one for each scene in the game. Each scene has a **.BMP** file associated with it, and some have music and sound clips. Here is a typical *Town* subclass:

```
class Town3 : public Town
{
public:
        Town3() : Town("town03.bmp", 4, 2) { }
        void look_left(int)  { start_director(typeid(Town2)); }
        void look_right(int) { start_director(typeid(Town10)); }
};
```

The *Town* constructor accepts as many as three arguments. The first argument is the name of the **.BMP** file that provides the scene's full-screen image. The second argument is a music clip, if one is to be played when the scene begins. The third argument is a sound clip, if one is to be played when the scene begins. These clip arguments are zero if no clip is to be played. The Town constructor parameters have default arguments of zero, so you can omit the argument values.

Navigating the Town

The *look_left* and *look_right* callback functions override the empty callback functions of the same name in the base *Town* class. There may also be *look_forward* and *look_back* callback functions. These functions specify what to do when the user presses an arrow key or clicks in a mouse region to move forward, backward, right, or left. In most cases, these functions call the *start_director* function, specifying the *typeid* of the *Town* subclass to be started. This action stops the current director and starts the specified director.

Planning the scenes involved figuring out where the user's viewpoint would be for each one. Then, from each such viewpoint, we had to determine which viewpoint would be activated depending on which way the user navigated with the keyboard or the mouse.

To make this analysis easier, we built a map of the town by moving the camera high in the sky and pointing it downward. Then we determined where the game's camera locations would be for each scene. Figure 8.8 is that map with the camera information added.

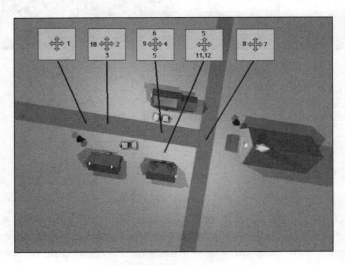

Figure 8.8 A map of the Town

Each of the camera legends in Figure 8.8 indicates the scene number when the camera is pointed in the direction of one of the arrows. From these legends we were able to determine where to place the camera to render each scene from the 3-D model and which scene to change to when the user moves away from the current scene in one of the four directions. Figure 8.9 is a montage of all 12 scenes from the Town game.

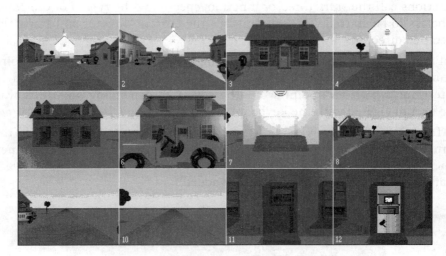

Figure 8.9 The Town scenes

Twelve scenes are not many for a complex game. Myst has more than 2500 scenes. This demo, however, shows you where to start when building games like this.

Playing a Video Clip

The *Town12* subclass does one thing that the others don't do: it plays a moving picture video clip during scene 12. The open door with a cat and a piano in scene 12 of Figure 8.9 is actually one frame of a video clip. The clip wags the cat's tail, rolls the piano roll, and moves the piano keys up and down. Here is the *Town12* class declaration:

```
class Town12 : public Town {
public:
        Town12() : Town("town11.bmp", 2) { }
        void display()
        {
                Town::display();
                show_video("room.avi", 132, 53, TRUE);
        }
        void hide()
        {
                stop_video();
                Town::hide();
        }
        void look_back()  { start_director(typeid(Town11)); }
        void iterate_director()
        {
                SceneryDirector::iterate_director();
                if (conductor->isconducting() &&
                        !conductor->music_clip_is_playing())
                    look_back();

        }
    };
```

This class uses the same **.BMP** scenery file that *Town11* uses. By projecting the video clip over the part of the screen that shows the door of the house, the scene seems to open the door and show the motion inside. The call to the base *Town* class's constructor specifies the scene and a music clip to play. The overriding *display* function starts a video clip by calling the *show_video* function. Its parameters are the name of the **.AVI** file, the X and Y coordinates of the upper-left corner where the video clip displays, and a true or false indicator to specify that the clip is to repeat or to play only once.

The overridden *iterate_director* function is called for each loop that the *Director* class processes to run the game. This function permits a game to insert frequent tests and processes that are not related to ticks of the clock. The *Town12* class uses this iteration function to see whether the music clip has finished playing. If it has, the function calls the *Town12::look_back* callback function to move to scene 11.

The TownApp Class

The *TownApp* class derives from *Theatrix* and contains pointers to all the subclasses:

```
class TownApp : public Theatrix
{
        Town1 *town1;
        Town2 *town2;
        Town3 *town3;
        Town4 *town4;
        Town5 *town5;
        Town6 *town6;
        Town7 *town7;
        Town8 *town8;
        Town9 *town9;
        Town10 *town10;
        Town11 *town11;
        Town12 *town12;
public:
        TownApp(HINSTANCE,int);
        ~TownApp();
};
```

The *TownApp* constructor builds instances of the scene objects using the *new* operator. The destructor deletes these objects. The program's *WinMain* function looks like the other *WinMain* functions listed in this chapter.

Theatris

Theatris uses random game pieces that fall into a pit. The player fits these pieces together by rotating and moving them with the keyboard. The game employs a grid matrix to implement the tiled pit into which the pieces fall.

We won't go into much detail about the game's implementation. You can read the code and see how most of it works. But several parts of Theatris are worthy of study. The menu is unique, so we describe it here. The implementation of the pit uses grid logic common to many games. The data structures that implement the game pieces are interesting. These details might not be obvious from reading the code, so we explain them here.

The Menu

The Theatris menu is different from other menus in that it indicates the current selection with an animated rotating game piece. Figure 8.10 shows the Theatris menu.

Figure 8.10 The Theatris menu

You can't tell by looking at Figure 8.10, but when you view the menu on the screen, the game piece just to the left of the current selection rotates. As you move the selection up and down with the arrow keys, the new selection's game piece starts rotating and the old one stops. The image frames of each piece on the menu are stored in a **.GFX** file dedicated to the piece. The *MenuItem* class manages the display of each game piece on the menu, and the *Menu* class manages the entire menu.

The *Menu* constructor instantiates three *MenuItem* objects and keeps track of which one is currently selected by receiving keyboard cues for the up and down arrow keys. The *Menu* object also gets a timer cue once every timer tick. The *Menu::on_timer* function manages the rotation, as shown here:

```
void Menu::on_timer()
{
        item[cur]->update();
        blt_window();
}
```

The *MenuItem::update* function, called by *Menu::on_timer*, computes the next frame to be displayed and displays it. When the *update* function returns, *on_timer* calls *VideoDirector::blt_window*; *update* makes its changes to the display buffer and that buffer needs to become visible:

```
void MenuItem::update()
{
        image=(image+1)%numimages;
        show_frame(x,y,image+1);
}
```

Each game piece on the menu is displayed from image frames taken from its own **.GFX** file. The *numimages* data member is the number of images in that file. The file contains exactly enough images to animate one complete rotation of the piece, so the expression on the right side of the assignment in the preceding code always computes the next frame number in the animation sequence.

The game pieces are similar to sprites in that they are animated. However, unlike sprites, the pieces display themselves by using the *VideoDirector::show_frame* function instead of the *VideoDirector::show_image* function. *VideoDirector::show_frame* does not check for transparent parts of the rectangle. The game piece images were rendered against the actual background so that their shadows would be projected onto the background.

The Pit

Figure 8.11 shows a Theatris game in progress. The game pieces fall into the pit, and the player fits the pieces together by rotating and moving them with the keyboard.

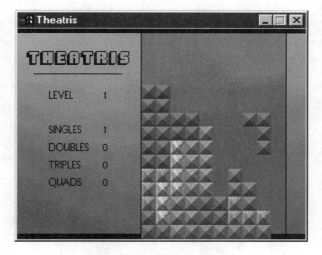

Figure 8.11 A Theatris game

The pit is implemented as a grid, represented by a logical two-dimensional array of tile positions. Each position contains a pointer to an object of type *Block*, a class that implements the game piece. When the pointer is null, the grid position is not filled with a part of a game piece. The outer array is an array of rows. Each row contains an inner array of tile positions and an indicator that says whether the row is fully occupied. Shown next is the organization of these arrays:

```
struct row_array
{
        Block* col[PIT_WIDTH];
        int is_full;
};

struct pit_grid
{
        row_array row[PIT_DEPTH];
};
```

Game Pieces

Theatris uses seven distinct game pieces. Each piece is made of four square tiles. Figure 8.12 shows the seven pieces.

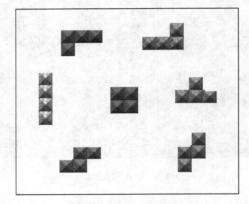

Figure 8.12 The Theatris game pieces

The game pieces are implemented by arrays of coordinates in a five by five grid of tiles. Coordinate 0/0 is the center tile. Tiles to the left of center are addressed as –1 and –2 on the X axis. Tiles to the right of center are addressed as -1 and -2 on the X axis. Tiles above center are addressed as –1 and –2 on the Y axis. Tiles below center are addressed as 1 and 2 on the Y axis.

Each game piece is represented in memory by four arrays of four coordinates. Each array represents the piece at one of its four rotations.

Each of the four coordinates in an array specifies a tiled position. These data structures are shown next:

```
struct point
{
        int x,y;
};

struct pointlist
{
        point pair[4];
};

pointlist blueblockinfo[4] =
  {
  {{ {-1,0},  {0,0}, {1,0}, {-1,1}, },},      //   XXX   XX    X  X
  {{ {-1,-1}, {0,-1},{0,0}, {0,1},  },},      //   X       X  XXX  X
  {{ {-1,0},  {0,0}, {1,0}, {1,-1}, },},      //            X       XX
  {{ {0,-1},  {0,0}, {0,1}, {1,1},  },},
  };
```

The *blueblockinfo* array is initialized with the data to construct an L-shaped piece in four different rotations. Each block style is implemented with an array like *blueblockinfo*.

Shootout

Shootout is an arcade game that includes many of the features that Theatrix supports. It is the most complex of the demo games, yet it has the simple, hand-drawn appearance of many arcade-style games.

Shootout uses an intro screen to introduce the game and to explain the underlying story. A menu guides users to the help screen, the options screen, and the action. The program is written at the highest level of abstraction, leaving most of the details to the hidden functions of the *SceneryDirector*, *SceneDirector*, and *Player* classes. Figure 8.13 shows the game as it plays out.

Shootout teaches several new lessons. First, the game demonstrates Theatrix's ability to support multiple sprites. Second, the sheriff's walk is animated using a smooth pace algorithm. Third, the other sprites use clipping to appear in windows, from doorways, and from behind buildings.

Figure 8.13 The Shootout game

Multiple Sprites

In addition to the seven players on the screen, each door on a building is a *Player* object, as is each digit in the scoreboard. To support Shootout, Theatrix must coordinate 13 sprites.

Smooth Animation

The sheriff's walking pace must seem natural. When a foot is firmly planted on the street, the rest of the body should move forward without having that foot slide in either direction. The *Sheriff* class implements walking animation with a five-frame sequence that we described in Chapter 3 under "Motion: One Frame at a Time." The *Sheriff::Walk* function implements that sequence:

```
void Sheriff::Walk()
{
    setinterval(walkinterval);
    if (++steps == 40)
    {
        steps = 0;
        forward ^= 1;
        incr = 1;
        of = 0;
        frame = 0;
        if (forward)
        {
            offset = 0;
            setx(FirstX);
        }
        else
            offset = 5;
    }
    else
    {
        if (forward)
            setx(getx() + walkincr[of]);
        else
            setx(getx() - walkincr[of]);
        if (++of == 4)
            of = 0;
    }
    frame += incr;
    if (frame == 5)
            incr = -1;
    else if (frame == 1)
        incr = 1;
    set_imageno(frame+offset);
}
```

The *Sheriff::Walk* function is executed once every other clock tick, or approximately nine times per second. The five frame images are numbered 1 through 5 in the .GFX library associated with the *Sheriff* object. The *steps* data member counts the steps. There are 40 steps across the screen, at which time the sheriff changes direction. Each step changes the object's X coordinate and image.

Clipping

When the townspeople and the bad guys come into view, they appear in one of the windows of a building, from out of a door, or from behind a building and down the alley to the street. Their images must be clipped to within the windows and doorframes and the edges of buildings. Except when they appear in windows, the clipping stops after they are in full view.

The *Shootout* class clips the images of the *BitPart* objects when they are about to enter the scene. Clipping is done by calling the *Player::clip* function with four coordinate points to define the rectangular screen region within which the *Player* object can display. The *BitPart* class is derived from the *Player* class, so this action clips the *BitPart* object to display within the window, doorway, or alleyway. Each such entrance is described by a *Portal* object that contains its coordinates.

When a *BitPart* object gets into full view, it unclips itself by calling the *Player::unclip* function. When the object is about to exit the scene, it clips itself to the portal through which it is going to exit.

THEATRIX REFERENCE MANUAL

This chapter is the reference manual to the Theatrix C++ class framework. You use it to look up details about the various components of the library. The chapter includes descriptions of:

- The Theatrix class library
- Theatrix macros
- Global values
- Global constants

Class Library Reference

This manual documents those parts of the Theatrix class library that represent its public interface. The material presented here is designed for readers who are using the Theatrix library to develop games. Because the framework internals are not discussed, this chapter reveals little about how the library works. The inner workings of Theatrix are discussed in Chapter 10.

The framework is covered on a class-by-class basis. A short description of the class is given, and then each public and protected member is discussed.

Director (director.h)

There is usually one *Director* object per screen in a game. The game play is one or more *Director* objects, the menu is another *Director* object, and so on. A game created with Theatrix must have at least one *Director*.

Constructor

```
Director()
```

Creates a new *Director* object. Because this constructor is protected, you can create a *Director* only by using derivation. Director is a large class, and so derivative classes should be created dynamically using the *new* operator.

take_over

```
virtual void take_over()
```

Runs the *Director*'s cue-dispatching loop. This member function is called automatically by Theatrix. The *take_over* function causes the *Director* to take control of the application. During the execution of *take_over*, all other *Director* objects in the game are idle.

Because *take_over* is called automatically by Theatrix, it is not necessary to call it. It is, however, often useful to override it. For example, overriding *take_over* is a way to ensure that a director runs in a certain keyboard mode (see *Hand::set_hotkeys*). In the overridden constructor, set the new mode, call *Director::take_over*, and then restore the mode.

display

```
virtual void display()
```

The *display* member function is called automatically by Theatrix when the *Director* is about to take over. By default, this routine does nothing, but it can be overridden to display backgrounds, initialize variables, and so forth.

hide

```
virtual void hide()
```

The *hide* member function is called automatically by Theatrix after the *Director* has given up control. By default, *hide* does nothing, but it can be overridden to clear the screen, display statistics, do a fancy fade-out, and so on.

iterate_director

```
virtual void iterate_director()
```

The *iterate_director* member function is called by *Director::take_over* once per cycle of the dispatching loop. You can override this member to perform tasks that must occur more often than a timer can provide. Note, however, that the member will be called at different rates depending on the speed of the processor.

get_next_director

```
virtual const Type_info& get_next_director()
```

Returns the type identification of the next director that should take control of the game. Theatrix calls this member function automatically after the *Director* has given up control. Unless a previous call to *set_next_director* has been made or the member function has been overridden, the type identification for *StopDirector* is returned, notifying Theatrix to terminate the application.

set_next_director

```
void set_next_director(const Type_info *dir)
```

Informs Theatrix which *Director* should follow the current one.

next_director_set

```
int next_director_set()
```

Returns 1 if a call to *set_next_director* has been made with other than a null pointer; otherwise, returns 0.

Hand (hand.h)

A *Hand* object is the basic unit in a game. As in a theatrical play, a *Hand* (a stagehand) may or may not be visible to the audience. A *Hand* has one or more tasks that it knows how to perform, and it relies on its *Director* for cues, which tell the *Hand* when to perform the task.

Constructor

```
Hand(Director* dir=0)
```

Creates a *Hand* object. This constructor, like the constructor for *Director*, is protected, which means that in order to use *Hand*, it is necessary to derive from *Hand*. Note that the *Director** parameter is optional. Although it is not mandatory to supply this parameter, a *Director* must be supplied for any cue members of the *Hand* object to operate. If a *Director* pointer is not supplied during construction, then it should be supplied later with a call to *set_director*. If any of the *Hand* class's member functions is invoked before a *Director* has been set (with either the constructor or the *set_director* member function), a fatal error occurs and the program terminates.

get_mouseposition

```
void get_mouseposition(int *x, int *y, int *b)
void get_mouseposition(int *x, int *y)
```

Retrieves information about the mouse pointer. The *x* and *y* parameters are pointers to variables where the data should go. The data values are the location of the mouse cursor in screen coordinates. The *b* parameter retrieves information about the mouse buttons. The *b* parameter will be set to one of these values:

0:	no buttons are down
LEFTMOUSEBUTTON:	left button is down
RIGHTMOUSEBUTTON:	right button is down

initialize

```
virtual void initialize()
```

Does nothing. The *initialize* member function is called automatically by Theatrix once and only once per execution of the game. The function is designed to be overridden and is used to perform initialization tasks that should occur only once, such as requesting cues or loading **.GFX** libraries and sound or music lists. In fact, these resources should be loaded only in overridden *initialize* members. This member is also useful for initializing variables.

mouse_cursorshape

```
void mouse_cursorshape(int cursor_resource)
```

Specifies what the mouse cursor should look like. The parameter should be a resource number for a cursor resource. Resource constants are usually defined in **resource.h** in the project directory.

my_director

```
Director* my_director()
```

Returns a pointer to the *Director* on which the *Hand* depends for cues. This is useful if the *Hand* is creating other *Hand*s and needs to supply a *Director* for the constructors.

post_message

```
void post_message(int msg, long data=0)
```

Posts the message *msg*. Theatrix delivers the message to any *Hand*s that either have requested a cue for the message *msg* or have included it in a shortcut macro. The *data* parameter is optional but can be used to send information, including pointers to more data.

post_netpack

```
void post_netpack(int netpack)
```

Sends a packet out on the network. The packet is received by a remote system, generating cues for *Hand*s on that system.

request_hotkey_cue

```
void request_hotkey_cue(int key, hotkeycallback cb)
```

Requests a cue when the hotkey *key* is pressed. Calling this routine tells Theatrix that when the user presses the key the callback function should be executed. The *key* parameter can be an uppercase ASCII value or a Windows virtual key code. ASCII values should be surrounded by single-quote characters. Although the ASCII values must be specified as uppercase, Theatrix will respond to both cases. The callback *cb* should have a return type of *void* and can take a single integer parameter. The parameter sent to the callback is the value *key*. The second parameter requires a cast. Here's an example:

```
request_hotkey_cue(VK_ENTER,
    (hotkeycallback)&MyHand::on_enter_key);
```

request_joystickbutton_cue

```
void request_joystickbutton_cue(int b, joystickbuttoncallback cb)
```

Requests a cue whenever a joystick button is pressed. Calling this routine is like telling Theatrix, "Whenever the user presses a button, execute the routine I have written called cb." The callback *cb* should have a return type of *void* and take two integer parameters. The two parameters are the distance from center that the joystick currently is. If the values are zero, the joystick is centered. The first value is the horizontal position, and the second value is the vertical position. The range for these values can be retrieved using *Theatrix::get_joystick_extremes*. The second parameter requires a cast. Here's an example:

```
request_joystickbutton_cue(BUTTON_ONE,
        (joystickbuttoncallback)&MyHand::on_fire_button);
```

request_joystickmove_cue

```
void request_joystickmove_cue(joystickmovecallback cb)
```

Requests a cue whenever the joystick is moved. Calling this routine is like telling Theatrix, "Whenever the user moves the joystick, execute the routine I have written called *cb*." The callback *cb* should have a return type of *void* and take two integer parameters. The two parameters are the distance from center that the joystick currently is. If the values are zero, the joystick is centered. The first value is the horizontal position, and the second is the vertical position. The range for these values can be retrieved using *Theatrix::get_joystick_extremes*. The parameter requires a cast. Here's an example:

```
request_joystickmove_cue(
        (joystickmovecallback)&MyHand::on_joystick_moved);
```

request_keystroke_cue

```
void request_keystroke_cue(int key, keystrokecallback cb)
```

Requests a cue when the keystroke *key* occurs. Calling this routine tells Theatrix that when the user presses the key, Theatrix should execute the callback function. The *key* parameter can be an uppercase ASCII value or a Windows virtual key code. ASCII values should be surrounded by single-quote characters. Although the ASCII values must be specified as uppercase, Theatrix will respond to both cases. The *cb* parameter is a member function that you write and should have a return type of *void* and take a single integer parameter. The second parameter requires a cast. Here's an example:

```
request_hotkey_cue(VK_ENTER,
        (keystrokecallback)&MyHand::on_enter_key);
```

request_message_cue

```
void request_message_cue(int message, messagecallback cb)
```

Requests a cue whenever the message *message* is posted. Calling this routine tells Theatrix that when the message *message* is posted, Theatrix should call the callback function. The callback *cb* should have a return type of *void* and take three integer parameters. The first parameter is the message value, and the two remaining integers contain any optional data sent with the message. The second parameter requires a cast. Here's an example:

```
request_message_cue(GAME_OVER_MSG,
    (messagecallback)&MyHand::on_gameover);
```

request_mouseclick_cue

```
void request_mouseclick_cue(int b, mouseclickcallback cb)
```

Requests a cue when a mouse button is pressed. Calling this routine is like telling Theatrix, "Whenever the user presses button *b* on the mouse, execute the routine I have written called cb." The *b* parameter can be either of the constants LEFTMOUSEBUTTON or RIGHTMOUSEBUTTON. The callback *cb* should have a return type of *void* and take three integer parameters. The first two parameters are the x and y, respectively, of the mouse position, and the final parameter is the button that was pressed. The second parameter requires a cast. Here's an example:

```
request_mouseclick_cue(LEFTMOUSEBUTTON,
    (mouseclickcallback)&MyHand::on_click);
```

request_mousemove_cue

```
void request_mousemove_cue(mousemovecallback cb)
```

Requests a cue whenever the mouse is moved. Calling this routine is like telling Theatrix, "Whenever the user moves the mouse, execute the routine I have written called *cb*." The callback *cb* should have a return of type *void* and take two integer parameters, which are the x and y positions of the mouse. The parameter requires a cast. Here's an example:

```
request_mousemove_cue(
    (mousemovecallback)&MyHand::on_mousemoved );
```

request_netpack_cue

```
void request_netpack_cue(int netpack, netpackcallback cb)
```

Requests a cue whenever a packet is received from a remote computer. Calling this routine is like telling Theatrix, "Whenever a packet is received, execute the routine I have written called *cb*." The callback *cb* must have a return type of *void* and take a single integer parameter. The second parameter requires a cast. Here's an example:

```
request_netpack_cue(YOU_WIN,(netpackcallback)&MyHand::I_win);
```

request_timer_cue

```
void request_timer_cue(int rate, timercallback cb)
```

Requests a cue every *rate* seconds. Calling this routine tells Theatrix, "At about *rate* times a second, call the callback function." The *rate* parameter can be an integer from 1 to 18. Using 1 means that the function *cb* is called once per second, and using 18 means that the function is called 18 times per second. The callback *cb* should have a return type of *void* and take no parameters. Here's an example:

```
request_timer_cue(18, (timercallback)&MyHand::on_timer);
```

set_director

```
void set_director(Director*)
```

This member function is used to tell a *Hand* which *Director* it should request its cues from. If you supply a *Director* pointer as a parameter to the *Hand* constructor, it is not necessary to call this member function.

set_hotkeys

```
void set_hotkeys(int on)
```

Turns the hotkey mode on and off. By default, the hotkey mode is off. Sending 1 or ON activates the hotkey mode. Sending 0 or OFF turns off the hotkey mode. Keystroke cues are delivered only when the hotkey mode is off, and hotkey cues are delivered only when the hotkey mode is on.

set_mouseposition

```
void set_mouseposition(int x, int y)
```

Forces the mouse pointer to the location specified by *x* and *y*.

start_director

```
void start_director(const Type_info& next)
```

Signals Theatrix to put the argument *Director* in control. Before doing so, Theatrix takes control away from the current *Director*.

stop_director

```
void stop_director()
```

Signals the *Director* to give up control. When the *stop_director* member function is called, the *Director* currently responsible for supplying cues relinquishes control to the Theatrix scheduling loop.

stop_hotkey_cue

```
void stop_hotkey_cue(int key, hotkeycallback cb)
```

Prevents future cues from occurring. The logical complement to *request_hotkey_cue*, this member function undoes what *request* does. The parameters should be identical to those used for *request_hotkey_cue*.

stop_joystickbutton_cue

```
void stop_joystickbutton_cue(int b, joystickcallback cb)
```

Prevents future cues from occurring. The logical complement to *request_joystickbutton_cue*, this member function undoes what *request* does. The parameters should be identical to those used for *request_joystickbutton_cue*.

stop_joystickmove_cue

```
void stop_joystickmove_cue(joystickmovecallback cb)
```

Prevents future cues from occurring. The logical complement to *request_joystickmove_cue*, this member function undoes what *request* does. The parameters should be identical to those used for *request_*joystickmove_*cue*.

stop_keystroke_cue

```
void stop_keystroke_cue(int key, keystrokecallback cb)
```

Prevents future cues from occurring. The logical complement to *request_keystroke_cue*, this member function undoes what *request* does. The parameters should be identical to those used for *request_keystroke_cue*.

stop_message_cue

```
void stop_message_cue(int message, messagecallback cb)
```

Prevents future cues from occurring. The logical complement to *request_message_cue*, this member function undoes what *request* does. The parameters should be identical to those used for *request_message_cue*.

stop_mouseclick_cue

```
void stop_mouseclick_cue(int b, mouseclickcallback cb)
```

Prevents future cues from occurring. The logical complement to *request_mouseclick_cue*, this member function undoes what *request* does. The parameters should be identical to those used for *request_mouseclick_cue*.

stop_mousemove_cue

```
void stop_mousemove_cue(mousemovecallback cb)
```

Prevents future cues from occurring. The logical complement to *request_mousemove_cue*, this member function undoes what *request* does. The parameters should be identical to those used for *request_mousemove_cue*.

stop_netpack_cue

```
void stop_netpack_cue(int netpack, netpackcallback cb)
```

Prevents future cues from occurring. The logical complement to *request_netpack_cue*, this member function undoes what *request* does. The parameters should be identical to those used for *request_netpack_cue*.

stop_timer_cue

```
void stop_timer_cue(int rate, timercallback cb)
```

Prevents future cues from occurring. The logical complement to *request_timer_cue*, this member function undoes what *request* does. The parameters should be identical to those used for *request_timer_cue*.

MusicHand (music.h)

MusicHand is not used as a base class for any of the classes in Theatrix. Although it is safe to assume that each graphical character in a game might make sounds, it is not safe to assume that each character might want to play music. *MusicHand* can be used as a base class for your own music-handling class. More often you will instantiate an object of *MusicHand* and use that object in one of your *Director* objects.

Constructor

```
MusicHand(char *sc)
```

Creates a *MusicHand* object. The *sc* parameter is the name of a **.TXT** file that contains a list of music clips (**.MID** files).

initialize

```
virtual void initialize()
```

Initializes the *MusicHand*. This member function is called automatically by Theatrix.

isconducting

```
int isconducting()
```

Returns 1 if music is supported. Otherwise, returns 0.

load_score

```
void load_score(char* fname)
```

Loads a new music list file. This file replaces any file specified at construction.

music_clip_is_playing

```
int music_clip_is_playing()
```

Returns 1 if a clip is currently being played; otherwise, returns a 0.

play_music_clip

```
void play_music_clip(int index)
```

Begins the music clip found at location *index* within the **.TXT** file supplied to the constructor. The *index* parameter is an integer value that must be greater than zero and less than or equal to the number of music clips in the **.TXT** file.

stop_music_clip

```
void stop_music_clip()
```

Interrupts a sound clip that is being played. If no clip is being played, the call is ignored.

Performer (perform.h)

Performer provides basic graphics support. Classes derived from *Performer* can load **.GFX** libraries and display bitmaps on the active video page.

Constructor

```
Performer(Director* dir=0)
```

Constructs a *Performer* object. If possible, it is recommended that the *Director** parameter be supplied here. If it is not supplied, *set_director* must be called *before* any cues are requested.

get_char_height

```
int get_char_height(char ch)
```

Returns the height (in pixels) of the character *ch*. Note that this value may vary depending on the active **.GFX** font.

get_char_width

```
int get_char_width(char ch)
```

Returns the width (in pixels) of the character *ch*. Note that this value may vary depending on the active **.GFX** font.

get_image_height

```
int get_image_height(int image_number)
```

Returns the bitmap height (in pixels) of the bitmap located at location *image_number* in the active **.GFX** library.

get_image_width

```
int get_image_width(int image_number)
```

Returns the bitmap width (in pixels) of the bitmap located at location *image_number* in the active **.GFX** library.

get_num_images

```
int get_num_images()
```

Returns the number of bitmaps contained in the active **.GFX** library.

load_gfxfont

```
void load_gfxfont(char* fontlibname)
```

Loads the **.GFX** font library *fontlibname* and makes it the active font for this *Performer*. A **.GFX** font file is a **.GFX** library with 36 bitmaps (the alphabet and 10 digits).

load_gfxlib

```
void load_gfxlib(char* libname)
```

Loads a **.GFX** file (a **.GFX** file created with GFXMAKE) into memory and marks it as the active library for this *Performer*. If *libname* has already been loaded by another *Performer*, it is not loaded again, but it is marked as the active library for this *Performer*. This member function should be called only in an *initialize* routine.

set_gfxfont

```
void set_gfxfont(char* fontlibname)
```

Marks *fontlibname* as the active font for this *Performer*. Note that it is necessary to call this member function only if the *Performer* needs access to more than one **.GFX** font library.

set_gfxlib

```
void set_gfxlib(char* libname)
```

Marks the active library for the *Performer* as *libname*. Note that it is necessary to invoke this member function only if the *Performer* needs to access images in more than one .GFX library.

show_clipped_image

```
void show_clipped_image(int x,int y,int image_number)
```

Displays the bitmap *image_number* of the currently active **.GFX** library at screen location *x,y*. The bitmaps in the **.GFX** library are numbered from 1. Unlike *show_image* and *show_frame*, *show_clipped_image* observes the current clipping boundaries. By default, the clipping boundaries are set to include the whole screen. The *show_clipped_image* member function supports transparency. The *x* and *y* parameters specify where the upper-left corner of the image will be placed.

show_frame

```
void show_frame(int x,int y,int image_number)
```

Displays the frame *image_number* of the currently active **.GFX** library at screen location *x,y*. The bitmaps in the **.GFX** library are numbered from 1. Unlike *show_image*, *show_frame* does not support transparency. Because of this, *show_frame* is faster than *show_image*. The *x* and *y* parameters specify where the upper-left corner of the image will be placed.

show_image

```
void show_image(int x,int y,int image_number)
```

Displays the bitmap *image_number* of the currently active **.GFX** library at screen location *x,y*. The bitmaps in the **.GFX** library are numbered from 1. The *show_image* function supports transparency (pixels with value zero are not drawn), so this is a typical routine for animation. The *x* and *y* parameters specify where the upper-left corner of the image will be placed.

show_number

```
void show_number(int x,int y,int number)
```

Displays the number *number* at *x,y*, using the active **.GFX** font. *x* and *y*, expressed in screen pixels, indicate where the upper-left corner of the number is to be placed. *number* should be positive.

show_print

```
void show_print(int x,int y,char* string)
```

Displays the string at *x,y* using the active **.GFX** font. *string* should contain only letters, digits, and spaces. *x* and *y* are expressed in screen pixels and refer to the upper-left corner of the text. The *x* and *y* parameters specify where the upper-left corner of the string is to be placed.

Player (player.h)

Player is used in conjunction with *SceneDirector*. By using a *SceneDirector* with several *Player* objects, you can animate multiple characters simultaneously.

Constructor

```
Player(char* gl=0,char* sl=0,int intv=1)
```

Creates a *Player* object. *gl* is the **.GFX** library in which the character's graphics are stored, and *sl* is the list of sound effects for the character. *intv* is the update interval for the character. This interval defaults to 1, which means that the *Player* is updated on every tick of the timer. A value of 2 means that the *Player* is updated every two timer ticks. The *intv* argument can be any positive number.

appear

```
void appear()
```

Causes the *Player* to become visible.

clip

```
void clip(int x1,int y1,int x2,int y2)
```

Activates clipping for the *Player*. *x1,y1* indicates the upper-left corner of the new clipping region, and *x2,y2* indicates the lower-right corner.

disappear

```
void disappear()
```

Causes the *Player* to become hidden.

get_imageno

```
short int get_imageno()
```

Returns the current image number for the *Player*.

getheight

```
short int getheight() const
```

Returns the *Player*'s current height in pixels.

getwidth

```
short int getwidth() const
```

Returns the *Player*'s current width in pixels.

getx

```
short int getx() const
```

Returns the *Player*'s current horizontal position.

gety

```
short int gety() const
```

Returns the *Player*'s current vertical position.

initialize

```
void initialize()
```

Loads the **.GFX** file for the player. This member function is called by Theatrix, but it is sometimes useful to override it to include other tasks.

isclipped

```
int isclipped()
```

Returns 1 if a clipping region is active; otherwise, returns 0.

isvisible

```
int isvisible()
```

Returns 1 if the player is visible; otherwise, returns 0.

set_imageno

```
void set_imageno(short int index)
```

Specifies the **.GFX** bitmap number. The *index* parameter specifies which image to use from the **.GFX** file. If the *Player* changes from frame to frame, this member function can be used to modify which image is used in the **.GFX** library to draw the character.

setinterval

```
void setinterval(short int inv)
```

Sets the *Player*'s update interval to *inv*.

setx

```
void setx(short int nx)
```

Sets the *Player*'s current x position to *nx*.

setxy

```
void setxy(short int nx,short int ny)
```

Sets the *Player*'s current x and y positions to *nx* and *ny*.

sety

```
void sety(short int ny)
```

Sets the *Player*'s current y position to *ny*.

stillframe

```
void stillframe(short int im,short int wait)
```

Displays image *im* at the current position and delays for *wait* ticks of the timer.

unclip

```
void unclip()
```

Deactivates the current clipping region. If no clipping region has been set, then the call is ignored.

update_position

```
virtual void update_position()
```

Does nothing. The intended purpose of this member function is to be overridden by a derived class. The new member function is then called by *SceneDirector* and should calculate a new position based on the *Player's* role in your game.

SceneDirector (scenedir.h)

SceneDirector is designed for use with *Player*. Using this combination, it is possible to animate multiple characters simultaneously.

Constructor

```
SceneDirector(char* scfile)
```

Constructs a *SceneDirector* object. *scfile* is a **.BMP** file that is used as a background for the scene. The image and the palette found in *scfile* are installed whenever the *SceneDirector* becomes active. If the **.BMP** file is too large or too small for the current window, the window is resized to accommodate the image.

display

```
void display()
```

Clears video, displays the background image, and requests internal cues. This member function is called automatically by Theatrix when the *Director* object first takes control, and it is sometimes useful to override it. When you do, your derived class's member function should call *SceneDirector::display* in addition to whatever the override does.

on_escape

```
void on_escape(int)
```

Stops the *Director*. If you don't want the *Director* to stop when the **Esc** key is pressed, then override this function with an empty version.

on_timer

```
void on_timer()
```

Updates the screen. This is called automatically by Theatrix once each clock tick. You can override the function to add behavior.

SceneryDirector (scenery.h)

SceneryDirector provides a basic, simple interface for displaying background scenery.

Constructor

```
SceneryDirector(char *bmpfile,int trans=ClearEveryTime)
```

Creates a *SceneryDirector* object. The *bmpfile* parameter is the name of the **.BMP** file for use as a background. The optional *trans* parameter defines how the *SceneryDirector* displays the background. The default value *ClearEveryTime* means that the window client area is cleared (to color zero) and then the **.BMP** file is displayed. Alternatively, using the value *NoTransition* causes *SceneryDirector* to display images without clearing video memory.

display_original_scenery

```
virtual void display_original_scenery();
```

Copies the contents of the background buffer to the screen buffer. The screen buffer's contents are overwritten.

get_next_director

```
virtual const Type_info& get_next_director()
```

Returns the ID of the next *Director*. Unless a previous call to *set_next_director* has been made, this member returns *NextDirector*. This member is called by Theatrix and can be overridden to return a specific *Director* identification of your choice.

refresh_display

```
virtual void refresh_display();
```

Flushes the contents of the display buffer to the screen. This is the same as calling *VideoDirector::swap_video_pages*.

Theatrix (theatrix.h)

Theatrix is the object that encapsulates the whole game. It is designed as a base class for an object that will be instantiated in the *WinMain* function of the program. Any *Director*-derived objects in the game should be created in the constructor of the *Theatrix*-derived class.

Constructor

```
Theatrix(char* str,HINSTANCE hInstance,int show)
```

Creates a *Theatrix* object. The *str* parameter is a string that appears on the window border. The *hInstance* and *show* parameters are sent to *WinMain* by Windows and should be passed on to the *Theatrix* constructor without modification.

enable_joystick

```
void enable_joystick()
```

Instructs Theatrix that the game uses the joystick. Among other things, this activates the joystick calibration sequence.

enable_netpacks

```
void enable_netpacks()
```

Activates the netpack event system. This is to be used if the game makes use of the serial communications abilities of Theatrix.

go

```
void go(int index=0)
```

This is the member function that makes it all happen. Theatrix initializes itself and puts in charge the *Director* indicated by *index*. The default 0 parameter causes the first *Director* created to be the first to be executed. Sending 1 causes the second *Director* created to be executed first, and so on.

go

```
void go(const Type_info& d)
```

This routine acts just like the previous version except that it starts the game with the *Director* specified as the parameter *d*.

joystick_extremes

```
void joystick_extremes(int *x1, int *y1, int *x2, int *y2)
```

Returns the extreme values that the joystick can return. Because the values returned by a joystick differ from one joystick to another (and from one computer to another), the extreme values that are retrieved during joystick calibration can be retrieved using this member.

VideoDirector (viddir.h)

Derived from *Director*, *VideoDirector* provides a set of routines that are useful in managing a graphical window. Specifically, *VideoDirector* controls the transfer of image data between image buffers and the window client area. *VideoDirector* is rarely used directly and is useful primarily as a base class for the *SceneryDirector*.

The *VideoDirector* class manages a display buffer and a background buffer. Before images become visible, they are prepared in the display buffer. The background buffer contains a bitmap that is used to repair the display buffer image. Both buffers are resized whenever the window size changes.

Constructor

```
VideoDirector()
```

Constructs a *VideoDirector* object. Because this is a protected constructor, it is possible to create such an object only by using derivation.

fill_background_buffer

```
void fill_background_buffer()
```

Copies the contents of the display buffer to the background buffer. Typically, this function is called after an image is loaded into the display buffer using *VideoDirector::show_bmp*.

blt_patch

```
static void flush_patch(int x1,int y1,int x2,int y2)
```

Copies a portion of the display buffer to the client area of the window. This is useful when an isolated change has been made to the display buffer and must be reflected on the screen. Use *blt_window* if the whole display buffer should be copied to the screen.

init_video

```
void init_video()
```

Clears both the display buffer and the background buffer to 0 (usually black).

restore_page

```
void restore_page()
```

Copies the contents of the background buffer to the display buffer. This returns the display buffer to its original state, erasing any sprites that have been drawn.

restore_patch

```
static void restore_patch(int x1,int y1,int x2,int y2)
```

Copies a portion of the background buffer to the display buffer. This is useful for erasing sprites drawn in the display buffer. Because a clean copy of the background is usually stored in the background buffer (with a call to *fill_background_buffer*), the restored patch looks like the original.

set_restore_patch

```
static int set_synch_patch(int x1,int y1,int x2,int y2)
```

Marks a patch (or rectangle) for restoration from the background buffer. Several of these patches can be marked in this manner, and then all of them can copied from the background buffer to the display buffer at once with a call to *restore_patches*.

show_bmp

```
static int show_bmp(char* bmpfile)
```

Reads *bmpfile* into the display buffer. The palette found in *bmpfile* is also installed. If *bmpfile* is missing or corrupted, *show_bmp* returns NOT_OK. If all goes well, it returns OK.

show_video

```
static void show_video(char* fname,int x,int y,int nonstop=FALSE)
```

Plays a **.AVI** file. The file name is specified by the *fname* parameter. *x* and *y* indicate where the upper-left corner of the video rectangle should appear in the window. The optional *nonstop* parameter can be set to TRUE if the video should be played in a continuous loop.

stop_video

```
static void stop_video()
```

Interrupts the **.AVI** file. If no file is playing, the call is ignored.

blt_window

```
void blt_window()    // protected
```

Copies the contents of the display buffer to the screen.

restore_patches

```
static int synch_patches()
```

Copies all the patches marked with *set_restore_patch* from the background buffer to the display buffer. The return value is the number of patches that were marked before the call. Once this member function is called, all the patches are unmarked.

video_playing

```
static int video_playing()
```

Returns 1 if a **.AVI** file is playing; otherwise, returns 0.

VocalHand (vocal.h)

The *VocalHand* class supports sound effects and voices by maintaining and playing sound clips. It is possible to derive directly from *VocalHand* and use the resulting class to do all the sounds for the game, or you can have each *Performer* play its own sounds. The latter is possible because *Performer* (the class that supports sprites) is derived from *VocalHand*.

Constructor

```
VocalHand(Director* d=0)
```

Creates a *VocalHand* object. The *Director** parameter should be supplied if any of *VocalHand's* cue functions are to be used.

get_num_clips

```
int get_num_clips()
```

Returns the number of sound clips in the active sound list.

get_sound_clip_length

```
int get_sound_clip_length(int clip_index)
```

Returns the length (in bytes) of the clip at the location *clip_index* in the active sound list.

load_sounds

```
void load_sounds(char* soundlist)
```

Loads the sound clip list *soundlist* (a **.TXT** file that contains the names of the **.WAV** files) into memory. This member function should be called only in an *initialize* routine.

play_sound_clip

```
void play_sound_cilp(int clip_index)
```

Plays the sound clip in the active sound list at the location *clip_index*. The clip is played until it is interrupted by another call to *play_sound_clip* or the end of the clip is reached.

set_cur_sounds

```
void set_cur_sounds(char* soundlist)
```

Sets *soundlist* as the active sound list for this *VocalHand*. It is necessary to call this member function only if a single *VocalHand* must play sound clips from more than one sound list.

sound_clip_is_playing

```
int sound_clip_is_playing()
```

Returns TRUE if a sound clip is currently being played, and FALSE if the sound card is idle.

stop_sound_clip

```
void stop_sound_clip()
```

Stops the sound card from playing the rest of a sound clip. If no sound is being played at the time of the call, the call is ignored.

Macros

Theatrix provides a set of macros to connect events to callbacks and to define mouse cursor screen regions. These macros define tables that the system uses to make the associations. Other miscellaneous macros are also discussed here.

The CUELIST (hand.h)

The CUELIST table associates events with callback functions. The program includes the DECLARE_CUELIST statement in a class declaration and puts a CUELIST declaration in the executable code within scope of the class declaration, as shown in this example:

```
class MyHand : public Hand  {
    // ...
    DECLARE_CUELIST
    void on_key_a();
    void on_timer();
};

CUELIST(MyHand)
    KEYSTROKE('a',on_key_a)
    TIMER(1,on_timer)
ENDLIST
```

This is the same as calling *request_keystroke_cue* and *request_timer_cue*. The CUELIST syntax is preferable because it improves readability and it doesn't require application-level type casting (the *request* functions do).

CUELIST

```
CUELIST(class_name)
```

Begins a CUE table definition. *class_name* is the name of the class that contains the cues.

DECLARE_CUELIST

```
DECLARE_CUELIST
```

Declares that a class will have a CUELIST table. This statement must appear in the class declaration.

ENDCUELIST

```
ENDCUELIST
```

Terminates the CUELIST table.

HOTKEY

```
HOTKEY(key,cue_function)
```

Defines a relationship between the key *key* and the function *cue_function*. This means that whenever the user presses *key*, Theatrix invokes *cue_function* automatically. The *cue_function* function should be provided without class specification and without parentheses.

JOYSTICKBUTTON

```
JOYSTICKBUTTON(b,cue_function)
```

Requests that *cue_function* be called whenever the button *b* is pressed on the joystick. The *b* argument specifies the button and may be BUTTONONE or BUTTONTWO. The *cue_function* callback should be provided without class specification and without parentheses.

JOYSTICKMOVE

```
JOYSTICKMOVE(cue_function)
```

Informs Theatrix that whenever the joystick is moved, *cue_function* should be invoked. The *cue_function* callback should be provided without class specification and without parentheses.

KEYSTROKE

```
KEYSTROKE(key,cue_function)
```

Establishes a connection between *key* and *cue_function*. When the user presses *key*, Theatrix invokes *cue_function*. The *cue_function* function should be provided without class specification and without parentheses.

MESSAGE

```
MESSAGE(msg,cue_function)
```

Instructs Theatrix to invoke the *cue_function* whenever the message *msg* is posted. *cue_function* should be provided without class specification and without parentheses.

MOUSECLICK

```
MOUSECLICK(button,cue_function)
```

Establishes a connection between the mouse button *button* and the *cue_function* callback. The *button* argument may be RIGHTMOUSEBUTTON or LEFTMOUSEBUTTON. When the user presses a mouse button, Theatrix invokes the *cue_function*. The *cue_function* callback should be provided without class specification and without parentheses.

MOUSEMOVE

```
MOUSEMOVE(cue_function)
```

Informs Theatrix that whenever the mouse moves, *cue_function* should be invoked. *cue_function* should be provided without class specification and without parentheses.

NETPACK

```
NETPACK(packet, cue_function)
```

Requests that if the *packet* is received at the serial port, *cue_function* should be called. *cue_function* should be provided without class specification and without parentheses.

TIMER

```
TIMER(rate,cue_function)
```

Instructs Theatrix to invoke *cue_function* at *rate* times per second. *cue_function* should be provided without class specification and without parentheses.

The CURSORLIST (scenery.h)

The CURSORLIST table associates events with callback functions. The program includes the DECLARE_MOUSECURSORS statement in a class declaration and puts a CURSORLIST declaration in the executable code within scope of the class declaration, as shown in this example:

```
class MyHand : public Hand  {
    // ...
    DECLARE_MOUSECURSORS
    void click_left();
    void click_up();
    void click_down();
    void click_right();
};

CURSORLIST(MyHand)
    MOUSE_CURSOR(  0,  0,105,239, LEFTARROWCURSOR,  click_left)
    MOUSE_CURSOR(106,  0,211,199, UPARROWCURSOR,    click_up)
    MOUSE_CURSOR(106,200,211,239, DOWNARROWCURSOR,  click_down)
    MOUSE_CURSOR(212,  0,319,239, RIGHTARROWCURSOR, click_right)
ENDCURSORLIST
```

CURSORLIST

```
CURSORLIST(class_name)
```

Begins a CURSOR table definition. *class_name* is the name of the class that contains the cursor list.

DECLARE_MOUSECURSORS

```
DECLARE_MOUSECURSORS
```

Declares that a class will have a CURSORLIST table. This statement must appear in the class declaration.

ENDCURSORLIST

```
ENDCURSORLIST
```

Terminates the CURSORLIST table.

MOUSECURSOR

```
MOUSE_CURSOR(x1,y1,x2,y2,cursorshape,callback)
```

Defines a mouse cursor region and a callback function to be called if the user clicks in that region. The *x1* and *y1* arguments define the upper-left screen coordinates. The *x2* and *y2* arguments define the lower-right screen coordinates. The *cursorshape* argument is an integer resource ID that corresponds to a cursor resource. The *callback* argument is the address of a function that Theatrix calls when the user clicks the left mouse button within the screen region defined by the coordinate arguments.

Assert (debug.h)

```
Assert(condition);
```

The *Assert* macro works just like the Standard C *assert* macro. Theatrix implements its own version to allow an assertion to find its way to the functions that make an orderly shutdown of the game runtime environment, including the release of Windows resources.

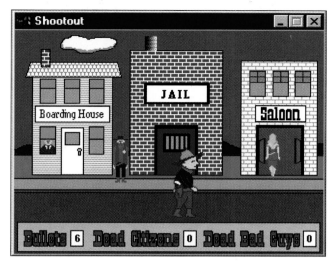

The CD-ROM includes everything that you need to write your own games. The Shootout demo (above) is an example of a complete game that uses animation, sound, and music. The object of the game is to shoot the wanted criminals without killing innocent bystanders. The Skater demo (below) illustrates the use of Z-order.

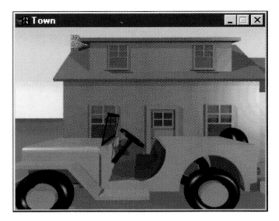

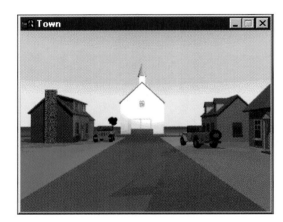

The Town demo (above and left) uses a Myst-like interface to create a ray-traced town that you can explore. The Planet demo (below) is a simple animation example.

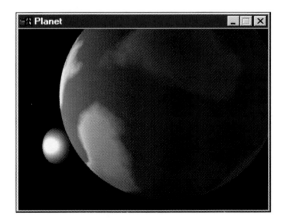

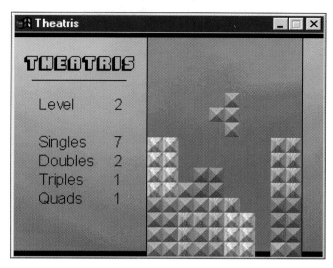

Theatris is a tetris clone that uses ray-traced graphics. The game (above) uses ray-traced game pieces. The Theatris menu (below) uses rotating 3-D game pieces to highlight the current selection.

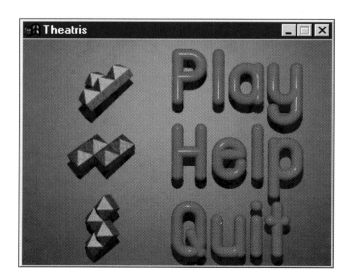

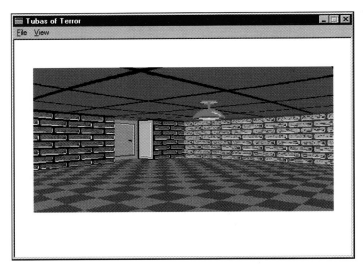

The Tubas of Terror demo (shown above and below) uses the RayCast engine included on the CD-ROM. The engine supports textured walls, floors and ceilings, and allows you to add moving and stationary sprites to your ray-casting game.

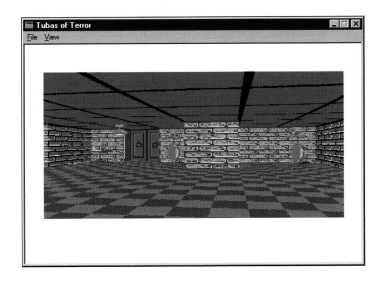

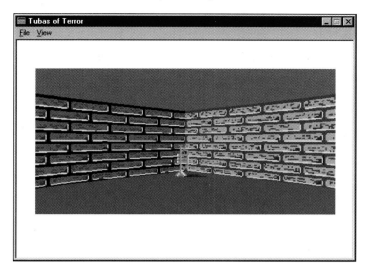

Tubas of Terror pits you against an irritable and dangerous tuba player. Your only chance for survival is to meet his attacks with trumpet blasts. Before you face the tuba player, it is a good idea to locate your trumpet (shown above). The final confrontation is shown below.

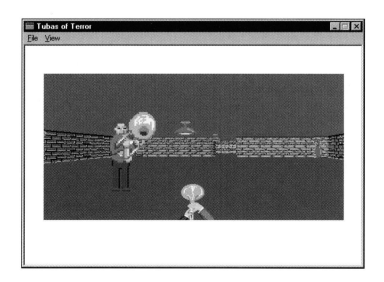

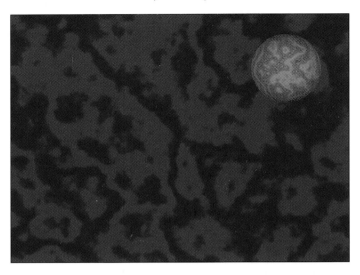

The CD-ROM includes a framework that uses the Microsoft Games SDK. Demos are provided that showcase each of the framework features. The Sprite demo (above) provides animation by bouncing a sprite around the screen. Multiple sprites can be animated with a little extra code. The Scroll demo (below) is a side-scrolling example, and uses a rotating sprite.

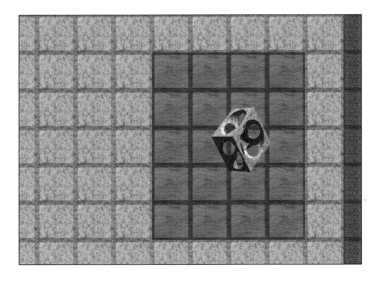

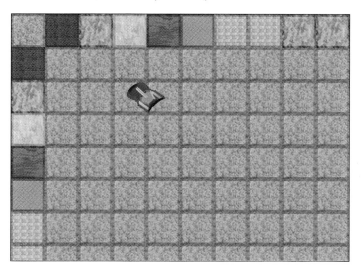

The TankTop demo (shown above and below) uses the Games SDK to provide fast, smooth animation and mixed sound effects. The demo uses a futuristic tank with a turret that can rotate and fire bullets. The TankTop demo uses hit detection to determine if any part of the tank has made contact with a wall.

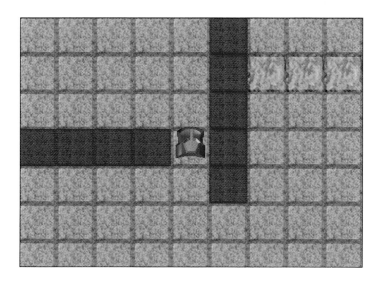

The Marble Fighter demo (above) is a simple fighting game. You can play against the computer, or against another player over a network. The Marble Fighter help screen appears below.

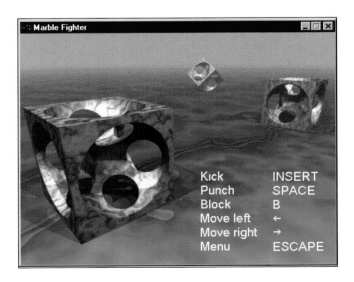

Adjusting Theatrix (settings.h)

The following constant values define ranges and operating limits for the library. For most games, the values assigned to these settings suffice, but a large or unusual game may need to change one or more of these values. In this case, modify the value and recompile Theatrix.

MAXDIRECTORS

Theatrix has a limit of 20 *Director*s to a game. If you need to use more, then increment this constant.

MAXHANDS

Theatrix has a limit of 250 *Hand*s to a game. If you find that this is not enough, then increment this constant.

MAXGFXLIBS

Theatrix allows a game to load as many as 30 **.GFX** libraries. If you require more, increment this constant.

MAXSOUNDLISTS

Theatrix allows a game to load as many as 10 sound clip lists. If you require more, increment this constant.

MAXMIDICLIPS

Theatrix allows each MIDI list to contain a maximum of 20 entries.

MAXMESSAGE

Theatrix allows messages ranging in value from 0 to 199. This value can be increased to allow higher values as messages.

MAXNETPACK

Theatrix allows netpack values (network messages) to range in value from 0 to 99. This value can be increased to allow more netpack values.

NUMPATCHES

Theatrix allows as many as 25 restore patches to be set at once (see *VideoDirector::set_restore_patch*). If you need more, increment this constant.

Keyboard Codes (winuser and keycodes.h)

The symbols shown in Table 9.1 are values that are useful for specifying key cues with the KEYSTROKE and HOTKEY macros and for testing key values. The codes prefixed with VK_ are defined in the **winuser.h** file (usually located in **\MSDEV\INLUCDE**). The other codes are from the **keycodes.h** file.

Table 9.1 Constants for KEYSTROKE and HOTKEY Cues

DEL	DN	DOWNARROW
END	ENTER	ESC
ESCAPE	HOME	INS
INSERT	LEFTARROW	LF
PGDN	PGUP	RIGHTARROW
RT	SPACE	SPACEBAR
UP	UPARROW	VK_ADD
VK_BACK	VK_CAPITAL	VK_CLEAR
VK_CONTROL	VK_DECIMAL	VK_DELETE
VK_DIVIDE	VK_DOWN	VK_EECUTE
VK_END	VK_ESCAPE	VK_F1
VK_F10	VK_F11	VK_F12
VK_F2	VK_F3	VK_F4

VK_F5	VK_F6	VK_F7
VK_F8	VK_F9	VK_HOME
VK_INSERT	VK_LCONTROL	VK_LEFT
VK_LSHIFT	VK_MENU	VK_MULTIPLY
VK_NET	VK_NUMLOCK	VK_NUMPAD0
VK_NUMPAD1	VK_NUMPAD2	VK_NUMPAD3
VK_NUMPAD4	VK_NUMPAD5	VK_NUMPAD6
VK_NUMPAD7	VK_NUMPAD8	VK_NUMPAD9
VK_PAUSE	VK_PRINT	VK_PRIOR
VK_RCONTROL	VK_RETURN	VK_RIGHT
VK_RSHIFT	VK_SCROLL	VK_SELECT
VK_SEPARATOR	VK_SHIFT	VK_SNAPSHOT
VK_SPACE	VK_SUBTRACT	VK_TAB
VK_UP		

Controller Button Symbols (standard.h)

The symbols shown in Table 9.2 define button values on the mouse and joystick and are used in statements in the CUELIST table.

Table 9.2 Mouse and Joystick Button Constants

CUELIST Statement	Symbol	Value
MOUSECLICK	LEFTMOUSEBUTTON	1
MOUSECLICK	RIGHTMOUSEBUTTON	2
JOYSTICKBUTTON	BUTTONONE	1
JOYSTICKBUTTON	BUTTONTWO	2

You can also use these symbols as arguments to Theatrix functions that expect button arguments.

THEATRIX TECHNICAL SPECIFICATIONS

This chapter explains the Theatrix internal class structure and data files. We assume that you understand Theatrix well enough to use it and that you are now interested in knowing more about how it works. This chapter is a technical discussion of the operation of the class library, which will be of interest to programmers who want to enhance or modify the library. It also provides insight into the best ways to take advantage of the framework when you design your games. You will learn about:

- How the classes operate
- How Theatrix uses data files

Classes and Data Structures

The implementation of Theatrix consists of several class hierarchies that combine to support the interface that you learned about in Chapters 6 and 8. Those chapters taught you how to use the Theatrix library, so they presented only the public interfaces of the exposed classes and the protected interfaces of the classes from which you derive to build your game. This chapter delves more deeply into how Theatrix works and what the underlying classes are.

Theatrix

You learned to build a game by first deriving a game class from the *Theatrix* class and then having your derived class encapsulate and instantiate the components of the game: scenery, players, directors, sound effects, music, and so on.

A game must instantiate one and only one object derived from the *Theatrix* class before constructing any of the other components of the game. The *Theatrix* constructor initializes a *current_game* global pointer to type *Theatrix* with its own address after asserting that the pointer is set to zero. This assertion ensures that no other *Theatrix* objects are instantiated. Other parts of the game use the *current_game* pointer to address the game object. Because the pointer is global, your instantiation of the object may be local. Some of the demo games instantiate in their *main* functions an *auto* object of a type derived from *Theatrix*.

List of Directors

The *Theatrix* class maintains an array of pointers to the directors that constitute the game. When an object of type *Director* or one derived from *Director* is constructed, the *Director* constructor adds the object's address to the *Theatrix* class's array of director pointers by calling the *Theatrix::add_director* function through the *current_game* pointer. This order of director object pointers in the array represents the logical order of directors in the game. This order figures prominently later.

Message Servers

The *Theatrix* class includes eight event *server* objects. These objects are part of the mechanism that dispatches event messages to components of the game.

The complex event sensing and message dispatching procedure spans several classes and uses several data structures. The complexity of this approach provides the most efficient mechanism to achieve the desired result.

The server objects cause the dispatching of messages to the callback functions for all game components that have requested cues for the specific events. The servers themselves do not dispatch the messages. This task is done by the *folder* mechanism in the *Director* class, but the event servers launch the folder functions that dispatch the messages.

There are event servers for events related to keystrokes, timers, generic messages, mouse clicks, mouse movements, joystick motion, key presses, and serial port network packets.

Event servers are declared *static* in the *Theatrix* class declaration. They would not need to be *static* to work properly, because only one *Theatrix* object can be instantiated at any one time. The *static* declaration is used for performance reasons. Event sensing runs constantly, testing event flags and launching message dispatching when events occur. By making the server objects *static*, we avoid the overhead added by the compiler to initialize and dereference the *this* pointer for each use of a server object.

Each of the event servers differs according to the device it polls, but they all operate in a similar fashion. The server classes are defined in the files shown in Table 10.1.

Table 10.1 Event Server Implementation Files

Server	Header File
Timer	timesrvr.h
Keystroke	keysrvr.h
Hotkey	kdsrvr.h
Message	msgsrvr.h
Mouse click	mcsrvr.h
Mouse movement	mmsrvr.h
Joystick	jssrvr.h
Network packet	netsrvr.h

Each of the header files has an associated **.CPP** file on the CD-ROM in **\THEATRIX\SRC\THEATRIX**.

Messages are dispatched to objects derived from the *Hand* class. The object receiving the dispatch must be associated with an object derived from the *Director* class, either by being derived from *Director* or by receiving cues from the current *Director* object in control of the game. Each *Director* object has tables of event registrations. You will learn more about these tables, which involve objects called *folders* and *handlers*, later in the discussion of the *Director* class.

Event servers report events by calling the *dispatch* function associated with a folder object that contains the registrations of *Hand* functions with events.

The keystroke server is a typical event server. We will discuss its operation, and you can apply that knowledge to your understanding of the other servers.

All server classes are derived from the *Server* abstract base class, which is declared in **server.h**:

```
class Server
{
    virtual void startup() { }
    virtual void shutdown() { }
public:
    virtual void check(Folder&) = 0;
};
```

Some servers override the virtual *startup* and *shutdown* functions if their devices have initialization and shutdown procedures that must execute before the servers can be used. The *KeystrokeServer* class, shown next, does not override these functions.

```
class KeystrokeServer : public Server
{
public:
    void check(Folder&);
    void log(int k);
private:
    int nextkey;
};
```

When a *Director* object runs a game, it has a dispatching loop from which it calls the check function for all the device servers. Your program does not concern itself with the dispatching loop. The *Director* class takes care of it. The *Director* class includes folder objects for each of the devices, and *Director* passes to the server's *check* function a reference to the folder object. As you will see later, folder objects are specialized for the devices they support. Here is the *KeystrokeServer::check* function.

```
void KeystrokeServer::check(Folder& fld)
{
    if (nextkey)
    {
        fld.dispatch(nextkey);
        nextkey=0;
    }
}
```

The *nextkey* flag is set whenever a new **WM_KEYDOWN** message is received from Windows. The *KeystrokeServer::check* function tests the flag. If a key has been pressed, the *dispatch* function—the one associated with the folder object that was passed by reference as an argument is called. The *check* function passes to the *dispatch* function the value that represents a keystroke.

The server senses only that the user has pressed a key. It is the folder's job to determine whether there are game components registered to receive a cue when the particular key is pressed.

System Startup

The game program calls the *Theatrix::go* function to launch the game. The *go* function sets things up so that the first instantiated *Director* object will run the game. To specify starting with a different *Director*, include its class *typeid* or its relative-to-zero position as an argument to the *go* function. The go(int index) member looks like this:

```
void Theatrix::go(int index)
{
    system_startup();

    Hand::initialize_hands();

    do
    {
        director[index]->reset();
        director[index]->display();
        director[index]->take_over();
        director[index]->hide();
        index=find_director_index(director[index]->get_next_director());
    } while (index>=0 && !quitflag);

    system_shutdown();
}
```

The *go* function calls the *startup* functions for each of the server objects, then calls the static *Hand::initialize_hands* member function to initialize all instantiated *Hand* objects. This is the only time that those objects' initialization function is called, so it is important that the program declare all instances of *Hand* objects for the entire game before calling the *go* function.

The function then runs a director-launching loop calling, in succession, *Director::display*, *Director::take_over*, and *Director::hide* for the *Director* object that is being given control. All the game activity for the scene being directed takes place from within these three function calls. When they return, the director-launching loop calls the old director's *get_next_director* function to compute an index to a new director to take over. The index is a subscript into the list of directors that the *Theatrix* class maintains. The director-launching loop continues until its call to *find_director_index* returns –1 or the *quitflag* is set.

System Shutdown

When a game is over, the *Theatrix* object shuts down the event devices in the reverse order in which it started them up. Each of the devices has a *shutdown* function that takes care of its own shutdown procedures.

System Abort

The *Theatrix* class includes *fatal* functions that do an orderly shutdown of the system before aborting. These functions, declared in **theatrix.h**, display message boxes after restoring system resources. One of the *fatal* functions accepts a *char** argument that points to the message to be displayed. This function is called from within the library when it finds exceptional conditions that require the program to stop.

The other *fatal* function supports the *Assert* macro defined in **theatrix.h**. The function accepts two strings and an integer. The first string is the error condition, the second string is the name of the source code file where the error was encountered, and the integer is the source code line number. The *Assert* macro replaces the Standard C *assert* macro to allow the game program to make an orderly shutdown of its devices prior to aborting due to a failed assertion.

Hands

The *Hand* base class exists to support the registration of derived class objects for event messages and to support mouse operations. Directors and other game components derive from *Hand* so that they can request and receive event messages.

The *Hand* base class has only three data members: a pointer to the *Director* object that is in charge of the *Hand* object (when the *Hand* object is itself a *Director*, this is a pointer to itself); a static count of instantiated *Hand* objects; and a static array of pointers to instantiated *Hand* objects.

When a *Hand* object is instantiated, its constructor accepts a pointer to the *Director* that directs the actions of the *Hand*. The object stores that pointer for later use and appends its own address (the *this* pointer) to the array of instantiated *Hand* objects.

Cue Registries

Most of the members of the *Hand* class support the registration of the *Hand* object to receive cues based on events. There are request and stop functions for each of the kinds of cues that a *Hand* can receive.

The **hand.h** file also defines the macros that implement the CUELIST table. When a derived class includes the DECLARE_CUELIST macro, the C++ preprocessor translates that statement into the declaration of a static array of structure objects that represent cues. Each element in the array contains an event code, a data byte, and the address of a callback function. The DECLARE_CUELIST macro also declares an inline function named *GetMessageMap* that returns the address of the array. This function overrides a virtual function in the base *Hand* class that returns a null pointer.

The CUELIST macro expands into the definition of the array that the DECLARE_CUELIST macro declares. There are several other macros (HOTKEY, TIMER, MESSAGE, KEYSTROKE, MOUSECLICK, MOUSEMOVE, JOYSTICKMOVE, JOYSTICKBUTTON, and NETPACK) that declare initializers to the array. The END_CUELIST macro declares the terminal entry and C++ tokens for the array.

The static *Hand::initialize_hands* function iterates through the static array of instantiated *Hand* objects and calls the *GetMessageMap* function of each one. If the function returns a non-null pointer, the program iterates through the array of event structures in the *Hand* object's message map. For each entry, the program requests the appropriate cue for the hand, specifying the callback function in the message map entry.

Directors

Objects of classes derived from *Director* run the game. The *Director* class is derived from the *Hand* class, so *Director* objects may request and receive cues.

One *Director* object at a time is in control of the game. As *Director* objects are constructed, they are added to the list of directors that the *Theatrix* class object maintains. Their order in this list represents their logical order of execution. By default, the first director in the list is the first director given control. When that director relinquishes control, the second director in the list gets control. When the last director in the list relinquishes control, the game is over. Directors relinquish control by calling the *Hand::stop_director* function. If a director wants to pass control to a specific director other than the next one in the list, the controlling director (or one of its other *Hand* objects) calls *Hand::start_director* and passes the *typeid* of the director object that will take control.

Folders

Each instantiated *Director* object has eight objects of classes derived from the *Folder* class, which is declared in **folder.h**. There is one folder for each of the event devices, and they are all derived from the *Folder* abstract base class. Each *Folder* class has a *dispatch* function that dispatches event cue messages to those *Hand* objects that have registered for the cues. The event servers previously discussed call the *Folder* classes' *dispatch* functions when events are sensed.

We will continue our explanation of events and messages by addressing the keystroke event. Each *Director* contains one *KeystrokeFolder* object, the essence of which is shown here. You can view the entire class in **folder.h** and **keyfold.h**.

```
class KeystrokeFolder : public Folder
{
public:
        KeystrokeFolder() : Folder(key, NUMKEYS) { }
        void register_key(Hand*,int key,callback);
        void unregister_key(Hand*,int key,callback);
        void reset();
        void dispatch(int, int, int);
private:
        EventHandler key[NUMKEYS];
        friend class KeystrokeServer;
};
```

The array of *EventHandler* objects in the *KeystrokeFolder* class is the dispatching table. There is one such object for each possible event. In this case, there is one *EventHandler* object for each possible keystroke. The *EventHandler* class is shown here.

```
class EventHandler
{
public:
        ~EventHandler()
                { reset(); }
        void add(Hand*,callback);
        void del(Hand*,callback);
        void delHand(Hand*);
        void execute_hotkey_callbacks(int);
        void execute_keystroke_callbacks(int);
        void execute_timer_callbacks();
        void execute_netpack_callbacks(int);
        void execute_message_callbacks(int,int,int);
        void execute_mouseclick_callbacks(int,int,int);
        void execute_mousemove_callbacks(int,int);
        void reset();
        int getnum();
        LinkedList<subscription> slist;
};
```

The EventHandler class has a different function for each type of event.

Each *EventHandler* object includes a linked list of *subscription* objects. The *subscription* class is declared in **handler.h**:

```
struct subscription
{
        Hand* hand;
        callback cb;
        subscription(Hand*h, callback c)
        {
                hand=h;
                cb=c;
        }
};
```

The *callback* type is a *typedef* declared in **hand.h** as shown here:

```
typedef void (Hand::*callback)();
```

Each *subscription* object contains the address of the *Hand* object that requested the event cue message along with the address of the *Hand* object's callback function. Figure 10.1 illustrates the relationship of directors, folders, event handlers, subscriptions, and callback functions.

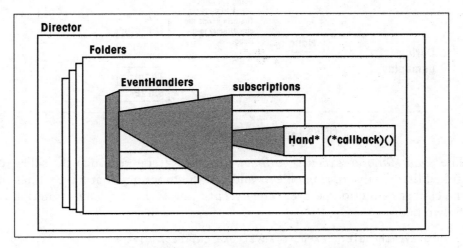

Figure 10.1 Event cue message data structures

A *Folder* object's *dispatch* function uses the data passed to it by the *Server* object's *check* function to determine which *EventHandler* table entry to access:

```
void KeystrokeFolder::dispatch(int k, int, int)
{
      key[k].execute_keystroke_callbacks(k);
}
```

The *KeystrokeFolder::dispatch* function uses the integer *key* parameters to vector into its array of *EventHandler* objects. In turn, the *EventHandler* executes the callbacks stored in its linked list.

Figure 10.2 illustrates the role of the Folder during the course of the game.

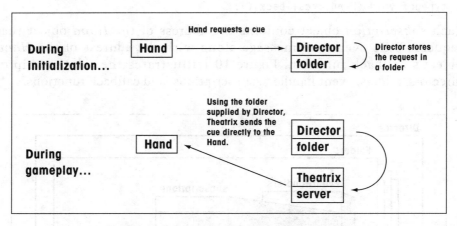

Figure 10.2 Event cue message logical flow

The *EventHandler::execute_callback* functions iterate through the selected linked list of *subscription* objects and call the functions that have values in the callback function pointer. The *execute_keystroke_callbacks* function is shown here:

```
void EventHandler::execute_keystroke_callbacks(int k)
{
        subscription *ptr=slist.FirstEntry();
        while (ptr)
        {
                Hand* h=ptr->hand;
                keystrokecallback cb=(keystrokecallback)ptr->cb;
                ptr=slist.NextEntry();
                (h->*cb)(k);
        }
}
```

During the cue request, the callback pointer is cast to the generic callback type. Before we can execute the callback, it is necessary to cast the pointer back to the proper type. In this example, the type used is *keystrokecallback*, which is defined this way:

```
typedef void (Hand::*keystrokecallback)(int);
```

VideoDirector

The *VideoDirector* class, declared in **viddir.h**, is derived from *Director* and handles video buffers and playing motion video clips. Some games might derive their director classes directly from *VideoDirector*, but most of them will use *SceneryDirector*, *SceneDirector*, or both. These two classes are discussed in the next section.

The main purpose of the *VideoDirector* class is to encapsulate the graphics portion of the framework. *VideoDirector* updates the window, loads **.BMP** files, plays **.AVI** motion video files, and provides functions to manage the display buffers.

Most of VideoDirector's functionality is provided by the Dib class. Dib encapsulates the Windows device independent bitmap (DIB) and provides an array of functions that manipulate the bitmap.

VideoDirector supports graphical buffer management with functions that copy whole and partial sections of the internal DIB. *VideoDirector* supports the display of sprites by providing a low-level patch facility. A *patch*, a rectangular subsection of the DIB, is usually used to define the space that a sprite occupies. A program can build a table of patch regions by calling the *set_restore_patch* function once for each patch. Later you can use the *restore_patches* function to copy the patch regions from the background buffer to the display buffer. You can also work with individual patches.

To use these functions, the programmer must understand the relationship between the display buffers and the DIB. Most of these details are hidden by the *SceneryDirector* and *SceneDirector* classes.

SceneryDirector

The *SceneryDirector* class, declared in **scenery.h**, supports the display of static scenes where animation is not involved. Game programs use this class to implement information screens, menus, and help screens. *SceneryDirector* is also useful for implementing Myst-like games that involve high-resolution, 3-D modeled, ray-traced scenes where game motion is superimposed over the scenery using **.AVI** sequences.

SceneryDirector implements most of the mouse operations that games use. The header file defines the DECLARE_MOUSECURSORS, CURSORLIST, MOUSE_CURSOR, and END_CURSORLIST macros. When a derived class includes the DECLARE_CURSORLIST macro, the C++ preprocessor translates this statement into the declaration of a static array of structure objects that represent screen regions. Each element in the array contains rectangle coordinates, a cursor resource index, and the address of a callback function. The DECLARE_CURSORLIST macro also declares an inline function named *GetMouseCursors* that returns the address of the array. This function overrides a virtual function in the base *SceneryDirector* class that returns a null pointer.

The CURSORLIST macro expands into the definition of the array that the DECLARE_CURSORLIST macro declares. The MOUSE_CURSOR macro declares initializers to the array. The END_CURSORLIST macro declares the terminal entry and C++ tokens for the array.

SceneDirector declares its own CUELIST table to be cued when the user presses **Esc**, **Spacebar**, or **Enter**. These actions cause the *SceneryDirector* object to call *stop_director* to relinquish control to the next director.

SceneDirector

The *SceneDirector* class is derived from *SceneryDirector*. *SceneDirector* adds support for animated sprite actions and is a companion class to the *Player* class. The *SceneDirector* object in control expects to manage all the currently active *Player* objects. To make that happen, you construct the *SceneDirector* object and then the *Player* objects that it owns. If a game has several animated scenes, you should instantiate the *SceneDirector*s and *Player*s together so that they are properly associated. To ensure that things work that way, instantiate the *Player* objects from within the constructor of the *SceneDirector* object.

The *SceneDirector* object maintains a list of the *Player* sprites that it controls. The order of this list implements the Z-order of the sprites when they are displayed on the screen, and sprites change their place in the list to change their Z-order as they move among one another. On each tick of the system timer, the *SceneDirector* object iterates through its list of *Player* objects and calls the *displayframe* function of each one so that the *Player*s can update their images and positions and copy the images into the display buffer. When all the sprites have done that, the *SceneryDirector* object copies the buffer contents to the client area of the window. Then the *SceneryDirector* object calls *VideoDirector::restore_patches*, which restores the active page to the original background without sprites, ready for the next timer tick and frame update cycle.

More Hands

All *Director* classes are derived from *Hand*. Other *Hand* classes implement sprites and play music. This discussion describes them and some of the classes that support them.

VocalHand

The *VocalHand* class, declared in **vocal.h**, is derived from the *Hand* class. *VocalHand* objects generate sound effects, and the *VocalHand* class gives the object the behavior needed to do that. The class's public interface includes functions to load sound effect lists, play and stop sound clips from these lists, and test to see whether a sound clip is playing.

The *VocalHand* class includes a static array of *soundlib* structures and an integer that specifies which soundlib the object is using. Because the array is static, there is only one copy, even if you instantiate multiple *VocalHand* objects. The integer index is not static, so each *VocalHand* has its own copy.

The *VocalHand* plays **.WAV** files from the list by indexing into the *soundlib* array to retrieve a file name. The name is used to call PlaySound. The call looks like this:

```
PlaySound(lib[curlib].clip[index-1].filename,
        NULL,SND_ASYNC | SND_FILENAME | SND_NODEFAULT);
```

Performer

The *Performer* class, declared in **perform.h**, is derived from the *VocalHand* class. *Performer* adds the ability to display on the screen graphical images selected from a library of images. A *Performer* object can make sounds and display images of itself.

The *Performer* class includes a static object of type *GraphicsMedia* and an integer that specifies which of several image libraries the object of the class is using. A Theatrix game maintains one *GraphicsMedia* object, which contains an array of *MediaLib* objects. At any given time, a *Performer* object is using one of these *MediaLib* objects from which to select images to display. A *Performer* object uses its *load_gfxlib* function to load its library of images into memory.

When the *Performer* object determines that an image frame is to be displayed, the object calls one of the image-displaying functions of its base *Performer* class. These functions rely on *VideoDirector* to copy the selected image into the display buffer.

Player

The *Player* class, declared in **player.h**, is used in combination with the *SceneDirector* class to give sprites the behavior of animation. The *Player* class is derived from the *Performer* class. *Player* maintains information about a sprite's current image number and screen position as well as whether the sprite is currently in view. *Player* also stores information about clipping parameters when a sprite is only partially in view.

A *Player* object assumes that it is being managed by a *SceneDirector* object. The *Player* constructor associates the *Player* object with the currently running *SceneDirector* object. When the *Player* object's *initialize* function is called from the *Hand::initialize_hands* function, the *Player* object loads its graphics and sound effect lists.

A *Player* object is programmed to refresh its screen image at a regular interval specified as a number of clock ticks. Once every clock tick, the *SceneDirector* calls the *Player::displayframe* function. The *SceneDirector* has prepared the active page to be updated with new sprite images, and *SceneDirector* calls *displayframe* for each sprite in Z-order sequence so that the nearest sprite is called last.

The *SceneDirector* and *Player* classes coordinate the display of the sprites on the background scenery. The game-dependent sprite classes derived from *Player* specify which images from their libraries are to be displayed and where on the screen they are to be displayed.

The *displayframe* function uses a countdown variable to see whether the *Player*'s refresh interval has expired. If it has, *displayframe* calls *update_position*. A class derived from *Player* must provide an *update_position* function that, based on the game's circumstances, establishes the image number and position by calling *Player::setxy* and *Player::set_imageno*. The only valid place to make these changes is from within the *update_position* function. If a sprite class calls these functions from outside the *update_position* function, the *Player* class makes note of that condition, saves the changed values, and applies them just before calling *update_position*.

MusicHand

The *MusicHand* class, declared in **music.h**, integrates MIDI music files into the game. *MusicHand* is derived from *Hand*, but *MusicHand* has no director. You usually instantiate an object of *MusicHand*, use that object to load a list of MIDI files, and play selections from the file. Playing, stopping, and testing for music clips is done with the Windows Media Control Interface (MCI).

File Formats

Theatrix uses four types of input files: **.BMP** files, **.GFX** files, and text files.

Scenery: BMP

The **.BMP** format supported by Theatrix uses no compression and uses at most 256 colors per image. The file consists of header data, a palette record, and an array of color bytes, with one byte per pixel.

Theatrix uses **.BMP** files for two purposes. They serve as background scenery, and they supply the palette. When *VideoDirector* displays a **.BMP** file, its palette is installed into the Windows palette manager.

Sprites: GFX

.GFX files are generated using the GFXMAKE utility found in the **\THEATRIX\BIN** directory of the included CD-ROM. A **.GFX** file stores a variable number of graphical bitmaps. Each record is an image stored as a binary stream. Figure 10.3 shows the format of a **.GFX** file.

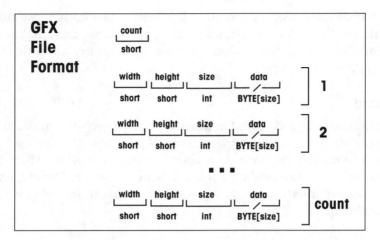

Figure 10.3 The .GFX file format

The first data item in the file is the number of images. This count is followed by the image records. Each record begins with the pixel width and height of the image when it is displayed on the screen. Next is an integer that contains the size of the image bitmap in bytes. This size field is followed by the image bitmap, consisting of one byte per pixel in the image. No palette data is stored in the **.GFX** file.

Sound Effects: Sound Lists

A *sound list* is an ASCII file with a variable number of sound clip names, each on a separate line. The files named should be **.WAV** files.

Music: Music Lists

Music lists are ASCII files with one or more file names. Each name specifies a **.MID** file. One name should appear on each line.

A C++ Ray-Casting Engine

Ray casting is a graphical scene-rendering technique that supports 3-D action games such as Wolfenstein and Doom. Unlike ray tracing, which slowly renders photo-realistic scenes to be used later in the development of a game, ray casting renders its scenes in real time—as the game is being played.

This chapter and the next explain how ray casting works, and they describe the RayCaster engine class library with demonstration programs and a reference manual. In this chapter, you will learn about:

- Ray-casting theory
- Designing the maze and its occupants
- Building the maze's graphical components
- Customizing the RayCaster engine to fit your games
- Writing programs to implement your 3-D maze games

Ray-Casting Theory

Ray casting works within a programmed model of a maze of rooms and hallways that are defined by walls and connected by doors. The game player moves through the rooms and hallways of the maze in any direction, viewing and interacting with the contents of each room and hallway.

The ray-casting algorithm makes certain assumptions about the maze: Walls are of a uniform height; walls are always parallel or perpendicular to one another when viewed from above; the viewer's line of sight is on a horizontal level exactly one-half the height of the walls; a wall's thickness is the same as its height; each wall's length is an even multiple of its height. Figure 11.1 represents a simple maze as viewed from overhead. The game player never sees this view, but the view helps you to understand the concept.

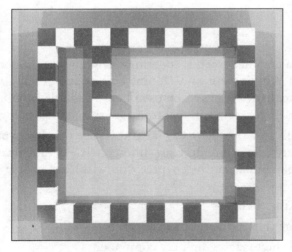

Figure 11.1 An overhead view of a 3-D maze

Each of the squares in the maze is a cube. The cubes' colors alternate so that you can distinguish them. The game player moves about in this maze, and the program renders views of it from within. Figure 11.2 represents the player's view from a position in the lower-right corner facing toward the upper-left corner.

Figure 11.2 is the last look you'll have of such a simple maze. The demonstration games that follow use a much more complex model. In fact, we did not render Figure 11.2 with a ray-caster. We built it with a ray-tracer program so that we could easily render the overhead view to illustrate the principle. Observe the shadows in Figures 11.1 and 11.2. A ray-tracer casts shadows. A ray-caster does not.

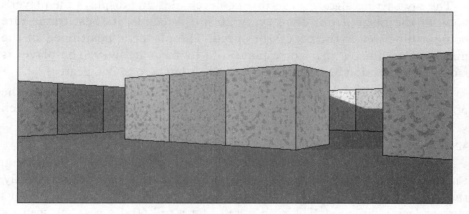

Figure 11.2 The interior view of a 3-D maze

The Ray-Casting Algorithm

The algorithm is called ray casting because the program scans the maze from left to right and renders each vertical slice of the picture in turn. Several popular books have explained the algorithm in detail. Probably the best such description is in *Gardens of Imagination*, by Christopher Lampton, The Waite Group, 1994.

We are not going to describe the inner workings of ray casting in much detail in this book for three reasons: First, the subject has been well visited in other works and, as a result, is widely understood. Second, a comprehensive description of the algorithm is a complete book in itself. Best of all, you do not need a detailed understanding of the underlying ray-casting mechanism to successfully build a 3-D maze game. The C++ class library presented here encapsulates the process and hides the details. You need to understand only these three things: how to build the engine's data structures; how to configure the engine; and how to use the public interfaces of the engine's class library in a C++ program.

If this brief description whets your appetite to know how the algorithm works in detail, then refer to Lampton's book. You'll need to sharpen your trigonometry skills to keep up.

The ray-casting algorithm in this book rebuilds and displays the player's view of the maze about once every 20 milliseconds, its best frame rate being a function of the processor speed. The player is positioned in the maze at coordinates that correspond to a room or hallway. The player is facing in a direction based on the compass—from zero to 360 degrees.

A set of memory arrays describes the 3-D maze. Two arrays define the positions of the wall cubes and doors in the maze, one array for each viewing axis: an X ray and a Y ray. Other arrays define the placement of sprites, props, and ceiling and floor tiles. More about tiles later.

The RayCaster engine assumes a viewing angle of 60 degrees, although you can modify that value by changing one of the engine's constants. Consequently, the horizontal scan of the maze starts at 30 degrees less than the player's current facing direction. The scan iterates for a full 60 degrees, one scan for each vertical line in the viewing window. Each iteration casts an imaginary ray forward from the player's position until the ray hits a wall. The effective degree of angle for each ray is a function of the width of the viewing window.

The algorithm uses a lot of trigonometry. The C/C++ standard math functions are not particularly efficient for real-time applications, even when the computer includes a math coprocessor. For this reason, the engine uses the screen dimensions and viewing angle to compute all possible results as integer values in tables. The runtime program uses these tables rather than call the trig functions. This strategy delivers a significant performance advantage, making ray casting possible on contemporary PCs.

The engine assumes that every wall unit is really a cube. Based on that assumption, the ray-caster does not need to examine every coordinate in the maze when it casts rays. The caster begins at the next coordinate in front of the player that is an even multiple of a wall unit's width. In this implementation, wall cubes are 64^3. As long as the caster finds no wall or door unit in that position in the maze array, the caster increments 64 units to look in the image cell position.

The caster casts two rays for each slice. One ray looks for wall surfaces that run north and south (X rays), and the second ray looks for walls that run east and west (Y rays). Each wall unit is a cube, so the same wall unit can be hit by both rays for a given slice. The shorter of the two rays represents that slice's hit. A Y ray that is cast due north or south (or close to one of these headings) but that is looking for east/west walls might go all the way to the edge of the maze without hitting anything. If the player is near an open door and there is nothing to hit all the way to the horizon, neither ray is treated as having hit anything.

The caster makes an additional top-down cast in those maze rooms that have floor and ceiling tiles to be rendered. Otherwise, the caster uses a solid color for floors and ceilings. When the player is outside the maze, the caster uses blue over green to suggest sky and grass. When the player is inside, the solid floor and ceiling colors are defined as constants.

While the caster is building the scene, a ray might hit sprite and prop elements in the maze. The caster stores these hits in a table and renders them after it has completely built the scene. Unlike walls and doors, sprites and props have transparent elements that cannot overwrite the scenery. Sprites and props are not cube objects, so they cannot be rendered in two axes. The player's view of a sprite or prop is always head-on. Each sprite has several bitmaps that represent its action as viewed from different angles. A prop is treated as a symmetrical object with one view only.

There is a lot more to know about the ray-casting algorithm, and we encourage you to read other works and even study the RayCaster engine's source code to learn more. For now, we will get on with the business of learning how to use the engine and build a 3-D maze game.

The RayCaster Engine

The ray-casting engine that this book provides goes several steps beyond what other books give you. Our engine supports all the visual components of a 3-D maze game: sprites, props, doors, ceilings, and floors. You can even go outside the maze. Furthermore, the engine is a Windows 95 C++ class library implemented with Visual C++ 4.0 using the application architecture of a Microsoft Foundation Classes program.

The Demo Game Programs

The rest of this chapter explains how to use the basic elements of the engine to build the shell of a 3-D maze game. There are four demo games. Each new game builds on the game that preceded it. Chapter 12 completes the project by building the Tubas of Terror demonstration game.

Demo 1: The Maze

The first demonstration game builds a maze and uses a small program that lets the player move around in the maze. This is about as far as most books on this subject go. As you will see, we go much further.

Building the Demo 1 Program from the CD-ROM

To prepare for these exercises, you must copy some files from the CD-ROM to your hard drive. We assume that you have Windows 95 running and Visual C++ 4.0 installed.

Make a subdirectory to hold copies of the demo files. For this discussion, we will call the subdirectory **tot**, for Tubas of Terror, the name of the game. The examples given here assume that your hard drive is **C:** and that your CD-ROM drive is **D:**. We use DOS commands to explain the procedure. You can achieve the same results by using Windows 95's file and folder copy procedures.

Copy all the files from the **Raycaste** subdirectory on the CD-ROM into your subdirectory as shown here:

```
c:
md \tot
cd \tot
copy d:\raycaste\*.*
```

Use **xcopy** to copy the first demo's files from the CD-ROM's **raycastd\demo1** subdirectory:

```
xcopy d:\raycastd\demo1\*.* /s
```

Be sure to use **xcopy** and to include the **/s** option on the command line. This procedure creates the **tot\res** subdirectory and copies the resource files that Visual C++ requires.

Before you compile and run the first demo program, we should discuss some of its components. You have the files copied to your hard drive, and every file that we discuss is in the **\tot** subdirectory. You can view them from the Visual C++ editor or Notepad as we proceed.

Designing a 3-D Maze

A 3-D maze is an array of wall units. You define the array in a text file. All the demo programs use a text file named **maze.txt**. Each demo has an enhanced version of the file, so you will be replacing it as we proceed to later demos. Figure 11.3 shows **maze.txt** for Demo 1.

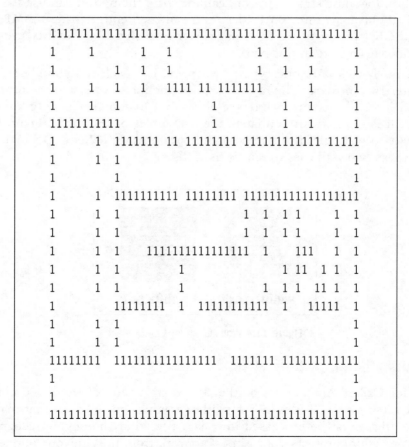

```
111111111111111111111111111111111111111111111111
1       1       1   1               1   1   1               1
1               1   1   1               1   1   1               1
1       1   1   1   1111 11 1111111                 1               1
1       1   1                           1                   1   1               1
11111111111                             1                   1   1               1
1               1   1111111 11 11111111 111111111111 11111
1               1   1                                                           1
1               1                                                               1
1               1   1111111111 11111111 1111111111111111111
1               1   1                           1   1   1 1           1   1
1               1   1                           1   1   1 1           1   1
1               1   1   1111111111111111   1       111     1   1
1               1   1           1                       1 11   1 1   1
1               1   1           1                   1   1 1 11 1   1
1                       11111111   1   11111111111   1       11111     1
1               1   1                                                           1
1               1   1                                                           1
11111111   111111111111111   1111111 111111111111
1                                                                               1
1                                                                               1
111111111111111111111111111111111111111111111111
```

Figure 11.3 Maze.txt for Demo 1

Each of the digits represents a wall unit. Each of the spaces represents open space in which the game player can navigate the maze. This demo has only one kind of wall unit, so all the digits are 1. A maze can be no wider and no deeper than 64 character positions.

Texture-Mapped Maze Tiles

Every wall unit in a maze is represented by a 64-pixel x 64-pixel bitmap that defines how the ray-caster renders each side of the cube. This bitmap is called the wall's *tile bitmap*. Tile bitmaps must be in the **.PCX** bitmapped graphic format. The Windows 95 Paint program can read **.PCX** files but, for some strange reason, cannot write them. You can use Paint to build tile bitmaps into **.BMP** files. You can then convert these **.BMP** files into **.PCX** files by using the Image Alchemy shareware utility program described elsewhere in this book.

Demo 1 uses only one type of wall tile, but each individual wall tile requires two bitmaps. The ray-caster uses one for X walls and the other for Y walls. Wall textures that are the same except for subtle shading differences dramatically enhance the 3-D effect of the maze. Figure 11.4 shows two wall tile files named **wall01.pcx** and **wall02.pcx**. Demo 1 uses only these two wall tiles to render its walls.

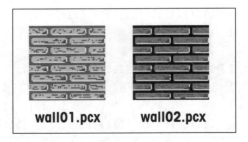

Figure 11.4 Wall tile bitmaps for Demo 1

Building the Maze Data Files

The RayCaster engine uses neither the text version of the maze nor the **.PCX** version of wall tiles (nor any other graphics bitmaps, for that matter). These files must be processed into data files that the engine recognizes. This procedure protects your games' artwork from mischievous tampering.

Two utility programs build the raw data files into the engine's proprietary format. These utility programs are on the CD-ROM in the **raycastu** subdirectory.

Before you can run the Demo 1 game, you must run these two programs as described next.

Bldmaze

The bldmaze program converts a text maze file into the format that the engine expects. You run it from the command line as shown here:

```
bldmaze maze.txt maze.dat
```

Maze.txt is the name of the text file. **Maze.dat** is the name of the converted maze data file. You can use other names. **Maze.dat** is specified in the game program's source code.

Gfxmake

The gfxmake program converts a set of **.PCX** graphics bitmap files into the RayCaster engine's **.gfx** format. Note that this program is not the same as the Theatrix utility program of the same name described elsewhere in this book. Also note that the format of the **.gfx** file is unlike the format of Theatrix **.gfx** files. The different formats and programs support the different requirements for the two game development environments.

You can run gfxmake by specifying the name of the **.gfx** file to be built followed by the names of the **.pcx** files to be used as shown here:

```
gfxmake tiles.gfx wall01.pcx wall02.pcx
```

You can also put the names of the **.pcx** files into a text response file and name it, instead of the files, on the command line:

```
gfxmake tiles.gfx @tiles.lst
```

This procedure is the preferred one. The sequence of file names is vital to the proper execution of the program. As you will soon learn, the program needs to know exactly which tile bitmap to use at any given time, and the position of the bitmap in the **.gfx** file is its identification.

All the demos include response files to build the **.gfx** files. Use either of the commands just shown to build **tiles.gfx** for Demo 1.

Showgfx

The showgfx program is a Windows 95 applet that displays the contents of a **.gfx** file. Its executable file is in the CD-ROM's **\raycastu** subdirectory. The program is handy for previewing tiles, doors, props, and sprites and for verifying the content of **.gfx** files and the sequence of bitmaps in those files. Figure 11.5 shows the showgfx program with one of Demo 1's wall tiles being displayed.

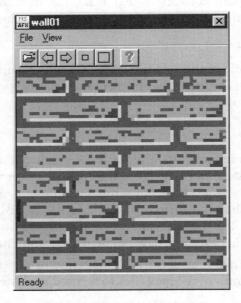

Figure 11.5 The showgfx program

The arrow buttons move back and forth through the bitmaps in the **.gfx** file. The box buttons zoom the display in and out.

Configuring the Engine

Each game gets its own custom compile of the engine. We chose this approach rather than use static or dynamic link libraries because the different characteristics of each game would involve performance considerations if they were processed as variable parameters and functions rather than as constants and inline functions. Consequently, when you design a new game, you redefine a set of constant expressions and recompile the engine. The demo programs include the engine's source code files directly in their own Visual C++ projects, which is why you copied those source code files from the CD-ROM into your own subdirectory.

Consts.h

The constants that you modify to configure the RayCaster engine are in the file named **consts.h**. Figure 11.6 shows the part of **consts.h** that concerns this demo. This figure shows only fragments of the file. View the actual file from your **\tot** subdirectory to get the complete picture.

```
const SHORT highwall = 2;  // highest assigned wall tile #

inline bool isWall(SHORT bmpno)
{
    bmpno = BmpNumber(bmpno);
    return bmpno == 1 || bmpno == 2;
}
```

Figure 11.6 Constants and functions in Consts.h for Demo 1

As you can see, there's not much to it. There are only two wall tile bitmaps, so the *highwall* constant is 2. The *isWall* function returns true if the bitmap number passed to it is 1 or 2.

The changes to **consts.h** become more complex as we add features in later demos.

Writing the Program

The game program is probably the easiest part of this exercise. All the hard parts are encapsulated in the engine's class library.

Game programs that use the RayCaster engine also use the Microsoft Foundation Classes (MFC) library. The game program is derived from *CWinApp* and uses the *CFrameWnd*-derived class for many of the user interactions. We assume here that you have a working knowledge of this architecture.

You could use AppWizard to build your program, but AppWizard insists on building a document-centric application with either a single- or multiple-document interface. You would have to strip the document and document view source files out of the project and then use trickery to coerce the project to forget about them. It's easier to use the model given here and build your application from it. You can still use the features of ClassWizard and the debugger to work with your program.

The CMainFrame Class

Figure 11.7 shows the class definition for *CMainFrame*, which is derived from the *CFrameWnd* class. Every MFC application has, at a minimum, a *CWndApp*-derived class and a *CFrameWnd*-derived class. We use *CMainFrame*, a *CFrameWnd*-derived class, to launch the game and handle the user interface.

The two *const*s at the top of the file define the height and width of the ray-caster's viewing window. The frame window is built around this viewport.

The class overrides the standard MFC functions *OnKeyDown* and *OnKeyUp* to process keystrokes. A game has different keystroke requirements than other applications have. The program must keep an eye on the ups and downs of all the keystrokes that control the game. The five BOOL members are used for that purpose.

A pointer to type *DemoMaze* is used to instantiate a data member object of type *DemoMaze*, which is the class that implements the ray-caster for this game. The class overrides *OnTimer* to control the game's timing and *OnCreate* to get things rolling.

```
class DemoMaze;
const int width = 480;
const int height = 240;

class CMainFrame : public CFrameWnd
{
    BOOL upkey, downkey, rightkey, leftkey, shiftkey;
    int cxframe;
    int cyframe;
    int windowwidth;     // window width
    int windowheight;     // window height
    DemoMaze* m_pDemoMaze;
public:
    CMainFrame();
    virtual ~CMainFrame();
protected:
    DECLARE_DYNCREATE(CMainFrame)
    afx_msg void OnKeyDown(UINT nChar, UINT nRepCnt, UINT nFlags);
    afx_msg void OnKeyUp(UINT nChar, UINT nRepCnt, UINT nFlags);
    afx_msg void OnTimer(UINT nIDEvent);
    afx_msg int OnCreate(LPCREATESTRUCT lpCreateStruct);
    DECLARE_MESSAGE_MAP()
};
```

Figure 11.7 The CMainFrame class declaration

Figure 11.8 is the *CMainFrame* constructor from **Mainfrm.cpp**, the source code file that implements the *CMainFrame* class.

```
CWnd* pCMainFrame; // extern pointer for VGA class to blt frames

CMainFrame::CMainFrame()
{
    pCMainFrame = this;  // must assign this to support VGA class;
    m_pDemoMaze = 0;     // pointer to game class
    // -- keyboard signals
    upkey    = FALSE;
    downkey  = FALSE;
    rightkey = FALSE;
    leftkey  = FALSE;
    shiftkey = FALSE;
    // --- compute window size
    cxframe = GetSystemMetrics(SM_CXFRAME) * 2;
    cyframe = GetSystemMetrics(SM_CYFRAME) * 2
                    + GetSystemMetrics(SM_CYCAPTION);
    windowwidth  = 540 + cxframe;      // window width
    windowheight = 380 + cyframe;      // window height
    RECT rc = {0, 0, windowwidth, windowheight};
    // ----- create the game window
    Create(0, "Demo 3-D Maze",
                        WS_BORDER      |
                        WS_CAPTION     |
                        WS_MAXIMIZE    |
                        WS_MINIMIZEBOX |
                        WS_SYSMENU     |
                        WS_VISIBLE,
                        rc);
}
```

Figure 11.8 The CMainFrame constructor

The *CMainFrame* constructor's first job is to initialize a global pointer to type *Cwnd* with the address of the *CMainFrame* object. This global pointer is always named *pCMainFrame*. You must declare it and initialize it for the ray-caster to work properly.

The constructor initializes its data variables and then computes the size of the application window. The program uses the Windows 95 SDK *GetSystemMetrics* function to compute the size of the window frames. Finally, the *CMainFrame* constructor creates the application window.

When an MFC window is created, MFC calls its *OnCreate* function. The demo game program overrides that function to create the game object. Figure 11.9 is the *CMainFrame::OnCreate* function.

```
int CMainFrame::OnCreate(LPCREATESTRUCT lpCreateStruct)
{
    if (CFrameWnd::OnCreate(lpCreateStruct) == -1)
        return -1;
    // --- player's initial position in maze
    const int x = 192;
    const int y = 192;
    // --- player's initial viewing angle (0 - 359)
    const int angle = 0;
    // -- compute viewport within window
    //       (width and height are the viewport dimensions in pixels)
    int leftcol = (windowwidth-cxframe-width) / 2;
    int toprow  = (windowheight-cyframe-height) / 3;
    ViewPort vp = { leftcol, toprow, width, height };
    // --- start the game
    m_pDemoMaze = new DemoMaze(x, y, angle, vp);
    if (!(m_pDemoMaze->isLoaded()))
        return -1;
    // ---- set timer to run the game
    SetTimer(1, 20, 0);
    return 0;
}
```

Figure 11.9 The CMainFrame::OnCreate function

The *CMainFrame::OnCreate* function establishes the player's starting position and orientation. If you were to implement a feature that allows players to save and restore games in progress, you would get these values and others from the saved game.

Observe the values of the player position and orientation. We'll discuss them after we've run the game program.

One way to save and restore game settings is to override the *CWinApp::InitInstance* function in your derived *CWinApp* class and use the Windows 95 SDK functions *GetProfileString*, *GetProfileInt*, *WriteProfileString*, and *WriteProfileInt*.

Using the window dimensions computed in the constructor, the function builds a *ViewPort* object that describes the ray-caster's viewing window— its position and size. Then the *OnCreate* function instantiates an object of type *DemoMaze*, which is the class that is derived from the *RayCaster* class to implement this game. The arguments to the *DemoMaze* constructor specify the player's position and the ray-caster's viewport.

If the *DemoMaze* object was successfully constructed, the *isLoaded* function returns a true value, and the game can proceed. The call to the Windows 95 *CWnd::SetTimer* function sets a timer that causes an automatic call to the *CWnd::OnTimer* function every 20 milliseconds. This mechanism manages the game's action through an override of the *CWnd::OnTimer* function. Figure 11.10 is the *CMainFrame::OnTimer* function.

```
void CMainFrame::OnTimer(UINT nIDEvent)
{
    // ----- test for player movement commands
    if (upkey)
        m_pDemoMaze->MoveForward();
    if (downkey)
        m_pDemoMaze->MoveBackward();
    if (rightkey)
        if (shiftkey)
            m_pDemoMaze->MoveRightward();
        else
            m_pDemoMaze->RotateRight();
    if (leftkey)
        if (shiftkey)
            m_pDemoMaze->MoveLeftward();
        else
            m_pDemoMaze->RotateLeft();
    // ------ render a frame
    m_pDemoMaze->DrawFrame();
    CFrameWnd::OnTimer(nIDEvent);
}
```

Figure 11.10 The CMainFrame::OnTimer function

The *CMainFrame::OnKeyDown* and *CMainFrame::OnKeyUp* functions set and clear the *upkey, downkey, rightkey, shiftkey,* and *leftkey* data members as the corresponding keys are pressed and released. This technique allows a program to watch all the keys at once and to respond to multiple key presses. The *CMainFrame::OnTimer* function, which executes every 20 milliseconds, tests these Boolean data members. If one of these members is true, the *OnTimer* function calls the corresponding *RayCaster* function through the derived class's pointer to move and rotate the player's position within the maze. This mechanism is how the player navigates the maze.

The *Move...* functions do not cause anything to be displayed. They only change the ray-caster's indicators that specify the player's position and orientation. The *OnTimer* function must then call the *RayCaster::DrawFrame* function to render a frame from the new information.

The Derived RayCaster Class

Demo 1 does very little in *DemoMaze*, the class that is derived from *RayCaster*. Figure 11.11 shows the entire class definition for Demo 1. We could have omitted it and used the *RayCaster* class directly. Including it, however, sets up the skeleton framework for later games. Our Tubas of Terror game in Chapter 12 does not use the *DemoMaze* class at all but instead provides custom classes to inherit and modify the ray-casting operations.

```
class DemoMaze : public RayCaster    {
public:
    DemoMaze(SHORT px, SHORT py, SHORT pangle, ViewPort vp);
    ~DemoMaze();
};
DemoMaze::DemoMaze(SHORT px, SHORT py, SHORT pangle, ViewPort vp) :
            RayCaster("maze.dat", "tiles.gfx", px, py, pangle, vp)
{
}
DemoMaze::~DemoMaze()
{
}
```

Figure 11.11 The DemoMaze class

Compiling and Running Demo 1

Now that you understand all the components, you are ready to build the Demo 1 program. Start the Visual C++ 4.0 Developer Studio and open the Project Workspace file in **c:\tot**. The file is named **DemoRaycaster.mdp**. Choose the **Rebuild All** command from Developer Studio's Build menu. When the command is finished, you can run the program and navigate the maze. Figure 11.12 shows the first thing you see when the program starts.

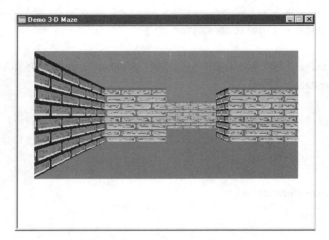

Figure 11.12 The Demo 1 program

Remember the initial values for the player's position and orientation? We established them in Figure 11.9 in the *CMainFrame::OnCreate* function. The x and y coordinates were both 192, and the orientation was 0. Refer now to the text representation of the maze in Figure 11.3. Each character position represents a square array of 64 by 64 coordinate points. The maze coordinates are zero-based, so 192/192 puts the player at the third character row and third character column. North is to the right in the maze text file, and east points downward. Therefore, the zero value for the player's initial orientation points the player to the right as viewed from above in the maze's text file. Figure 11.13 shows the southwest corner of the maze with a "greater than" symbol indicating the player's position and orientation.

```
1111111111111111111111
1>      1         1
1              1    1
1        1    1    1
1        1    1
11111111111
1          1    1111111111
```

Figure 11.13 Player position in the maze

Demo 2: Doors

The boring maze in Demo 1 represents what most books on this subject provide in the way of a demo. A 3-D maze game needs doors to open and close. Many games include doors that the player cannot open until a key object has been found somewhere else in the maze. We'll add doors to the maze in Demo 2.

To build Demo 2, log into your **\tot** subdirectory in an MS-DOS window and execute the following commands from the DOS command line.

```
copy d:\raycastd\demo2\*.*
bldmaze maze.txt maze.dat
gfxmake tiles.gfx @tiles.lst
```

It is necessary to rerun bldmaze and gfxmake; the maze for Demo 2 includes doors and therefore needs a modified **maze.txt** and some additional bitmap tiles. Figure 11.14 shows the new **tiles.lst** file, which identifies the two new tiles for the demo. Remember that their order in the file is important and must correspond to changes that we make to **consts.h** later in this discussion.

```
wall01.pcx
wall02.pcx
doorjam1.pcx
door01.pcx
```

Figure 11.14 Tiles.lst for Demo 2

Doors in the Maze

The maze from Demo 1 had nothing except wall tiles. To add doors, you put characters in the maze that represent door tiles. By convention, digits in the maze are reserved for wall tiles. The letters *D* and *d* represent doors; soon we'll see why we need two letters. Figure 11.15 shows **maze.txt** for Demo 2.

```
11111111111111111111111111111111111111111111111
1      1      1   1              1   1   1        1
1    d  1   1   1              1   1   1        1
1    1   1   1   1111D11 1111111   d   1        1
1    1   1        1              1   1        1
11111111111              1              1   1        1
1      1  1111111D11D11111111D1111111111111D11111
1      1  1                                        1
1    d  1                                        1
1      1  1111111111D11111111D11111111111111111111
1      1  1              1  1 11      1 1
1      1  1              1  1 11      1 1
1      1  1   11111111111111111  1    111   1 1
1      1  1        1           d 1 11  1 1 1
1      1  1        1              1  1 1 11 1 1
1    d  11111111  1  11111111111  1    11111   1
1      1  1                                        1
1      1  1                                        1
11111111  111111111111111111D11111111D11111111111111
1                                                  1
1                                                  1
111111111111111111111111111111111111111111111111111
```

Figure 11.15 Maze.txt for Demo 2

Each *D* in **maze.txt** represents a door on an east-west facing wall. Each *d* represents a door on a north-south facing wall. Remember that north is to the right in this coordinate system. By using different codes, we tell the ray-caster how to cast the door.

Door Tiles

Each door is represented by two 64x64 door tiles: one for the door itself and one for the doorjamb. Doors open by sliding from side to side. Instead of having them slide into the texture of a wall tile, we provide doorjamb bitmaps to set the doors off. Figure 11.16 shows the door bitmap tiles for the doors in Demo 2.

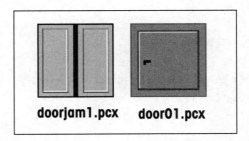

doorjam1.pcx   door01.pcx

Figure 11.16 Door and doorjamb bitmap tiles for Demo 2

Changes to Const.h for Demo 2

Const.h must be changed to recognize the door bitmaps. Figure 11.17 shows the pertinent changes to **const.h** for Demo 2.

```
const SHORT doorjam1 = highwall+1; // bitmap # for doorjamb
const SHORT door1    = highwall+2; // bitmap # for door1
const SHORT highdoor = highwall+2; // highest assigned door tile #
inline bool isXDoorCell(char cell)
{
    return islower(cell);
}
inline bool isDoorCell(char cell)
{
    // -- modify this function if doors are added
    cell = tolower(cell);
    return cell == 'd';
}
inline SHORT DoorTile(char cell)
{
    // -- modify this function if doors are added
    cell = tolower(cell);
    return cell == 'd' ? door1 : 0;
}
inline SHORT DoorJamTile(char cell)
{
    // -- modify this function if doors are added
    cell = tolower(cell);
    return cell == 'd' ? doorjam1 : 0;
}
```

Figure 11.17 Changes to const.h for Demo 2

Opening a Door: Another Key to Intercept

Displaying doors is one thing, but a player must also be able to open them. Otherwise, you'd be stuck in that small room in the southwest corner of the maze. Figure 11.18 shows how one small modification to the *CMainFrame::OnKeyUp* function takes care of that problem.

```
void CMainFrame::OnKeyUp(UINT nChar, UINT nRepCnt, UINT nFlags)
{
    switch (nChar)     {
        case VK_UP:     upkey    = FALSE; break;
        case VK_DOWN:   downkey  = FALSE; break;
        case VK_RIGHT:  rightkey = FALSE; break;
        case VK_LEFT:   leftkey  = FALSE; break;
        case VK_SHIFT:  shiftkey = FALSE; break;
        case VK_SPACE:  m_pDemoMaze->OpenCloseDoor(); break;
    }
    CFrameWnd::OnKeyUp(nChar, nRepCnt, nFlags);
}
```

Figure 11.18 The CMainFrame::OnKeyUp function for Demo 2

The VK_SPACE case is new for Demo 2. When the player presses and releases the **Spacebar**, the function calls the *RayCaster::OpenCloseDoor* function. If the player's position is facing a door and close enough to the door, the ray-cast engine opens that door if it is closed and closes that door if it is open. Doors close themselves automatically after they have been open a short time.

Compiling and Running Demo 2

Use the same procedure that you used with Demo 1 to build the program from within the Visual C++ 4.0 Developer Studio. Be sure to use the **Rebuild All** command on the Build menu. The new **const.h** file from the CD-ROM will be older than the object files that you built for Demo 1, so a **Rebuild All** is necessary.

Figure 11.19 shows the game's opening display from Demo 2.

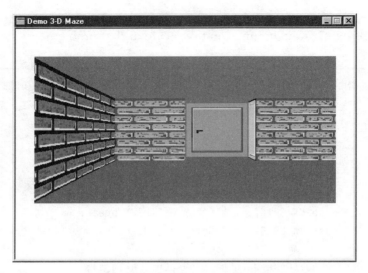

Figure 11.19 The Demo 2 program

Figure 11.20 shows a partially open door.

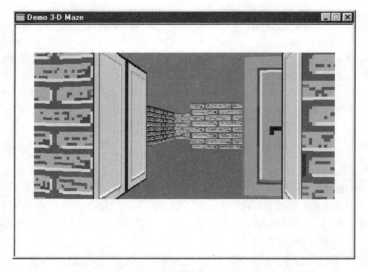

Figure 11.20 Partially open door

Demo 3: Props

A *prop* is a stationary graphical item that can occupy any space in the maze that is not occupied by a wall or door tile. Demo 3 adds props to the 3-D maze program we've been developing.

As the player moves through the maze, props represent objects through which the player cannot pass. Players have to go around a prop unless it is defined as being passable. Examples of passable props are ceiling fixtures and objects that the player picks up by stepping into the space where the object is positioned.

To build Demo 3, log into your **\tot** subdirectory in an MS-DOS window and execute the following commands from the DOS command line.

```
copy d:\raycastd\demo3\*.*
bldmaze maze.txt maze.dat
gfxmake tiles.gfx @tiles.lst
```

It is necessary to rerun bldmaze and gfxmake; the maze for Demo 3 includes props and therefore needs a modified **maze.txt** and some additional bitmap tiles. Figure 11.21 shows the new **tiles.lst** response file, which identifies three new tiles for the demo. Remember that the order of the tiles in the response file is important and must correspond to changes that we make to **consts.h** later in this discussion.

```
wall01.pcx
wall02.pcx
doorjam1.pcx
door01.pcx
flowrpot.pcx
light.pcx
table.pcx
```

Figure 11.21 Tiles.lst for Demo 2

Props in the Maze

You add props to the maze by assigning letter values to the props and putting these letters in the **maze.txt** file. Figure 11.22 shows the maze with props added.

```
1111111111111111111111111111111111111111111111111
1   G1         1  1T             T1   1   1   G1
1   d  1  1  1       L       1  1  1       1
1   1  1  1    1111D11 1111111   d   1   L  1
1   1  1  1            1        1  1      1
11111111111                     1        1  1   G1
1       1  1111111D11G11111111D11111111111D11111
1   1  1                           T          1
1  L  d  1       T T                           1
1       1  1111111111D11111111D11111111111111111
1       1  1                1 1 11      1 1
1T      1  1                1 1 11      1 1
1       1  1  L 1111111111111111   1     111   1  1
1       1  1        1        d  1 11  1 1  1
1       1  1        1           1 1 1  11 1  1
1  L  d  11111111  1  11111111111  1   11111   1
1       1  1                                  1
1       1  1                                  1
11111111  1111111111111111D11111111D1111111111111
1                                             1
1G                    T                        G
1111111111111111111111111111111111111111111111111
```

Figure 11.22 Maze.txt for Demo 3

The *G* characters in Figure 11.22 represent flowerpots. *T* characters are tables. *L* characters are overhead lights.

Prop Tiles

Each prop is represented by a 64x64 bitmap tile. A prop has transparent parts through which the player can see the walls, doors, and other objects in the background. You define transparent parts of a prop by using the zero color value. This value is the color offset byte to the palette and not the actual color. It helps to assign solid black to color zero so that you can see the transparent regions more readily. Figure 11.23 shows the three prop bitmap tiles that Demo 3 uses.

Figure 11.23 Prop bitmap tiles

Changes to Const.h for Demo 3

Const.h must be changed to recognize the prop bitmaps. Figure 11.24 shows the pertinent changes to **const.h** for Demo 3.

Observe the definition for the inline *isPassable* function. You must modify this function to specify all passable prop objects. In this program, only the overhead light is passable.

```
const SHORT flowerpot = highdoor+1; // bitmap # for flowerpot
const SHORT light     = highdoor+2; // bitmap # for light fixture
const SHORT table     = highdoor+3; // bitmap # for table
const SHORT highprop  = highdoor+3; // highest assigned prop tile
inline bool isPassable(SHORT bmpno)
{
    bmpno = BmpNumber(bmpno);
    return bmpno == light;
}
inline bool isPropCell(WORD cell)
{
    // ---- modify this function if props are added
    return cell == 'G' || cell == 'L' || cell == 'T';
}
inline SHORT PropTile(char cell)
{
    // ---- modify this function if props are added
    return cell == 'G' ? flowerpot :
           cell == 'L' ? light     :
           cell == 'T' ? table     :
           0;
}
```

Figure 11.24 Changes to const.h for Demo 3

Compiling and Running Demo 3

Use the same procedure that you used with Demos 1 and 2 to build the program from within the Visual C++ 4.0 Developer Studio. Remember to use the **Rebuild All** command.

Figure 11.25 shows the game's opening display from Demo 3. You can move through the maze now to view all the props.

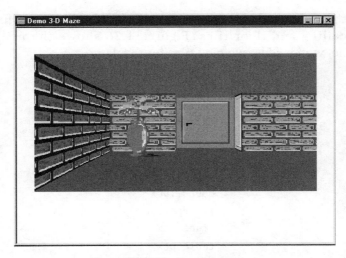

Figure 11.25 The Demo 3 program

Demo 4: Ceilings and Floors

Adding ceiling and floor tiles to a maze implies more than just adding the components. There is a significant performance penalty for processing floors and ceilings. The basic ray-casting algorithm does one set of X/Y casts per vertical line on the screen. Casting floors and ceilings requires vertical casts for each horizontal position from the edge of the viewport to the bottom of the nearest wall. Consequently, you want to be judicious about using this feature.

Don't use ceiling and floor casting in large rooms and hallways. Don't use the feature in a game that will run on an old, slow machine (assuming that you port this code to a 16-bit platform). The algorithm knows enough not to cast ceiling and floor rays in a room that does not use them, but it cannot disable itself if the platform is too slow to support it.

To build Demo 4, log into your **\tot** subdirectory in an MS-DOS window and execute the following commands from the DOS command line.

```
copy d:\raycastd\demo4\*.*
bldmaze maze.txt maze.dat
gfxmake tiles.gfx @tiles.lst
```

It is necessary to rerun bldmaze and gfxmake because the maze for Demo 4 includes ceiling and floor tiles. Figure 11.26 shows the new **tiles.lst** response file, which adds two new tiles for the demo.

```
wall01.pcx
wall02.pcx
floor1.pcx
ceiling1.pcx
doorjam1.pcx
door01.pcx
flowrpot.pcx
light.pcx
table.pcx
```

Figure 11.26 Tiles.lst for Demo 4

Adding Floor and Ceiling Entries to the Maze

To specify ceiling and floor tiles, you build a second copy of the maze for that purpose in **maze.txt**. Figure 11.27 shows the addition to **maze.txt** for Demo 4.

The text in Figure 11.27 follows the text for the rest of the maze. The pound sign (#) indicates the end of the main maze text and the beginning of the floor/ceiling maze. The *1* characters are unnecessary; they are there to help you orient yourself as you add ceiling characters. The only significant characters in this part of the maze are the *C* characters, which tell the ray-caster which rooms have ceilings and floors.

```
#

CCCCCCC11111111111CCCCCCCCCCCCCCCC1111111CCCCCCCC
CCCCCCC         1   CCCCCCCCCCCCCCCC   1   CCCCCCCC
CCCCCCC   1   1   CCCCCCCCCCCCCCCC   1   CCCCCCCC
CCCCCCC   1   1   CCCCCCCCCCCCCCCC       CCCCCCCC
CCCCCCC   1                 1             1   CCCCCCCC
CCCCCCC1111                 1             1   CCCCCCCC
1         1   1111111 11 11111111 1111111111CCCCCCCC
1         1 1                                       1
1         1                                         1
1         1   1111111111 11111111 111111111111111111
1        1 1                   1  1  1 1      1  1
1         1 1                   1  1 1 1      1  1
1         1 1     1111111111111111  1     111    1  1
1         1 1           1             1 11   1 1  1
1         1 1           1             1  1 1  11 1  1
1             11111111   1  11111111111   1    11111   1
1         1 1                                       1
1         1 1                                       1
11111111   1111111111111111 11111111 1111111111111
1                                                   1
1                                                   1
111111111111111111111111111111111111111111111111111
```

Figure 11.27 Maze.txt for Demo 4

Floor and Ceiling Tiles

Each floor/ceiling configuration consists of two 64x64 bitmap tiles: one for the floor and one for the ceiling. If a room has a ceiling, it must also have a floor. Figure 11.28 shows the floor and ceiling tiles for Demo 4.

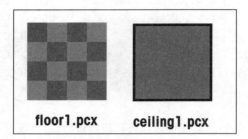

floor1.pcx   ceiling1.pcx

Figure 11.28 Floor and ceiling bitmap tiles

Changes to Const.h for Demo 4

Const.h must be changed to recognize the floor and ceiling bitmaps. Figure 11.29 shows the pertinent changes to **const.h** for Demo 4.

```
const SHORT floor1   = highwall+1; // bitmap for floor/ceiling 1
const SHORT highfloor = highwall+2; // highest floor/ceiling tile #
inline bool isCeilingCell(WORD cell)
{
    // ---- modify this function if ceiling tiles are added
    return cell == 'C';
}
inline SHORT CeilingTile(char cell)
{
    // ---- modify this function if ceiling tiles are added
    return cell == 'C' ? floor1 : 0;
}
```

Figure 11.29 Changes to const.h for Demo 4

Compiling and Running Demo 4

Use the same procedure that you used with the other demos to build the program from within the Visual C++ 4.0 Developer Studio. Remember to use the **Rebuild All** command.

Figure 11.30 shows the game's opening display from Demo 4.

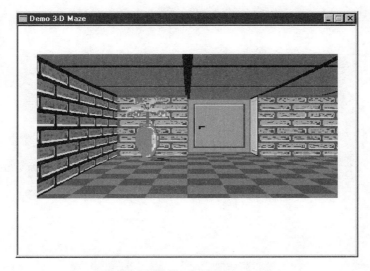

Figure 11.30 The Demo 4 program

What Next?

The four demo programs in this chapter show how to build a basic 3-D maze model with walls, doors, props, ceilings, and floors. In Chapter 12, we enhance this simple model so that it is a full-fledged 3-D maze game. We add sprites, weapons, a resizable viewport, a menu, center-opening doors, more wall, floor, and ceiling bitmap tiles, a speed control, and the ability for the player to venture outside the maze. Chapter 12 also presents a comprehensive reference guide to the RayCaster class library.

TUBAS OF TERROR:
A 3-D MAZE GAME

This chapter adds many features to the demo game of Chapter 11, turning it into Tubas of Terror, a full-fledged 3-D maze game. The game is not a world-beater; it is easy to play and win. But it represents the start of a full-fledged 3-D maze game. You could add components and levels of play and turn this relatively simple demonstration into a professional-quality product, or you could use it as a model for building your own unique game. In this chapter you will learn about:

- Sprites
- Viewport size
- Menus
- New doors, walls, ceilings, and floors
- Controlling the player's speed of motion
- Sound effects

Building the Game

To build the Tubas of Terror game, you must copy the files from Chapter 11's four demo programs onto your hard drive. If you skipped this procedure, return to Chapter 11 and copy into **C:\tot** the files for the RayCaster engine and Demo 1 through Demo 4, in that order.

Log into the **\tot** subdirectory and execute the following commands from the DOS command line:

```
copy d:\raycastd\demo5\*.*
bldmaze maze.txt maze.dat
gfxmake tiles.gfx @tiles.lst
gfxmake sprites.gfx @sprites.lst
```

It is necessary to rerun bldmaze and gfxmake, because the new maze includes new prop, wall, door, ceiling, and floor tiles as well as weapon tiles. The second run of gfxmake builds the **.gfx** file for the sprite images. Figures 12.1 and 12.2 show the **tiles.lst** and **sprites.lst** response files.

```
wall01.pcx
wall02.pcx
wall03.pcx
wall04.pcx
wall05.pcx
wall05.pcx
floor1.pcx
ceiling1.pcx
floor2.pcx
ceiling2.pcx
doorjam1.pcx
doorjam2.pcx
door01.pcx
door02.pcx
door03.pcx
door04.pcx
door05.pcx
door06.pcx
door07.pcx
door08.pcx
door09.pcx
flowrpot.pcx
light.pcx
table.pcx
clrtable.pcx
trumpet.pcx
trumpet1.pcx
trumpet2.pcx
```

Figure 12.1 Tiles.lst for Tubas of Terror

```
tuba100.pcx
tuba101.pcx
tuba102.pcx
tuba103.pcx
tuba104.pcx
tuba105.pcx
tuba106.pcx
tuba107.pcx
tuba200.pcx
tuba201.pcx
tuba202.pcx
tuba203.pcx
tuba204.pcx
tuba205.pcx
tuba206.pcx
tuba207.pcx
tuba300.pcx
tuba301.pcx
tuba302.pcx
tuba303.pcx
tuba304.pcx
tuba305.pcx
tuba306.pcx
tuba307.pcx
tuba400.pcx
tuba500.pcx
tuba501.pcx
```

Figure 12.2 Sprites.lst for Tubas of Terror

An Extended Maze

The **maze.txt** file for Tubas of Terror includes more ceiling and floor indicators, more wall tiles, and a door to the outdoors. Figure 12.3 shows the complete **maze.txt** for Tubas of Terror.

```
1111111111111111111111111111111111111111111111111
1      1      1  1                1   1   1        1
1  L   d   1   1   1              1   1   1        1
1      1   1   1   1111D11G1111111     d   1   L   1
1T     1   1               1          1   1        1
11111111111                1          1   1        1
13333331   1111111D11G11111111D11111111111D11111
13     31  1                                       1
13  L  d   1                                       1
13     31  1111111111G11111111D111111111111111111111
13t    31  1                1   1  1 1     H1   1
13333331   1                1   1  1 1          1   1
15555551   1     111111111111111   1   d  111      1   1
15t    51  1           1             d  1  11   1 1   1
15     51  1           1                1  1  11 1 1   1
15  L  d   11111111   1  11111111111   1    11111   1
15     51  1                                       1
15555551   1                                       1
11111111   1111111111111111   1111111D111111111111
1                                                  1
1                                                  1
11111111111111111111D1111111111111E1111111111111111
           1G   T   T   G   1G       G1
           1           L        1           1
        1111111                 1       111
        1       1                   1t      T1
        1           L   L   L   d       L  e
        1       1                   1t      G1
        1111111                 1       111
           1           L        1           1
           1G              G   1G       G1
           1111111111111111111111111111
```

#end (Ceiling tile specs follow)

Figure 12.3 Maze.txt for Tubas of Terror

```
ccccccc11111111111CCCCCCCCCCCCCCCC1111111CCCCCCCC
ccccccc        1   CCCCCCCCCCCCCCC    1   CCCCCCCC
ccccccc    1   1   CCCCCCCCCCCCCCC    1   CCCCCCCC
ccccccc    1   1   CCCCCCCCCCCCCCC    d   CCCCCCCC
ccccccc    1           1              1   CCCCCCCC
ccccccc1111            1              1   CCCCCCCC
ccccccc    1111111D11111111111D1111111111CCCCCCCC
ccccccc    1                                     1
ccccccc    1                                     1
ccccccc    1111111111111111111D111111111111111111
ccccccc    1               1   1  1 1      1  1
ccccccc    1               1   1  1 1      1  1
ccccccc    1    1111111111111111   1  d 111    1  1
ccccccc    1        1          d  1 11  1 1  1
ccccccc    1        1          1  1 1   11 1  1
ccccccc    11111111  1  11111111111  1    11111  1
ccccccc    1                                     1
ccccccc    1                                     1
ccccccc    1111111111111111   1111111D1111111111111
1                                                1
1                                                1
11111111111CCCCCCCCCCCCCCCCCCCCCCCCCCCCCC11111111111
              1              CCCCCCCCCC
              1              CCCCCCCCCC
          1111111            CCCCCCCCCC
          1                  CCCCCCCCCC
          1                  CCCCCCCCCC00
          1                  CCCCCCCCCC
          1111111            CCCCCCCCCC
              1              CCCCCCCCCC
              1              CCCCCCCCCC
              1111111111111111111CCCCCCCCCC

#
```

Figure 12.3 Maze.txt for Tubas of Terror (continued)

This maze is much more complex than the ones in Chapter 11. A two-room wing has been added to the east side of the maze. The northern room in the new wing has a door to the outside. Represented by the *e* character, this door is different from the routine one that the other demos use. Elsewhere in the maze is an *E* character representing the same new door on an east-west facing wall. The new door opens from the center rather than slide from side to side.

The two south rooms in the main part of the maze have new wall tiles (*3* and *5*) inside the usual *1* wall tiles. They are built as inner walls so that the outside view of these walls retains the texture of wall tile *1*. Remember that wall tiles come in sets of two for the 3-D effect, and the maze contains only the odd-numbered tile of each of these sets. If the maze had no door leading outside, the new wall tiles could be used in place of the *1* tiles, and the rooms could be the same size they were in the other demos.

The *t* cell in one of the thick-walled rooms represents another table prop for variety.

The south rooms of the main maze have new ceiling and floor tiles. The stoop of the door that leads outside has *O* characters to indicate to the ray caster that the player is now outdoors.

An *H* cell in a small room in the north center part of the main maze represents a weapon that the player can retrieve and use. In this game, weapons are musical instruments.

More Props, Doors, Walls, Floors, and Ceilings

Tubas of Terror has many more graphical elements than do the demos of Chapter 11. A trumpet stands on the floor. One room contains an empty table. There is a center-opening door. There are new walls, floors, and ceilings. Figure 12.4 is a montage of the new tiles that the game adds to the maze.

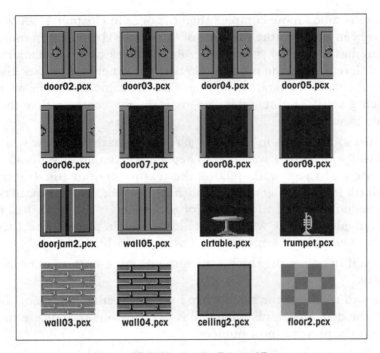

Figure 12.4 New tiles for Tubas of Terror

The center-opening door is represented by eight bitmap tiles: **door02.pcx** through **door09.pcx**. The black space between the door panels is the zero color value representing the transparent parts of the door. These eight tiles animate the door's opening and closing. There is an implied ninth tile that you do not have to provide—the fully open door, which is completely transparent. You can use this technique for doors that open in many interesting ways—the shutter on a camera, jagged edges that fit together as in a TV starship, doors that slide up or down, and so on.

Notice that there is only one tile, **wall05.pcx**, for the paneled wall. There was no visual advantage to using two tiles with subtle shading differences. However, the engine requires walls to be represented by sets of two, so **tiles.lst** in Figure 12.1 contains two entries for **wall05.pcx**.

In the black and white figure the new ceiling and floor tiles look just like the others, but they have different colors.

A Weapon

The **trumpet.pcx** tile in Figure 12.4 is a prop that stands on the floor in a hidden room. This prop is set in **consts.h** to be passable, which means that the player can move into the space occupied by the prop. The game program assigns the trumpet weapon to the player and deletes the prop from the maze.

When a player holds a weapon, the weapon is displayed at the bottom and in the center of the viewing window. The weapon seems to point in the direction that the player is facing. The program selects the player's weapon by calling the *RayCaster::SetWeapon* function. Weapons are selected by bitmap tile number from the tiles loaded from the **.gfx** file by the *RayCaster* constructor.

Figure 12.5 shows the tiles that display the game player's trumpet weapon.

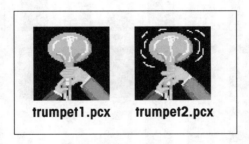

trumpet1.pcx   trumpet2.pcx

Figure 12.5 Weapon bitmap tiles

The two weapon tiles display under control of the game program. The engine does not automate their selection except to display whatever tile has been named as the current weapon. In this case, there are two tiles: one to represent the weapon being held and one to represent the weapon being fired (blown).

Sprites

Tubas of Terror contains one sprite: a tuba player that paces up and down in the large room in the east wing of the maze. The sprite's current position, orientation, and action are controlled by the application program. An *rcSprite* class encapsulates the behavior of sprites. The game derives a specialized *TubaPlayer* class from *rcSprite* and puts an instance of that class into the class that is derived from *RayCaster*.

A sprite is represented by 27 bitmap tiles. Each bitmap tile is 32 pixels wide by 64 pixels high. Twenty-four of these tiles animate the walking action as three poses viewed from eight angles. Eight of the 24 walking tiles also serve to render the sprite in a standing pose. Another tile renders the sprite's firing action, and two more tiles animate the sprite's dying action. Figure 12.6 shows the 27 bitmap tiles that represent the tuba player in Tubas of Terror.

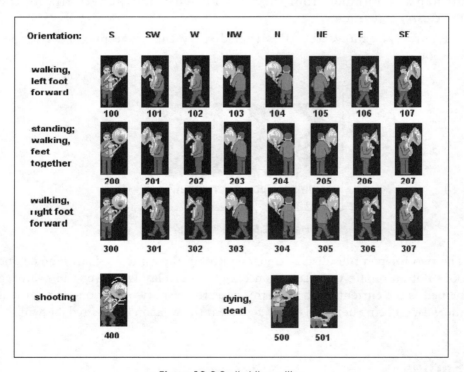

Figure 12.6 Sprite bitmap tiles

The tiles in Figure 12.6 are numbered to correspond to their **.pcx** file names. For example, tile 100 is **tuba100.pcx**. The names themselves have no significance to the program; we used this naming convention because it is convenient to work with. However, the order of names in **sprites.lst**

(Figure 12.2) is important. The *rcSprite* class computes which tile to render based on what the sprite is doing (walking, standing, shooting, pausing, dying, dead), the direction in which the sprite is facing, and the direction in which the player is facing. The figure shows the sprite's orientation at the top of the columns of tiles for standing and walking poses when the player is facing north.

In the shooting pose, the sprite is always facing the player. The engine assumes that a sprite shoots only at the player. The pausing pose uses the south-facing standing pose; a game uses the pausing pose between shots. The dying and dead poses also face the player. As the player walks around a dead sprite, its feet, in this example, are always toward the player.

Consts.h for Tubas of Terror

There are many changes to **consts.h** to support these new features. Figure 12.7 shows the principal changes.

```
const SHORT highwall  = 6;   // highest assigned wall tile #
// ======= floors ========
const SHORT floor1    = highwall+1;   // bitmap for floor/ceiling 1
const SHORT floor2    = highwall+3;   // bitmap for floor/ceiling 2
// add floor tiles here
const SHORT highfloor = highwall+4;   // highest floor/ceiling tile #
// ======= doors ========
const SHORT doorjam1  = highfloor+1;  // bitmap # for doorjam
const SHORT doorjam2  = highfloor+2;  // bitmap # for doorjam
const SHORT door1     = highfloor+3;  // bitmap # for door1
const SHORT door2     = highfloor+4;  // bitmap # for door2
const SHORT highdoor  = highfloor+11; // highest assigned door tile
// ======= props =========
const SHORT flowerpot = highdoor+1;   // bitmap # for flowerpot
const SHORT light     = highdoor+2;   // bitmap # for light fixture
```

Figure 12.7 Consts.h for Tubas of Terror

```
const SHORT table       = highdoor+3;    // bitmap # for table
const SHORT emptytable  = highdoor+4;    // bitmap # for empty table
const SHORT trumpet     = highdoor+5;    // bitmap # for trumpet
const SHORT highprop    = highdoor+5;  // highest assigned prop tile #
// ====== sprites ==========
const SHORT tuba        = highprop+1;  // bitmap # for tuba sprite
const SHORT highsprite  = highprop+1;  // highest assigned sprite tile #
// ===== other tiles =========
const SHORT outdoors    = highsprite+1;  // maze identifier for outdoors
// ===================================================================
inline bool isPassable(SHORT bmpno)
{
    bmpno = BmpNumber(bmpno);
    return bmpno == light || bmpno == trumpet;
}
inline bool isCenterDoor(SHORT bmpno)
{
    return BmpNumber(bmpno) >= door2;
}
inline bool isPropCell(WORD cell)
{
    // ---- modify this function if props are added
    return cell == 'G' ||
           cell == 'L' ||
           cell == 'T' ||
           cell == 't' ||
           cell == 'H';
}
inline bool isCeilingCell(WORD cell)
{
    // ---- modify this function if ceiling tiles are added
    return cell == 'C' || cell == 'c' || cell == '0';
}
```

Figure 12.7 Consts.h for Tubas of Terror (continued)

```
inline bool isDoorCell(char cell)
{
    // ---- modify this function if doors are added
    cell = tolower(cell);
    return cell == 'd' || cell == 'e';
}
inline SHORT PropTile(char cell)
{
    // ---- modify this function if props are added
    return cell == 'G' ? flowerpot  :
           cell == 'L' ? light      :
           cell == 'T' ? table      :
           cell == 't' ? emptytable :
           cell == 'H' ? trumpet    :
                    0;
}
inline SHORT CeilingTile(char cell)
{
    // ---- modify this function if ceiling tiles are added
    return cell == 'C' ? floor1 :
           cell == 'c' ? floor2 :
           cell == 'O' ? outdoors : 0;
}
inline SHORT OutdoorTile(char cell)
{
    return cell == 'O' ? outdoors : 0;
}
inline SHORT DoorTile(char cell)
{
    // ---- modify this function if doors are added
    cell = tolower(cell);
    return cell == 'd' ? door1  :
           cell == 'e' ? door2  :
```

Figure 12.7 Consts.h for Tubas of Terror (continued)

```
                0;
    }
    inline SHORT DoorJamTile(char cell)
    {
        // ---- modify this function if doors are added
        cell = tolower(cell);
        return cell == 'd' ? doorjam1 :
               cell == 'e' ? doorjam2 :
               0;
    }
    inline SHORT SpriteTile(char cell)
    {
        // ---- modify this function if sprites are added
        return cell == 'Z' ? tuba : 0;
    }
```

Figure 12.7 Consts.h for Tubas of Terror (continued)

Resizing the Viewport

Tubas of Terror permits the player to change the size of the viewport. There are many initial computations related to the viewport's size, and these values must be recalculated if the size changes. Therefore, the program deletes the derived *RayCaster* object, changes the *ViewPort* object, and constructs a new *RayCaster* object.

In the demonstration, the program makes no attempt to save the program's state except for the player's current position and orientation. In a real game you would save the state of all variables: the position and orientation of all sprites, their conditions (dead, alive), the player's health, weapons, ammunition, treasure collections, and so on.

A Menu

Tubas of Terror adds a Windows 95 menu to the application window. The menu includes commands to save and restore the game, zoom the viewport, and change the speed of the player's movement and rotation. The save and restore commands don't do anything, however; that's for you to do.

Speed Control

Changing the player's speed is a matter of calling the *RayCaster::Faster* and *RayCaster::Slower* functions. The menu has commands that execute *CMainFrame* functions to make these calls. Each call modifies the number of maze increments and the number of degrees of rotation by plus or minus one until the player's speed reaches a programmed minimum or maximum.

Sound Effects

Sound effects are implemented through a *SoundEffects* class that encapsulates the Windows SDK MCI functions to play **.wav** files. Playing sound effects is not part of the ray-casting algorithm, but a 3-D maze game without sound effects would be less than effective. The engine provides some support; it calls virtual functions at those times when sound effects would be appropriate. The virtual functions have empty implementations in the *RayCaster* and *rcSprite* classes. You can override each sound effect's corresponding virtual function in your classes derived from the *RayCaster* and *rcSprite* classes, or you can allow the empty implementations to stand.

The SoundEffects Class

The *SoundEffects* class has a constructor and a *Play* member function. The constructor takes a *CWnd* pointer as an argument to point to the *CWnd* object that receives notification when a sound effect is completed. The *Play* member function accepts a pointer to the name of a **.wav** file that is to be played.

The MM_MCINOTIFY Message

To use the *SoundEffects* class, you must provide a handler for the MM_MCINOTIFY message that the MCI functions send when a sound effect has completed playing. This handler must close the device that played the sound effect. Such messages can be sent only to window classes. Inasmuch as the only window class in Tubas of Terror is *CMainFrame*, this class receives and processes the MM_MCINOTIFY message. Override the *CWnd::WindowProc* function in the *CMainFrame* class declaration with the following statement:

```
virtual LRESULT WindowProc(UINT message, WPARAM wParam, LPARAM lParam);
```

Implement the overridden function with the following code:

```
LRESULT CMainFrame::WindowProc(UINT message,WPARAM wParam,LPARAM lParam)
{
    if (message == MM_MCINOTIFY)
        mciSendCommand(lParam, MCI_CLOSE, 0, 0);
    return CFrameWnd::WindowProc(message, wParam, lParam);
}
```

Tubas of Terror: The Game

Tubas of Terror is implemented by deriving the *TubasOfTerror* class from the *RayCaster* class, and the *TubaPlayer* class from the *rcSprite* class. As with the demos in Chapter 11, the *CMainFrame* class instantiates the game objects and processes player actions. As before, we use figures to show fragments of the program listings rather than the complete source code files. You should view **mainfrm.h**, **mainfrm.cpp**, **tubas.h**, and **tubas.cpp** in your programmer's editor to see the big picture during these discussions.

CMainFrame::OnCreate

Figure 12.8 is the *CMainFrame::OnCreate* function, which launches the game by setting everything up.

```
int CMainFrame::OnCreate(LPCREATESTRUCT lpCreateStruct)
{
    if (CFrameWnd::OnCreate(lpCreateStruct) == -1)
        return -1;
    const int x = 192;
    const int y = 192;
    const int angle = 0;
    size = 1; // initial viewport size (0, 1, 2 == small, medium, big)
    if (ChangeViewPort(swidth[size], sheight[size], x, y, angle) == -1)
        return -1;
    return 0;
}
```

Figure 12.8 CMainFrame::OnCreate

There are two principal differences between this *OnCreate* function and those of earlier demos. First, this *OnCreate* function calls *ChangeViewPort* instead of *BuildMaze* to instantiate the game. Second, this *OnCreate* uses the medium values from the *swidth* and *sheight* arrays, rather than constants, as size arguments for the viewing window. These arrays allow the program to change viewport sizes when the player issues zoom in and zoom out commands.

CMainFrame::ChangeViewPort

Figure 12.9 is the *CMainFrame::ChangeViewPort* function.

```
int CMainFrame::ChangeViewPort(int width, int height,
                               SHORT nx, SHORT ny, SHORT nangle)
{
    SHORT x = nx, y = ny, angle = nangle;
    if (m_pTubasOfTerror != 0) {
        m_pTubasOfTerror->GetPosition(x, y, angle);
        delete m_pTubasOfTerror;
        m_pTubasOfTerror = 0;
        RECT rcClient;
        GetClientRect(&rcClient);
        InvalidateRect(&rcClient, TRUE);
    }
    int leftcol = (windowwidth-cxframe-width) / 2;
    int toprow  = (windowheight-cyframe-height) / 3;
    ViewPort vp = { leftcol, toprow, width, height };
    return BuildMaze(x, y, angle, vp);
}
```

Figure 12.9 CMainFrame::ChangeViewPort

The *ChangeViewPort* function is used for the first instantiation of the object of the class derived from *RayCaster* and for subsequent deletes of that object and reinstantiations of new viewport sizes.

CMainFrame::BuildMaze

The *CMainFrame::BuildMaze* function does what it does in the earlier demos except that it instantiates an object of type *TubasOfTerror* instead of type *DemoRayCaster*.

CMainFrame::OnKey...

The *CMainFrame::OnKeyUp* and *CMainFrame::OnKeyDown* functions are the same as their earlier counterparts except that they sense the condition of the **Ctrl** key, which the game uses to blow the trumpet weapon.

CMainFrame::OnViewZoom...

The *CMainFrame::OnViewZoomIn* and *CMainFrame::OnViewZoomOut* functions execute when the player chooses the zoom in and zoom out commands. Figure 12.10 shows these functions. Both actions change the viewport's size by calling *CMainFrame::ChangeViewPort*. This function deletes the current derived *RayCaster* object and, consequently, the derived *rcSprite* object. *ChangeViewPort* builds a new game, preserving only the player's position and orientation.

```
void CMainFrame::OnViewZoomIn()
{
    if (size < maxsize-1)  {
        size++;
        ChangeViewPort(swidth[size], sheight[size]);
    }
}
void CMainFrame::OnViewZoomOut()
{
    if (size > 0)  {
        --size;
        ChangeViewPort(swidth[size], sheight[size]);
    }
}
```

Figure 12.10 Zooming the viewport

Other Commands

Figure 12.11 shows the *CMainFrame::On...* functions for changing the player's speed through the maze and for opening and closing doors. Previous demos used the *OnKeyUp* function to sense that the player was pressing the **Spacebar**. We changed it here to use the MFC feature that dispatches command functions based on accelerator-key presses.

```
void CMainFrame::OnViewFaster()
{
    m_pTubasOfTerror->Faster();
}
void CMainFrame::OnViewSlower()
{
    m_pTubasOfTerror->Slower();
}
void CMainFrame::OnOpendoor()
{
    m_pTubasOfTerror->OpenCloseDoor();
}
```

Figure 12.11 CMainFrame::On... command functions

CMainFrame::OnTimer

Figure 12.12 is the *CMainFrame::OnTimer* function, which executes every 20 milliseconds. This function works much as it does in the other demos but adds some operations. When the player has been destroyed by the sprite, the *OnTimer* function calls the *RayCaster::FadeScreen* function to process a sequence of screen fadeouts and then returns. Nothing else is permitted if you lose the game.

A call to *TubasOfTerror::FixWeapon* every cycle restores the weapon bitmap to the nonfiring image in case the player has fired the weapon (tooted the trumpet).

A call to *TubasOfTerror::StepSpriteForward* every cycle lets the game use the timer event to manage the movements of the sprite.

```
void CMainFrame::OnTimer(UINT nIDEvent)
{
    if (m_pTubasOfTerror->isAlive() == false)      {
        m_pTubasOfTerror->FadeScreen();
        return;
    }
    // ---- test for player movement commands
    if (upkey)
        m_pTubasOfTerror->MoveForward();
    if (downkey)
        m_pTubasOfTerror->MoveBackward();
    if (rightkey)
        if (shiftkey)
            m_pTubasOfTerror->MoveRightward();
        else
            m_pTubasOfTerror->RotateRight();
    if (leftkey)
        if (shiftkey)
            m_pTubasOfTerror->MoveLeftward();
        else
            m_pTubasOfTerror->RotateLeft();
    m_pTubasOfTerror->FixWeapon();
    if (ctrlkey)
        m_pTubasOfTerror->Shoot();
    // --- manage sprite movement
    m_pTubasOfTerror->StepSpriteForward();
    //----- cast and Blt the frame
    m_pTubasOfTerror->DrawFrame();
    CFrameWnd::OnTimer(nIDEvent);
}
```

Figure 12.12 CMainFrame::OnTimer

The TubasOfTerror Class

Figure 12.13 is the *TubasOfTerror* class, which is derived from the *RayCaster* class. *TubesOfTerror* specializes the ray-casting engine to the needs of this particular game. It adds a sprite, a weapon, and sound effects.

```
class TubasOfTerror : public RayCaster    {
    TubaPlayer* m_pTubaPlayer;
    SHORT spriteno;
    SHORT stepctr;
    SHORT shotcounter;
    SHORT health;
    bool alive;
    bool haveweapon;
    SoundEffects sound;
    void OpenDoorSoundEffect();
    void CloseDoorSoundEffect();
    void TootSoundEffect();
public:
    TubasOfTerror(SHORT px, SHORT py, SHORT pangle,
                                      ViewPort vp);
    ~TubasOfTerror();
    void StepSpriteForward();
    void Shoot();
    bool isAlive() const
        { return alive; }
    void MoveForward();
    void FixWeapon();
    void PlaySound(char* wav);
};
```

Figure 12.13 The TubasOfTerror class

The TubasOfTerror Constructor

Figure 12.14 is the *TubasOfTerror* constructor. Its function header calls the constructors for the base *RayCaster* class and the embedded *SoundEvents* object. The *TubasOfTerror* constructor instantiates one sprite object of the *TubaPlayer* class, which is derived from the *rcSprite* class.

```
// ----- initial tuba player sprite position within maze
static SHORT tx = 15*64+32, ty = 27*64+32;


TubasOfTerror::TubasOfTerror(SHORT px, SHORT py, SHORT pangle,
                             ViewPort vp) :
        RayCaster("maze.dat", "tiles.gfx", px, py, pangle, vp),
        sound(pCMainFrame)
{
    m_pTubaPlayer = 0;
    if (isLoaded())      {
        m_pTubaPlayer = new TubaPlayer(this, tx, ty);
        if (m_pTubaPlayer->isLoaded())
            spriteno = AddSprite(m_pTubaPlayer);
    }
    stepctr = 0;
    shotcounter = 0;
    health = 3;
    alive = true;
    haveweapon = false;
}
```

Figure 12.14 TubasOfTerror constructor

Observe the two integer expressions that specify where in the maze the sprite is initially positioned. The first value in each expression is the maze cell coordinate, which corresponds to a character position in the maze text file. The expression multiplies the maze cell coordinate by 64 to convert it into a maze coordinate and then adds 32 to position the sprite in the center of the cell.

This technique allows you to use your programmer's editor to determine maze cell coordinates. Load the maze text file into your editor. Put the cursor on the relevant cell and observe its line and column number in the text file. The line number is the cell's one-based Y coordinate, and the column number is the cell's one-based X coordinate. Subtract one from these values to get zero-based maze cell coordinates.

TubasOfTerror::Shoot and TubasOfTerror::FixWeapon

These two functions, shown in Figure 12.15, support the player's weapon operations. The *Shoot* function is called when the player presses **Ctrl** to fire the weapon. *Shoot* sounds the firing sound effect by calling *TootSoundEffect*, sets the weapon bitmap to the firing bitmap by calling RayCaster::SetWeapon, and calls *RayCaster::inSights* to see whether a sprite is in the sights of the player's weapon. If it is, and if the sprite is still alive, the *Shoot* function calls *rcSprite::Die* to tell the sprite that it has been hit.

The *FixWeapon* function is called once every cycle of the clock. If the player is in possession of a weapon, *FixWeapon* sets the weapon's bitmap by calling *RayCaster::SetWeapon*.

```
void TubasOfTerror::Shoot()
{
    if (haveweapon)  {
        TootSoundEffect();
        SetWeapon(28);
        rcSprite* tp = inSights();
        if (tp != 0 && tp->isAlive())
            tp->Die();
    }
}
void TubasOfTerror::FixWeapon()
{
    SetWeapon(haveweapon ? 27 : 0);
}
```

Figure 12.15 The game player's weaponry

TubasOfTerror::MoveForward

The *TubasOfTerror* class overrides the *RayCaster::MoveForward* function, which *CMainFrame* calls when the player presses the up arrow key. Figure 12.16 shows the overriding function. Its purpose is to see whether the player has moved to the maze cell spot where the trumpet weapon is stored. If it has, the function posts the weapon possession to the object and calls *RayCaster::DeleteProp* to delete the trumpet prop from the maze.

```
void TubasOfTerror::MoveForward()
{
    RayCaster::MoveForward();
    if (!haveweapon) {
        // ------ test to see if player has found trumpet
        SHORT x, y, angle;
        GetPosition(x, y, angle);
        x /= 64;
        y /= 64;
        if (x == 44 && y == 11)   {
            // ------ found trumpet
            haveweapon = true;
            DeleteProp(x, y);
        }
    }
}
```

Figure 12.16 TubasOfTerror::MoveForward

TubasOfTerror::StepSpriteForward

Figure 12.17 shows the *TubasOfTerror::StepSpriteForward* function, which *CMainFrame* calls once each clock cycle. *StepSpriteForward* manages the position of the *TubaPlayer* sprite.

```
void TubasOfTerror::StepSpriteForward()
{
    ASSERT(m_pTubaPlayer);
    if (!m_pTubaPlayer->isAlive())
        return;
    SHORT dist = m_pTubaPlayer->GetDistance();
    if (dist < 128)  {
        if (shotcounter < 10)
            m_pTubaPlayer->Shoot();
        else
            m_pTubaPlayer->Pause();
        if (++shotcounter == 30)  {
            if (--health == 0)
                alive = false;
            shotcounter = 0;
        }
    }
    else {
        shotcounter = 0;
        m_pTubaPlayer->ResumeWalking();
        if (stepctr == 10 * (tilewidth / stepincrement))
            m_pTubaPlayer->AboutFace();
        if (stepctr == 20 * (tilewidth / stepincrement))    {
            m_pTubaPlayer->AboutFace();
            stepctr = 0;
        }
        m_pTubaPlayer->StepForward();
        MoveSpriteRelative(spriteno,m_pTubaPlayer->CurrXIncrement(),0);
        stepctr++;
    }
}
```

Figure 12.17 TubasOfTerror::StepSpriteForward

If the sprite is no longer alive, the function ignores it. Otherwise, if the sprite is closer than 128 maze units away from the player, *StepSpriteForward* initiates the sprite's firing sequence by calling *rcSprite::Shoot*. The firing sequence is completely under the control of *StepSpriteForward*. Ten clock cycles after calling *Shoot*, the function calls *rcSprite::Pause* to display the second frame in the two-frame shooting sequence. Thirty cycles later, *StepSpriteForward* restarts the sequence. If the sequence repeats three times, the *TubasOfTerror::alive* flag is cleared to indicate that the sprite has defeated the player.

When the player is out of the sprite's firing range, *StepSpriteForward* maintains a back-and-forth pacing pattern, calling the *TubaPlayer::AboutFace* function every 10 steps. Each step involves a call to *TubaPlayer::StepForward* to manage the walking animation and a call to *RayCaster::MoveSpriteRelative* to advance the sprite in its X coordinate position. The number of elements to advance and the direction, plus or minus, are determined by the value returned from the *TubaPlayer::CurrXIncrement* function.

TubasOfTerror Sound Effects

The functions shown in Figure 12.18 implement sound effects for the various player actions. The *PlaySound* function provides access to the sound system for the *TubaPlayer* object. The *OpenDoorSoundEffect* and *CloseDoorSoundEffect* functions override empty versions of these functions in the *RayCaster* class. *RayCaster* calls these functions when a door is about to be opened and when the door is closed. They use the *SoundEffects* object to play **.wav** files.

The *TootSoundEffect* function plays the weapon-firing **.wav** file when the *TubasOfTerror* object receives the fire event (**Spacebar**) from the player.

```
void TubasOfTerror::PlaySound(char* wav)
{
    sound.Play(wav);
}
void TubasOfTerror::OpenDoorSoundEffect()
{
    sound.Play("dooropen.wav");
}
void TubasOfTerror::CloseDoorSoundEffect()
{
    sound.Play("doorcls.wav");
}
void TubasOfTerror::TootSoundEffect()
{
    sound.Play("toot.wav");
}
```

Figure 12.18 TubasOfTerror sound effects

The TubaPlayer Class

The *TubaPlayer* class is derived from the *rcSprite* class. *TubaPlayer* implements the specialized behavior of a tuba player sprite. Figure 12.19 shows the *TubaPlayer* class declaration.

```
class TubaPlayer : public rcSprite    {
    SHORT xincr;
    SHORT yincr;
    SHORT stepctr;
    TubasOfTerror* ptot;
    void ShootSoundEffect();
public:
    TubaPlayer(TubasOfTerror* ptt, SHORT tx, SHORT ty);
    void StepForward();
    void AboutFace();
    SHORT CurrXIncrement() const
        { return xincr; }
};
```

Figure 12.19 The TubaPlayer class

The TubaPlayer Constructor

The *TubaPlayer* constructor calls its base *rcSprite* constructor by passing the 'Z' maze cell identifier and the name of the .**gfx** file that contains the sprite's bitmap tile images. The *TubaPlayer* constructor uses *rcSprite::SetPosition* and *rcSprite::SetPose* to set the sprite's initial position and pose.

```
TubaPlayer::TubaPlayer(TubasOfTerror* ptt, SHORT tx, SHORT ty) :
                        rcSprite('Z', "sprites.gfx")
{
    SetPosition(tx, ty);
    SetPose(rcSprite::walking);
    xincr = stepincrement;
    yincr = 0;
    stepctr = 0;
    ptot = ptt;
}
```

Figure 12.20 The TubaPlayer constructor

TubaPlayer Motion Functions

Figure 12.21 shows the *TubaPlayer::StepForward* and *TubaPlayer::aboutFace* functions. The first function counts the steps and calls *rcSprite::Step* every other step to change the sprite's walking pose bitmap image. The *AboutFace* function calls *rcSprite::RotateRight* four times and changes the sign of the data member that specifies how far and in what direction to change the X coordinate for each step.

```
void TubaPlayer::StepForward()
{
    if (stepctr & 1)
        Step();
    stepctr++;
}
void TubaPlayer::AboutFace()
{
    RotateRight();
    RotateRight();
    RotateRight();
    RotateRight();
    xincr = -xincr;
}
```

Figure 12.21 Walking the sprite

TubaPlayer::ShootSoundEffect

Figure 12.22 is the *TubaPlayer::ShootSoundEffect* function, which overrides *rcSprite*'s empty function of the same name. The function calls *TubasOfTerror::PlaySound* to play a **.wav** file when the sprite fires its weapon (the tuba) at the player.

```
void TubaPlayer::ShootSoundEffect()
{
    ptot->PlaySound("blast.wav");
}
```

Figure 12.22 TubaPlayer::ShootSoundEffect

Building and Playing the Game

Use the same procedure that you used with the demos in Chapter 11 to build the program from within the Visual C++ 4.0 Developer Studio. Remember to use the **Rebuild All** command.

Run the game and move thoughout the maze until you find the trumpet in the corner of a small room. Figure 12.23 shows what that object looks like.

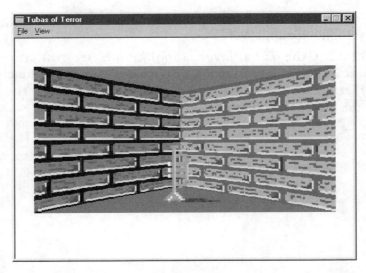

Figure 12.23 Finding a weapon

Move forward over the trumpet object to pick it up. Move backward and turn around to leave the room. The trumpet object is no longer on the floor, and you now have a trumpet in your hands and pointed forward, as Figure 12.24 shows.

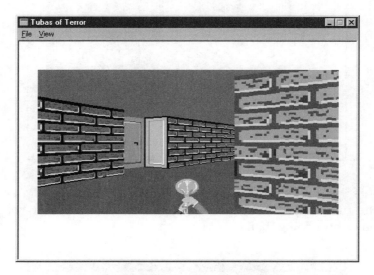

Figure 12.24 Armed and dangerous

To blow the trumpet, press **Ctrl**. You can blow the horn as often as you want to. There is no counted measure of ammunition in this game; it assumes that you never run out of breath.

Search through the maze until you find the big room where the tuba player sprite is pacing up and down. You can watch and follow him as long as you keep your distance. If you get too close, he senses your presence and turns to face you, as Figure 12.25 shows.

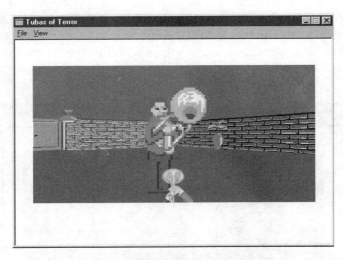

Figure 12.25 Facing the enemy

When the tuba player is close enough, he blows his tuba at you. Figure 12.26 shows him doing that.

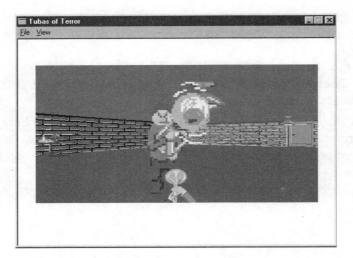

Figure 12.26 Getting shot at

Don't let the tuba player blow at you three times. If you do, the viewing window fades to white and the game is over. Instead, back away until you are out of range.

You can eliminate the tuba player by blowing your trumpet at him. Your range is farther than his, so you can get him from a distance; you must be pointed at him. Figure 12.27 shows the trumpet being blown and the tuba player being knocked backward by the blast.

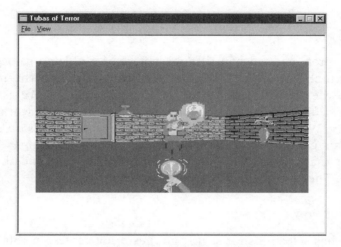

Figure 12.27 Shooting back

After hitting the tuba player, you can walk around the maze without fear of further assaults. Figure 12.28 shows the tuba player down for the count.

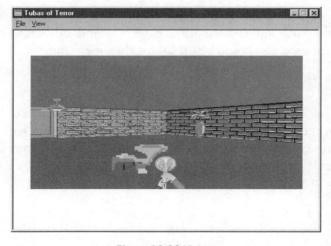

Figure 12.28 Victory

Improving Tubas of Terror

Tubas of Terror is a simple demonstration of the use of the ray-casting engine in a 3-D maze game. There are many things that you can do to improve this game.

Better Artwork

The sprite, prop, and weapon tiles are not bad for a demo game, but they could be much better. The more skilled the artist and the more time devoted to the artwork, the better the graphics will be. We assembled a primitive set of graphical components to demonstrate the working of the class library. With more attention to shading and the precision placement of parts, this game's visual components could be significantly improved. Remember that the software doesn't care how good or bad the artwork images are. They are just bitmaps to the program.

Saving and Restoring Games

The menu has selections for saving and restoring games. In this game you would save the player's position, orientation, health, and weapon ownership and the current position, orientation, and alive status of the sprite. In restoring a game, you would restore these values before launching the game. If the player had the weapon, you would delete the trumpet prop from the maze.

A more complex game would have more items to save and restore. You might want to save and restore different games under different names. The MFC *CDocument* class could be useful for this operation.

More Sprites

The Tubas of Terror maze has one sprite that is easy to eliminate. You could add other tuba players and sprites of other kinds. To a trumpet player, banjo players can be every bit as threatening as tuba players are. So can booking agents. Instead of blowing a horn, the agent could lie a lot and run off with the money.

Rewards and Treasures

The player could score points by finding hidden treasures such as the original score to "Trumpeter's Lullabye" or the Lost Chord.

More Weapons

You could add a trombone and a clarinet to the weapons that the player can find. The player could carry this arsenal and select one depending on the current foe. You could make a trumpet blast less lethal if it followed a trombone blast, because the player's chops (embochure) would be more fatigued. Chops could be the Tubas of Terror's answer to the expenditure of ammunition found in more violent 3-D maze games.

Health Aids and Miracles

The player's health declines with every blast from the tuba. Three blasts and the player is a goner. You could add health-giving props to the maze. For example, an autographed picture of Dizzy Gillespie could add enough inspiration to allow the player to endure more tuba blasts. You could allow some number of miracles to resurrect the player and continue the game after the tuba player blasts the player.

More Sound Effects

Add sound effects when the player goes outdoors or finds a weapon or treasure. The more sound effects you add, the better the game will be.

Door Keys

All the doors in Tubas of Terror open when the player presses the **Spacebar**. You could make some doors accessible only when a related goal had been achieved. For example, access to the union hall would require a union card.

Keeping Score

You could add a scoreboard of past games with the names of the players and their levels of achievement.

Levels of Play

Requiring higher skill levels after lower levels are completed would make this game more interesting. You could make the maze more complex with more enemies and obstacles at successively higher levels.

RayCaster Engine Reference Manual

This section is the RayCaster engine's reference manual. It includes a description of the public interface for the class library and explanations of the configuration options.

The RayCaster Class

The *RayCaster* class encapsulates the operation of the ray-casting algorithm. You derive a class from this one to implement your specialization of the class. An object of your specialized class can be embedded in your application class to run the ray caster.

Constructor

Call the constructor to instantiate the ray-casting engine. The constructor does not launch the game. The program uses the constructed object to move the player around and to draw scene frames based on user input.

```
RayCaster(char* mazename, char* gfxlibname,
    SHORT px,
    SHORT py,
    SHORT pangle,
    ViewPort vp = fullscreenviewport);
```

mazename	A pointer to the file name of the maze data file built by the bldmaze utility program.
gfxlibname	A pointer to the file name of the **.gfx** file built by the gfxmake utility program to contain bitmap tiles.
px, py	The maze coordinates where the player is positioned when the game starts. Both coordinates range from 0 to 64^2.
pangle	The direction (0–359) in which the player faces when the game starts.
vp	A *ViewPort* object that specifies the size and position of the game's viewing window within the application window.

AddSprite

Adds a sprite to the maze.

```
SHORT AddSprite(rcSprite* sp);
```

sp   Points to an object of type *rcSprite* that is to be added to the maze.

Returns: A sprite identification number to be used in other functions associated with sprites.

CloseDoorSoundEffect

Override this virtual function in the *RayCaster* class to provide a sound effect when a door closes.

```
virtual void CloseDoorSoundEffect();
```

DeleteProp

Deletes a prop from the maze. Typically used to remove an item that the player has picked up.

```
void DeleteProp(SHORT x, SHORT y);
```

x, y   The maze cell coordinates (0 - 64) where the prop is positioned.

DeleteSprite

Deletes a sprite from the maze. Following this call, no view of the sprite is rendered anywhere in the maze.

```
void DeleteSprite(SHORT spriteno);
```

spriteno   The sprite identification number returned by *RayCaster::AddSprite*

DrawFrame

Renders the current scene from the position and viewing orientation of the player.

```
void DrawFrame();
```

FadeScreen

Called when the game is over to fade the screen.

```
void FadeScreen();
```

Faster

Increases the player's speed of movement and rotation by one maze increment and one degree. If the current movement speed is already at the *fastspeed* constant value defined in **consts.h**, this function has no effect.

```
void Faster();
```

GetPosition

Returns the player's current position and viewing angle.

```
void GetPosition(SHORT& px, SHORT& py, SHORT& pangle);
```

px, py	The maze coordinates where the player is positioned. Both coordinates range from 0 to 64^2.
pangle	The direction (0–359 degrees) in which the player faces.

inSights

Called to determine whether a sprite is in the player's weapon sights. If a ray-cast from the player's position—in the direction the player is facing — hits a sprite object in the maze, the sprite is considered to be in the player's sights.

```
rcSprite* inSights();
```

Returns:	A pointer to the *rcSprite* object for the sprite that is in the player's sights. Returns zero if no sprite is in the sights.

isLoaded

Determines whether the *RayCaster* object was successfully initialized by its constructor. Failure to initialize could occur for several reasons. Usually it means that the maze data file or tile graphics library file does not exist.

```
bool isLoaded();
```

Returns:	True if the object successfully initialized. False otherwise.

MoveForward, MoveBackward, MoveLeftward, MoveRightward

Moves the player one increment within the maze relative to the player's current orientation. An increment is defined by the *mediumspeed* constant in **consts.h**. The constant specifies the number of maze coordinates to move the player for each call to one of the *Move...* functions. This value is incremented and decremented by calls to the *RayCaster::Faster* and *RayCaster::Slower* functions.

```
void MoveForward();
void MoveBackward();
void MoveLeftward();
void MoveRightward();
```

MoveSprite, MoveSpriteRelative

Moves a sprite within the maze. *MoveSprite* moves the sprite to an absolute position. *MoveSpriteRelative* moves the sprite to a position relative to its current position.

```
void MoveSprite(SHORT spriteno, SHORT newx, SHORT newy);
void MoveSpriteRelative(SHORT spriteno, SHORT newx, SHORT newy);
```

spriteno	The sprite identification number returned by *RayCaster::AddSprite*.
newx, newy	Maze coordinates (0–64^2). The new sprite position for *MoveSprite*. The values to be added to the sprite's current coordinates for *MoveSpriteRelative*.

OpenCloseDoor

Opens or closes a door in the maze when the player is facing a door and when the player's distance from the door is no farther than the value specified in the *doordistance* constant defined in **consts.h**.

```
void OpenCloseDoor();
```

OpenDoorSoundEffect

Override this virtual function in the *RayCaster* class to provide a sound effect when the player opens a door.

```
virtual void OpenDoorSoundEffect();
```

RotateRight, RotateLeft

Rotates the player's orientation right or left.

```
void RotateRight(SHORT degrees = 0);
void RotateLeft(SHORT degrees = 0);
```

degrees   The number of degrees to rotate. If *degrees* is zero, the rotation uses the *mediumrotation* constant value from **consts.h**. This value is incremented and decremented by calls to *RayCaster::Faster* and *RayCaster::Slower* .

SetPosition

Changes the player's position and viewing angle.

```
void SetPosition(SHORT px, SHORT py, SHORT pangle);
```

px, py   The new maze coordinates where the player is positioned. Both coordinates range from 0 to 64^2.

pangle   The new direction (0–359) in which the player faces.

SetWeapon

Sets a weapon for the player to wield. After this function is called, the selected weapon displays in the center of the viewing window at the bottom border. Also use this function to fire a weapon by selecting a bitmap of the weapon in firing order.

```
void SetWeapon(SHORT wno);
```

wno   The tile number of the weapon's bitmap tile in the **.gfx** library file loaded by the *RayCast* constructor. When this argument is zero, the engine removes the current weapon from the next frame display.

Slower

Decreases the player's speed of movement and rotation by one maze increment and one degree. If the current movement speed is already set to the *slowspeed* constant value defined in **consts.h**, this function has no effect.

```
void Slower();
```

The rcSprite Class

The *rcSprite* class encapsulates the behavior of a sprite in a 3-D maze game. A game program typically instantiates objects of classes derived from *rcSprite* as embedded objects in the game's derived *RayCaster* class.

enum Pose

An enumerated type that represents a sprite object's current pose.

```
enum Pose { standing, walking, shooting, pausing, dying, dead };
```

Constructors

Construct a sprite object

```
rcSprite(char code, const char* glib);
rcSprite(rcSprite& sp);
```

code	A character code that identifies the object in the maze as a sprite. This code corresponds to entries that are configured in **consts.h**.
glib	Points to the **.gfx** file that contains the bitmap tiles for the sprite.
sp	In the copy constructor, a reference to an existing *rcSprite* object. This usage allows the game program to share *rcSprite* resources, mainly the stored graphical bitmap tiles, among sprite instances that use the same graphical representation.

Die

Tells the sprite to enter its two-frame death sequence. After this call, the sprite accepts no further motion or action commands.

```
void Die();
```

DieSoundEffect

Override this virtual function in the *rcSprite* class to provide a sound effect when you call the *rcSprite::Die* function. Use *DieSoundEffect* to start playing the **.wav** file associated with the sprite's expiration. Typical sound effects are a scream or a thud.

```
virtual void DieSoundEffect();
```

GetAngle

Returns the direction in which the sprite is facing.

```
SHORT GetAngle() const;
```

Returns: Sprite's current direction. Always 0, 45, 90, 180, 225, 270, or 315.

GetDistance

Gets the distance from the player to the sprite.

```
SHORT GetDistance() const;
```

Returns: The distance in maze units.

GetPose

Gets the sprite's current pose.

```
Pose GetPose() const;
```

Returns: The current pose as a *Pose* enumerated type.

GetPosition

Gets the sprite's current position in the maze.

```
void GetPosition(SHORT& px, SHORT& py) const;
```

px, py   Maze coordinates (0–64^2) of the sprite's current position.

isAlive

Tests whether the sprite has been killed by a call to *rcSprite::Die*.

```
bool isAlive() const;
```

Returns: True if the sprite is still alive. False otherwise.

isLoaded

Determines whether the *rcSprite* object was successfully loaded.

```
bool isLoaded();
```

Returns: True if the sprite was successfully loaded. False otherwise.

Pause

Tells the sprite to assume its pausing pose following its shooting pose. The program typically cycles a sprite between shooting and pausing until the sprite is finished shooting at the player.

```
void Pause();
```

ResumeWalking

Tells the sprite to resume its walking sequence following a shooting-pausing sequence.

```
void ResumeWalking();
```

RotateLeft, RotateRight

Rotates the sprite 45 degrees.

```
void RotateLeft();
void RotateRight();
```

SetAngle

Sets the sprite's current orientation (direction facing) in degrees.

```
void SetAngle(SHORT ang);
```

ang   The new orientation. Always 0, 45, 90, 180, 225, 270, or 315.

SetPose

Sets the sprite's current pose.

```
void SetPose(Pose ps);
```

ps   The pose. Must be walking or standing. Other poses are set by other functions.

SetPosition

Sets the sprite's current position in the maze.

```
void SetPosition(SHORT px, SHORT py);
```

px, py   Maze coordinates (0–64^2) of the sprite's new position.

Shoot

Tells the sprite to initiate its shooting sequence.

```
void Shoot();
```

ShootSoundEffect

Override this virtual function in the *rcSprite* class to provide a sound effect when you call *rcSprite::Shoot* . Use *ShootSoundEffect* to start playing the **.wav** file associated with the sprite's shot.

```
virtual void ShootSoundEffect();
```

Step

Tells the sprite to sequence to the next frame in its walking sequence. This function does not change the sprite's location. It only operates the walking sequence. To animate the sprite's motion, the program must combine this call with calls to *SetPosition* and the *Rotate...* and *SetAngle* functions.

```
void Step();
```

The SoundEffects Class

The *SoundEffects* class implements sound effects by playing **.wav** files through the Windows 95 MCI functions.

Constructor

Constructs the *SoundEffects* object with the address of a window that receives notification when each sound effect is completed.

```
SoundEffects(CWnd* pWnd);
```

pWnd   Points to a window that receives an MM_MCINOTIFY message when sound effects
                played by the *SoundEffects::Play* function are finished.

Play

Plays a sound effect.

```
void Play(LPSTR lpszWAVEFileName);
```

lpszWAVEFileName   Points to the file name of the **.wav** file.

The ViewPort Structure

The *ViewPort* structure specifies the viewing window's position relative to the application window. It also specifies the viewing window's size. An object of this structure is passed as an argument to the *RayCaster* constructor. If you omit the argument, the constructor provides a default argument.

```
struct ViewPort {
    SHORT x, y;                      // upper left origin
    SHORT viewwidth, viewheight; // viewport dimensions
};
```

Configuration Constants

Following is a list of constant values defined in **consts.h**. Change these values and recompile the RayCaster engine to change the way the engine works. The tables provide the constant identifiers, their values as initialized in the published version of **consts.h**, and a brief description of their meaning.

The Viewing Window

viewangle	60	viewing angle
defx	0	default x position of viewing window
defy	0	default y position of viewing window
defviewwidth	320	default viewing window width
defviewheight	200	default viewing window height

The *viewangle* value represents the number of degrees of the player's viewing angle. The wider the angle, the more of the maze is visible in the viewing window.

The *defx*, *defy*, *defviewwidth*, and *defviewheight* constants define the default viewing window position and dimensions within the application window. These values are used to initialize the default *ViewPort* object argument to the *RayCaster* constructor.

Maze Occupants

maxprops	100	maximum props in the maze
maxsprites	25	maximum sprites in the maze

These values are used as the dimensions for arrays that hold instances of props and sprites.

Player Hit Values

closestprop	48	minimum distance cast to prop
mindistance	10	minimum distance cast to wall
maxdistance	2048	maximum distance cast to wall

The *closestprop* value specifies the minimum distance from a prop that the ray caster will render the prop's image. This approach prevents the prop's image from dominating the scene and slowing the rendering process when the prop is passable.

Door Opening Controls

openinterval	8	pixels per open interval
autoclose	25	frames until auto door close

The *openinterval* value specifies how many pixels a door shifts for each opening frame. Higher values make the doors open faster. This value also synchronizes the display of the multiple frames of a center-opening door.

Maze and Tile Dimensions

mazewidth	64	maze width
mazeheight	64	maze height
tilewidth	64	bitmap tile width
tileheight	64	bitmap tile height

The *mazewidth* and *mazeheight* values specify the dimensions of the maze expressed in maze character cells. The *tilewidth* and *tileheight* values specify the dimensions of a tile surface in pixels.

Player Speed

fastspeed	10	maximum increments per step
mediumspeed	12	default increments per step
slowspeed	14	minimum increments per step
mediumrotation	4	number of degrees per rotation

The speed values affect the number of maze increments that are changed by a call to a *RayCaster::Move...* function. Lower speed values translate to greater increment jumps, which gives the illusion of faster movements. When the current effective speed value is decremented to increase the speed of movement, the current number of degrees of rotation is incremented.

Solid Colors

ceilingclr	24	interior ceiling
floorclr	139	interior floor
skycolor	53	exterior sky
grndcolor	2	exterior ground

These values assume the standard palette, which we used to build all the demo programs. These values specify the colors used for solid floors, the ceiling, the ground, and the sky when the room or hallway does not use texture-mapped floor and ceiling tiles.

Corridor Length

```
#define LONGCORRIDORS      // initially commented out
```

When this macro is defined, the ray caster permits long corridors that stretch the full diagonal size of the maze. Because this option involves some floating-point math for every ray, there is a performance penalty for using it. If you see streaked vertical lines in your maze only from certain positions and orientations, try defining this macro to see if the problem goes away. Instead, you might try shortening the length of the corridors where the problem occurs.

GAMES SDK OVERVIEW

According to the help file that comes with the Microsoft Games SDK, the SDK allows the development of games that "rival or exceed performance on MS-DOS-based platforms and console-system platforms." This is quite a claim, especially considering how poorly Windows 3.1 supports games. Even MS-DOS games, which typically are faster than Windows games, don't rival game console platforms.

The Microsoft Games SDK is a set of low-level development tools designed to provide the fastest, most flexible foundation possible for high-performance Windows 95 applications. The Games SDK is perhaps misnamed, because it can support the development of many different kinds of software. Applications such as communications software, graphic modelers, and networked simulators can all benefit from the Games SDK. The SDK also addresses application installation.

This chapter is a broad discussion of the Games SDK. Much of the information found here is also in the help files that come with the SDK. Some of the discussion concerns GDKapp, the framework that is implemented with the SDK. In this chapter we use the terms *Games SDK* and *SDK* interchangeably. You will learn about:

- Hardware acceleration
- The Games SDK components
- GDKapp implementation issues

Performance

Game consoles have traditionally offered better performance than PC games, because console game systems use special hardware to provide high-performance graphics and sound. Today the average multimedia PC has similar hardware, but until recently this hardware was typically used for video playback. The Games SDK allows you to exercise fine control over this hardware. The resulting games run significantly faster than MS-DOS games, and their performance rivals that of console systems.

The technique of off-loading work to special hardware is known as *hardware acceleration*. The graphics and sound portions of the Games SDK use hardware acceleration whenever possible. On most 64-bit video cards, SDK-based games run at 60 to 72 frames per second in video modes such as 640 by 480. This performance compares favorably to 20 to 30 frames per second at 320 by 240, which is typical for MS-DOS-based games. Computers that are not equipped with hardware-accelerated devices will run games written with the SDK, but performance will be poor.

The COM Specification

The DirectPlay, DirectSound and DirectDraw components of the Games SDK are written using the component object model (COM). The COM specification of the Games SDK is designed to supply C++ class-like interfaces. In C, COM allows some of the features that make C++ so powerful. The GDKapp framework hides the details of the COM specification from the games programmer.

The SDK documentation refers to COM-based objects as *interfaces*. In this chapter we will use the term *classes*, but it is important to remember that COM classes differ from C++ classes.

The Games SDK Components

The Games SDK composed of the following components: DirectDraw, DirectSound, DirectPlay, DirectInput, DirectSetup, DirectX, and AutoPlay. A discussion of each component of the SDK follows.

DirectX

DirectX is the portion of the SDK that must be installed on the PC in order for Games SDK games to run. DirectX can be distributed with your game and installed on the user's computer using the DirectSetup component of the SDK. Once DirectX has been installed on a computer, SDK-based games will run without this installation.

DirectDraw

DirectDraw is the graphics component of the Games SDK. The largest of the APIs, DirectDraw is made up of four COM classes: *DirectDraw*, *DirectDrawSurface*, *DirectDrawPalette*, and *DirectDrawClipper*. The *DirectDraw* class represents the video card. The *DirectDrawSurface* class represents memory buffers containing bitmaps. *DirectDrawPalette* and *DirectDrawClipper* objects can be attached to instances of *DirectDrawSurface* and serve to change the appearance and the behavior of the surface.

To use DirectDraw, you use the *DirectDrawCreate* function to create an instance of the *DirectDraw* class. Instances of *DirectDrawSurface*, *DirectDrawPalette*, and *DirectDrawClipper* can then be created using the DirectDraw instance. DirectDraw also includes the *GetCaps* member function, which you can use to determine which if any features are supported by the installed video card.

You can create as many surfaces as memory permits, but only the *primary surface* is visible. The primary surface is usually accompanied by a surface known as a *backbuffer*. The contents of the primary buffer and its backbuffer can be exchanged by calling the *Flip* member of *DirectDrawSurface*. This technique, known as *page-flipping*, provides an instantaneous method of updating the screen.

You can copy nonprimary surfaces to the backbuffer using the *BltFast* member of DirectDrawSurface. By repeatedly updating the backbuffer and flipping the primary surface, you can animate images.

The DirectDrawPalette class dictates how the pixel values are displayed. Attaching a *DirectDrawPalette* object to the primary surface causes the palette represented by the *DirectDrawPalette* object to be installed into the system palette.

The DirectDrawClipper interface is used to manage *cliplists*. A cliplist specifies portions of a surface that are not to be drawn. You can also attach a *DirectDrawClipper* object to a window handle. The surface attached to such a *DirectDrawClipper* will then appear correctly even if it is partially obstructed by another application.

GDKapp uses DirectDraw for its graphics support. The *DirectDraw* class is created by the framework's application class, which creates a primary surface with a single backbuffer as well as the sprites used in the game. The framework composes scenes in the backbuffer and then flips the primary surface. Once the new image is displayed, the framework begins to build another scene.

The *DirectDraw* class is destroyed when the application class gets deleted. Before the destruction, the *RestoreDisplayMode* member function is called.

DirectSound

DirectSound provides support for high-performance audio playback. The DirectSound API consists of two COM classes: *DirectSound* and *DirectSoundBuffer*. The *DirectSound* class represents the sound card. The *DirectSoundBuffer* interface, which represents audio data that can be played on the sound card.

The *DirectSound* class is created by using the *DirectSoundCreate* function. Buffers are then created using the *CreateSoundBuffer* member of the *DirectSound* interface. There are two types of *DirectSoundBuffer*: primary and secondary. The *primary* buffer is the buffer that the sound card plays. *Secondary* buffers are played only after they have been mixed into the primary buffer. Applications that require fine control of the sound device create primary buffers explicitly, but a primary buffer can be created implicitly by creating one or more secondary buffers.

DirectSound buffers can be static or streaming buffers. *Static* buffers are reusable sounds that do not change after they have been loaded. To improve performance, *DirectSound* tries to move static buffers to RAM on the sound card. Buffers located on the sound card do not burden the CPU during playback. *Streaming* buffers are accessible during playback, so audio data can be generated and placed into the primary buffer while the buffer is being played.

GDKapp uses DirectSound in its *SoundCard* class. The *DirectSound* object is created by the *SoundCard* constructor. Secondary buffers are created for each sound clip required by the game. All the buffers are specified as static so that *DirectSound* will make as much use of hardware assistance as possible. The *Play* member function of *DirectSoundBuffer* is used to start playback. GDKapp specifies that the sound is to be played asynchronously so that games do not stop during playback. The *DirectSound* object is destroyed by the *SoundCard* destructor.

DirectPlay

DirectPlay is the SDK component that allows you to add network support to your games. The API consists of one COM class: *DirectPlay*. The *CreateDirectPlay* function creates an instance of the class, and the member functions allow network sessions to be created and manipulated. Once a connection is made, packets can be sent and received between games. DirectPlay provides your games with information about players, such as their names and preferences, supporting as many as 256 players at a time.

GDKapp uses DirectPlay for network support. The *DirectPlay* object is created by the application class. If a connection is made, game-specific messages are routed to the game classes during the game.

DirectInput

DirectInput is a high-performance API for joysticks. It looks just like the Win32 joystick API. DirectInput can support as many as 16 digital joysticks or two analog joysticks at a time. The API also applies to devices such as light pens, tablet controls, and virtual reality helmets.

GDKapp supports the keyboard and the mouse as input devices but does not use DirectInput.

DirectSetup

The DirectSetup API allows you to install the *DirectX* components on the user's machine. The entire installation is performed with a single call to the *DirectXSetup* function.

DirectSetup is not used by GDKapp.

AutoPlay

The AutoPlay feature is built into Windows 95 and allows users to install or play CD-ROM applications by placing the CD-ROM disk in the drive. For games, this means that PC games are as easy to play as home game systems. Enabling a game for AutoPlay requires that a file called **autorun.inf** be in the root directory of the CD-ROM. This file specifies AutoPlay settings, including the name of a program that is to be run whenever the CD-ROM is inserted.

The CD-ROM included with this book is not AutoPlay-enabled.

GDKAPP USER'S GUIDE

This chapter introduces and discusses the GDKapp class framework. In this chapter you will learn about:

- The Framework's features
- GDKapp classes
- Application structure
- The utilities

GDKapp Features

The GDKapp class framework supports the construction of sprite-based games. The framework supports static and scrolling backgrounds and provides optional hit detection for sprites of any size and shape. GDKapp uses the DirectDraw and DirectSound portions of the Games SDK.

Unlike the Theatrix framework, GDKapp does not employ a stage performance metaphor. Terms such as *application*, *sprite*, *background*, and *sounddevice* are used to describe and implement games. The TankTop demo, built with GDKapp, is described in Chapter 16.

Multiple Scenes

A game is more than a collection of sprites that move around on the screen. Games usually greet you with an intro screen and then display a menu. Most games also have some sort of help screen, even if it is only a list of commands. In GDKapp, each of these screens is called a *scene*. Your game can have as many scenes as memory permits.

Scrolling Backgrounds

The framework supports static and scrolling backgrounds.

Hit Detection

Sprite-based games involve characters that move about the screen and interact. This interaction is different for every game but usually involves contact between the sprites. A rocket might smash into the side of an enemy vehicle, for example, or a character might collect power-ups. Determining when sprite contact has been made is called *hit detection*.

GDKapp supports rectangular and pixel-based hit detection. Rectangular detection is fast and works well for some types of games, but it is not very accurate because only the sprite's location and dimensions are taken into consideration. Pixel-based hit detection considers the shape of the sprite; the detection is accurate, but it is slower than rectangular detection. The method you should use for your game depends on the game. Try both approaches and see what works best. You can specify which strategy to use, and you may decide not to use any hit detection.

Sound Support

DirectSound is used to implement the GDKapp sound support. This allows your games to play multiple sounds simultaneously. The *SoundDevice* class encapsulates the DirectSound API and provides a simple interface with members such as *Play* and *Loop*.

The Class Hierarchy

A class hierarchy illustrates how classes are related in terms of inheritance. Figure 14.1 is the GDKapp class hierarchy.

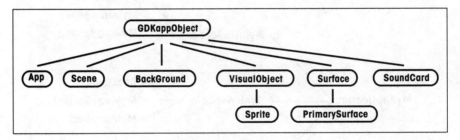

Figure 14.1 GDKapp class hierarchy

Each GDKapp game is represented by the *App* class. Game applications should have one and only one *App* instance. Your application object uses *App* as a base class, inheriting *App*'s ability to manage game components. In particular, *App* manages instances of the *Scene* class.

Each *Scene* manages one instance of the *BackGround* class and one or more instances of the *Sprite* class. The *BackGround* class provides support for static and scrolling scenery. *Sprite* provides support for the display and movement of partially transparent images over the background. *Sprite* also provides hit detection.

The *VisualObject, Surface,* and *PrimarySurface* classes are used in the GDKapp implementation but won't appear in your code.

Application Structure

An inheritance tree such as the one in Figure 14.1 does not tell us much about how an application written with the framework should be constructed. An object owner tree illustrates how the classes are related in terms of which classes own or contain other classes. Owner trees are valuable when you're learning a new framework, because they resemble the application being constructed. Figure 14.2 is an owner tree for a typical GDKapp application.

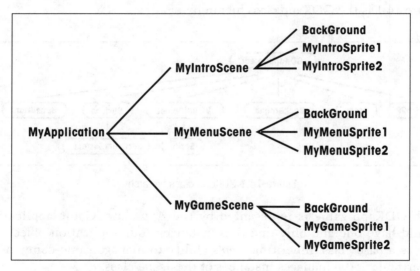

Figure 14.2 A typical GDKapp owner tree

Most of the classes appearing in the chart are classes that you provide. They aren't difficult to write, because each one is derived from a class in the framework. The chart relates directly to the order of execution in the game. The *App*-derived class (*MyApplication*) is created first. It in turn creates three *Scene*-derived objects. Each *Scene* object creates a background and a number of sprites. When the game application terminates, the *App* class is deleted and it deletes its three *Scene*s. Each *Scene* deletes its background and sprites. It is because the objects in the chart create and destroy each other that they are said to "own" each other.

You decide what the owner tree looks like for your game. Because you are providing most of the classes in the diagram, you are free to name the classes any way you like. Also, the number of scenes and sprites may vary depending on your game's requirements. Here are some rules for a GDKapp owner tree:

- It must have one and only one *App*-derived object.
- Each *App*-derived object must own at least one *Scene*-derived object.
- Each *Scene*-derived object must own one instance of the *BackGround* object.
- *App*-derived objects should not own backgrounds or sprites.

The App Class

The *App* class is designed to be used as a base class for your application class. By deriving from *App*, your application class inherits the ability to manage scenes and to launch and run the application. Your program creates an instance of the application class in the *WinMain* function. Assuming that we are building the application in Figure 14.2, *WinMain* would look like this:

```
int PASCAL WinMain(HINSTANCE hInstance,HINSTANCE,LPSTR,int show)
{
    MyApplication* app=new MyApplication(hInstance,show);
    int r=app->Run();
    delete app;
    return r;
}
```

The entire application is launched and executed in this function. When the *Run* member function returns, the application object is deleted and the application terminates. Let's look at how *MyApplication* is defined:

```
class MyApplication : public App
{
public:
    MyApplication(HINSTANCE hInstance,int show) :
                     App(hInstance,show,"MyApplication")
    {
        scene[0]=new MyIntroScene;
        scene[1]=new MyMenuScene;
        scene[2]=new MyGameScene;
    }
    ~MyApplication()
    {
        delete scene[2];
        delete scene[1];
        delete scene[0];
    }
private:
    Scene* scene[3];
};
```

MyApplication uses *App* as a base class. The *MyApplication* constructor creates three *Scene* objects, and the destructor deletes them. Notice that the parameters that are sent to the *MyApplication* constructor are passed to the *App* constructor. The third *App* constructor argument is a string that contains the name of the application.

The Scene Class

The *Scene* class manages backgrounds and sprites in much the same way that *App* manages scenes. Lets look at how the *MyIntroScene* class is defined:

```
class MyIntroScene : public Scene
{
public:
    MyIntroScene() : Scene("intro.pal")
    {
        background=new BackGround("intro.gfx");
        sprite[0]=new MyIntroSprite1;
        sprite[1]=new MyIntroSprite2;
    }
    ~MyIntroScene()
    {
        delete sprite[1];
        delete sprite[0];
        delete background;
    }
    void Update()
    {
        if (KeyDown(ESCAPE))
            StopApp();
        if (KeyDown(VK_F2))
            RunNextScene();
    }
    BackGround* background;
    Sprite* sprite[2];
};
```

MyIntroScene is derived from *Scene*. You can pass the name of a palette file to the *Scene* constructor. The supplied palette is installed whenever the scene is displayed. If you don't supply a palette, *Scene* will create and use a default grayscale palette. The *MyIntroScene* constructor creates a background and two sprites.

Notice the *Update* function. The *Scene::Update* function is called by GDKapp each time a scene is being constructed. We've overridden *Update* to inquire about the game player's actions. If the player has pressed the **Esc** key, the *Scene* member function *StopApp* is called and the application exits. If the player presses **F2**, the next scene is signaled to take control of the application. If no scene is found, the application exits. The *Update* function uses the *KeyDown* member function to ask GDKapp whether the **Esc** or **F2** key is being pressed.

Each *Scene* controls how long it runs and what happens after it gives up control. *Scene* provides a set of member functions that allow you to specify the scene that is to appear next:

```
void RunNextScene();
void RunPrevScene();
void RunScene(int scene);
void RunScene(const type_info& sceneid);
```

Chapter 15 discusses these functions in detail.

The BackGround Class

The *BackGround* class provides support for static and scrolling backgrounds. Each *Scene* must create one and only one *BackGround* object. Recall the *MyIntroScene* constructor:

```
MyIntroScene() : Scene("intro.pal")
{
    background=new BackGround("intro.gfx");
    sprite[0]=new MyIntroSprite1;
    sprite[1]=new MyIntroSprite2;
}
```

We create an instance of *BackGround* and pass the name of the **.GFX** file that contains the background image. You will learn more about **.GFX** files in this chapter in the section titled "The GDKapp Utilities."

BackGround includes two functions that control hit detection. By default, hit detection is disabled. The functions are:

```
void SetTileHitDetection(BOOL b);
void SetSpriteHitDetection(BOOL b);
```

To enable full hit detection, both functions should be called with TRUE as an argument.

Scrolling Backgrounds

The *BackGround* constructor takes an optional second parameter that is used to specify a **.MAP** file. A **.MAP** file is an ASCII file that defines a tile map to describe a scrolling background. The background for the TankTop demo is created this way:

```
TankTopScene() : Scene("tanktop.pal")
{
background=new BackGround("tiles.gfx","maze1.map");
    // ...
}
```

When a map file is specified, *BackGround* expects the supplied **.GFX** file to contain a set of tiles instead of a single background image. Here's an example of a map file:

```
10 10
2 2 2 2 2 2 2 2 2 2
2 1 1 1 1 1 1 1 1 2
2 1 1 1 1 1 1 1 1 2
2 1 1 1 1 1 1 1 1 2
2 1 1 1 3 3 1 1 1 2
2 1 1 1 3 3 1 1 1 2
2 1 1 1 1 1 1 1 1 2
2 1 1 1 1 1 1 1 1 2
2 1 1 1 1 1 1 1 1 2
2 2 2 2 2 2 2 2 2 2
1 e 0
2 s 50
3 s 100
```

This map file specifies a scrolling background that is made up of 100 tiles arranged in a square. The size of the tiles is determined by the size of the images in *BackGround*'s **.GFX** file. At the end of the map file is a tile legend that contains one line per tile. In our example, there are three different types of tiles. The entries that contain an *s* or *S* as the second field are solid tiles. (The first field is the tile number.) The sprites in your game will be notified when they come in contact with solid tiles. Tiles with an *e* or *E* are empty; they can be traversed freely by sprites.

The third field in the tile legend is the Z-order value of the tile. The value specifies the order in which GDKapp draws the graphics for each frame in a game. The lower the number, the earlier the tile is drawn. Tiles drawn early are covered by sprites drawn later and appear to be farther away. Because the tiles do not overlap, the Z-order of the tiles makes a difference only when sprites are animated across the background.

An important *BackGround* member function is *FocusOn*. Let's take a closer look at the *TankTopScene* constructor:

```
TankTopScene() : Scene("tanktop.pal")
{
    background=new BackGround("tiles.gfx","maze1.map");
    tank=new Tank;
    tank->SetZ(TANKZ);
    background->FocusOn(tank);
    // ...
}
```

After the *BackGround* and *Tank* objects are created, a pointer to the *Tank* object is passed to the *FocusOn* member function. This action causes the background to scroll according to the movements of the *tank* object. The *FocusOn* function must be called for games using scrolling backgrounds but is not required for static backgrounds.

The Sprite Class

With the exception of backgrounds, all the graphical elements in a GDKapp game are instances of *Sprite*. The *Sprite* class provides functionality that makes it easy to implement animation and respond to player actions. As with *BackGround*, the *Sprite* constructor takes a **.GFX** file name as a parameter. Let's look at the *MyIntroSprite1* class:

```
class MyIntroSprite1 : public Sprite
{
public:
    MyIntroSprite1() : Sprite("isprite1.gfx")
    // ...
};
```

MyIntroSprite is derived from *Sprite*. The name of the **.GFX** file that contains the sprite's image is passed to the *Sprite* constructor. By default, the first image is used to display the *Sprite*. The current image can be changed by using the *SetCurFrame* member function. Multiple sprites can use the same **.GFX** file, but only one copy of each **.GFX** file is loaded by the framework.

A sprite's visibility can be controlled by using the *Show* and *Hide* member functions. Calling the *Hide* function stops the sprite from being drawn by the framework, and calling *Show* indicates that the sprite should be drawn. A sprite's state can be determined using the *IsHidden* function. *IsHidden* cannot be used to determine whether a sprite is on the screen or whether it is covered by another sprite.

Another feature that *Sprite* provides is Z-order. A sprite's Z-order is specified using the *SetZ* member function and can be retrieved with the *GetZ* member function. The Z-order affects the sprite in the same way that tiles are affected by the Z-order values specified in the tile legend or the map file. You can animate a sprite to appear in front of some tiles and behind others by specifying a Z-order value that falls between the Z-order values of the tiles.

Like *Scene*, *Sprite* has an *Update* member function that is called by the framework once per screen update. The *Update* function can be overridden in your sprite. The sprite's location, the current frame number, and the sprite's visibility can be adjusted within the *Update* function. For example, to design a sprite that is to move across the screen from left to right, you might write this code:

```
void LeftRightSprite::Update()
{
    short x,y;
    GetLoc(x,y);
    if (x<640)
        x++;
    SetLoc(x,y);
}
```

Suppose we wanted to write code for a light that blinks about once every 30 frames. We would render a background that shows the light off and render a sprite shows that the light is on. We might write the following:

```
void BlinkingLight::Update()
{
    static UINT count=0;
    if (count<30)
        count++;
    else
    {
        if (IsHidden())
            Show();
        else
            Hide();
        count=0;
    }
}
```

You can use *KeyDown* member function to poll the state of the keyboard. The following code is from the TankTop demo:

```
void Tank::Update()
{
    if (KeyDown(UP)==1 && speed<TANKTOPSPEED)
        SetSpeed(++speed);
    if (KeyDown(DOWN)==1 && speed>-TANKTOPSPEED)
        SetSpeed(--speed);
    // ...
}
```

The *KeyDown* member function returns zero when queried about a key that is not currently being pressed. Otherwise, the return value is the number of times that the key has been queried since the key was first pressed. *KeyDown* returns 1 if a new keystroke has occurred. The preceding code tests for new **Up** and **Down** arrow keystrokes.

The *SetHitDetection* member function controls the level of hit detection that the sprite should perform. The function is defined this way:

```
void SetHitDetection(short setting);
```

The *setting* parameter can be one of three constants: HD_NONE, HD_RECT, or HD_FULL. By default, *Sprite* uses HD_FULL, the most accurate hit-detection setting. These settings have no effect if hit detection is not enabled by the *BackGround* instance that appears with the sprites.

The *Sprite* class provides two member functions that are used to notify the *Sprite* that a collision has been detected:

```
virtual void OnTileHit(Sprite* s);
virtual void OnSpriteHit(Sprite* s);
```

The first function is called by GDKapp if the sprite has collided with a solid tile. The function supplies a pointer to the tile that was hit. The pointer can be used to inquire about the tile's attributes. The second member function is called when the sprite collides with another sprite.

GDKapp detects hits regardless of Z-order settings. If the sprites overlap on the screen, a hit is detected. If your game requires that Z-order affect hit detection, the sprites should check for similar Z-order values as soon as they are notified of a collision.

The SoundDevice Class

Sound support is provided by GDKapp in the form of the *SoundDevice* class. Each *SoundDevice* instance is created with a file name that contains the names of the .WAV files to be loaded. For example, you can prepare a file called **sounds.txt**. The contents might look like this:

```
blast.wav
explode.wav
melt.wav
fry.wav
smash.wav
```

In your game, create a *SoundDevice* instance:

```
SoundDevice* sounddev=new SoundDevice("sounds.txt");
```

Any of the sounds can be played by passing the index of the .WAV file to the *Play* member function. The indices start at 1. The first .WAV file can be played like this:

```
sounddev->Play(1);
```

Your game can also inquire whether a sound is currently being played. The *IsPlaying* member function takes an index as a parameter. If the sound is being played, TRUE is returned.

```
if (sounddev->IsPlaying(1))
    // ...
```

The GFXMAKE Utility

GDKapp includes a set of bitmap utilities. Some of the tools are optional; their use is not required by the framework. The GDKapp utilities are similar to the Theatrix framework utilities, so some of the information found here is duplicated in Chapter 7. Separate versions of the utilities are included with each framework on the CD-ROM. (All three frameworks include utilities called GFXMAKE, but each version of GFXMAKE is different. Be sure to use the correct version for the framework that you are using.)

GFXMAKE is an image librarian utility. The graphical GDKapp classes deal with **.GFX** files exclusively, so all the images in your game must be processed with GFXMAKE. Bitmaps are supplied to GFXMAKE in the form of **.BMP** files. There are two ways to use GFXMAKE: The file names can be included on the command line, or a *list file* can be supplied that contains a list of the **.BMP** files to be included.

Let's say that we are going to write a game in which a character moves around the screen in four directions. We'll need four bitmaps of our character: one with the character moving up, one moving down, one moving left, and one moving right. The construction of the images is up to you. Whatever your source is, you need to produce each image in the **.BMP** format. Almost any format can be converted to the **.BMP** format using Image Alchemy. See Appendix A for more information on Image Alchemy.

Once you have the four **.BMP** files of the character moving in four directions, place the four images in the same directory. Then, in that same directory, execute this command:

```
GFXMAKE test.gfx up.bmp down.bmp left.bmp right.bmp
```

Make sure that GFXMAKE is in the command path. If all goes well (and you've named your **.BMP** files **up.bmp**, **down.bmp**, and so on), GFXMAKE will create a **.GFX** file called **test.gfx** that contains four images. To use the **.GFX** file, create a *Sprite*-based object and supply the file name as the first parameter:

```
class MySprite : public Sprite
{
public:
    MySprite() : Sprite("test.gfx")
        {
            // ...
        }
};
```

By default, the sprite is drawn with the first image in the **.GFX** file. Other images can be displayed by calling the *SetCurFrame* member function:

```
void MySprite::Update()
{
    SetCurFrame(2);
}
```

This line will cause the second image (**down.bmp**) of the **test.gfx** file to appear when *MySprite* is displayed.

Palette Management Utilities

GDKapp provides a suite of palette management utilities that allow you to display any number of images simultaneously even if the images use different palettes. Because these utilities allow the process of palette management to be virtually automated, it isn't necessary to understand every detail of palette theory or of the Windows palette manager. We will go over the basics.

Every **.BMP** file includes a palette, which is a list of colors. There are usually 256 colors in the palette (for 256-color **.BMP** files, which are the only type the utilities handle). The **.BMP** file also includes an array of bytes that represents the actual image. Each byte of the image array contains an index into the palette. The color indicated by this index is used in the image at that particular location.

Each **.BMP** file often has a different palette. This is especially true with ray-traced images. In order for multiple **.BMP** files to be displayed at the same time, each must use exactly the same palette.

Briefly, the palette utilities are as follows:

- GETPAL extracts the palette portion of a **.BMP** file.
- GENPAL creates new palettes by merging old ones.
- CVTPAL installs new palettes into **.BMP** files.

Each of these utilities deals with palette files, which have a **.PAL** extension. (The **.PAL** files are regular ASCII files and can be viewed and edited with any text editor, such as Windows Notepad.) These utilities are described in detail shortly, but first let's outline the procedure for preparing a set of **.BMP** files for use in a GDKapp game:

1. Produce all the **.BMP** images that will appear on the same screen. Usually, this means a background (either one large image or a set of tiles) and multiple sprites. If the sprites have multiple frames, or poses, those files must also be included.

2. Extract the palette from each **.BMP** file using GETPAL. If there are more than 10 files or so, select samples from the total collection. The samples should include the background and at least one pose from each sprite. Large images and images with unusual or striking color make good choices.

3. Create a master palette with GENPAL, using the extracted palettes as input. It may take several tries using different settings to produce a palette of the right size. Any output from GENPAL can be used, but if the output palette contains more than 256 colors, the remaining colors are ignored. It is better to produce a palette with slightly fewer than 256 colors. The master palette is saved as **NEW.PAL**.

4. Using CVTPAL, convert all the files (including those not used as samples) to use **NEW.PAL**.

Now all that remains to be done is to produce **.GFX** files with your new sprite images and supply the names of the **.GFX** and **.PAL** files to the framework. Because the background and the sprites now share the same palette, they will each appear correctly.

The palette utilities are discussed in more detail next.

GETPAL

GETPAL extracts palettes from **.BMP** files. The resulting **.PAL** file can be used with GENPAL and CVTPAL. GETPAL is used this way:

```
GETPAL picture1.bmp
```

This command causes GETPAL to create a palette file called **picture1.pal**. By default, GETPAL names the output file after the input file. A name can be supplied for the output file:

```
GETPAL picture1.bmp pal1.pal
```

If file extensions are not supplied, GETPAL assumes the typical extensions.

GENPAL

GENPAL merges multiple palettes and produces a master palette. The command looks like this:

```
GENPAL 0 first.pal second.pal third.pal ...
```

The first argument (zero in the example) is the tolerance level. Zero means that GENPAL will omit only exact color matches. Increasing this number means that more colors will be omitted and that a smaller palette will be produced. This setting should be used to create palettes with as close to 256 colors as possible.

Each specified palette is used to create the new palette. The palettes should be named in order of priority, the most important ones appearing first. The new palette is saved as **new.pal**.

CVTPAL

CVTPAL installs palettes into **.BMP** files. CVTPAL performs two steps: It replaces the existing palette, and it adjusts the image to match the new palette. CVTPAL adjusts the image as much as possible, but if the new and old palettes are radically different, the image quality will decay. CVTPAL is used like this:

```
CVTPAL picture1.bmp pal1.pal
```

This command causes CVTPAL to replace the existing palette in **picture1.bmp** with the palette in **pal1.pal**.

Miscellaneous Utilities

There are two remaining utilities. These tools are useful but are not necessary to use GDKapp.

PASTE

PASTE creates images by pasting or merging two images together. PASTE is useful for laying text or lettering over a complex background. PASTE allows you to prepare a separate image, containing only the text, and paste the text over the background image. If you decide to change the text color or move the text, you make the change in the text image and rerun PASTE. PASTE copies anything that is not color 0 (usually black). The two input images must have the same dimensions. The command looks like this:

```
PASTE scene.bmp text.bmp
```

The first file is treated as the background, and the second file is pasted onto the first. This command produces a file named **OUT.BMP** unless a third argument is supplied. The output image uses the palette from the background image.

REGION

REGION extracts image portions. For example:

```
REGION big.bmp small.bmp 100 100 199 199
```

This command extracts a region of **big.bmp** and saves it as **small.bmp**. The upper-left corner of the extracted region is located at 100/100, and the lower-right region is at 199/199.

GDKapp Reference Manual

This chapter is the reference manual for the GDKapp C++ class framework. You use it to look up classes and member functions as you develop your game. The chapter covers the following:

- The class library
- Macros
- Adjusting the library
- Keyboard codes

Class Library Reference

This manual documents those parts of the GDKapp class library that represent its public interface. The material presented here is designed for readers who are using the GDKapp library to develop games. The framework internals are not discussed. The framework is covered on a class-by-class basis. A short description of the class is given, and then each public and protected member is documented.

App (app.h)

App is the object that encapsulates the whole game. *App* is designed as a base class for an object that will be instantiated in the *WinMain* function of the program. All the *Scene*-derived objects in your game should be created in the constructor of the *App*-derived class.

Constructor

```
App(HINSTANCE hInstance,int show,LPCSTR appname);
```

Creates an *App* object. The *hInstance* and *show* parameters are sent to *WinMain* by Windows and should be passed to the *App* constructor unmolested. The *appname* parameter is a string that contains the name of your application. Windows 95 uses this string to identify your program in the desktop tray.

virtual int Run()

```
int Run();
```

Launches and executes that game application. The *Run* member function is called after the *App*-derived class has been constructed in the *WinMain* function. *Run* returns 0 if the application executes and terminates correctly, and 1 if an error occurs.

BackGround (backgr.h)

GDKapp provides the *BackGround* class to manage background images. Each *Scene* creates an instance of *BackGround* and supplies the constructor with the **.GFX** file that contains the background image or images.

Constructor

```
BackGround(const char* gfx,const char* map=0);
```

Creates a *BackGround* object. The *gfx* parameter is the name of the **.GFX** file that contains the background image or images. The optional *map* parameter is the name of a map file that should be supplied for scrolling games. If a map file is specified, GDKapp assumes that the **.GFX** file contains a set of tiles and not a single background image.

FocusOn

```
void FocusOn(Sprite* focalsprite);
```

Indicates the sprite that the scrolling background should follow, usually the sprite that represents the game player. When a static background is used, this function has no effect. The function must be called for scrolling backgrounds.

GetSize

```
void GetSize(short& w,short& h);
```

Returns the size of the background. For static backgrounds, the function returns the size of the background image (usually the same as the display mode dimensions). For scrolling backgrounds, the values depend on the size of the grid defined in the map file and on the size of the tiles supplied in the **.GFX** file.

SetTileHitDetection

```
void SetTileHitDetection(BOOL b);
```

Enables or disables tile hit detection. When tile hit detection is enabled, sprites are notified when they collide with solid tiles in the background. By default, tile hit detection is disabled. This function has no effect for static backgrounds.

SetSpriteHitDetection

```
void SetSpriteHitDetection(BOOL b);
```

Enables or disables sprite-to-sprite hit detection. When this function is enabled, sprites are notified when they collide. By default, sprite hit detection is disabled.

Scene (Scene.h)

There is usually one *Scene* object per screen in a game. The game play takes place in one or more *Scene* objects, the menu is another *Play* object, and so on. A game created with GDKapp must have at least one *Scene*.

Constructor

```
Scene(const char* palfile=0);
```

Creates a new *Scene* object. *Scene* is designed to be used as a base class. The *palfile* parameter points to the name of a **.PAL** file that was created with the GENPAL utility (see Chapter 14). The palette defined in *palfile* will be installed when the scene is displayed. If no parameter is supplied, *Scene* creates and uses a grayscale palette.

AnyKeyDown

```
BOOL Scene::AnyKeyDown();
```

Returns TRUE if the user is pressing any key (or detectable keys at least), otherwise FALSE. This function has a higher performance overhead than the *Scene::KeyDown* member function, so it is best for use with intro and exit screens.

Hide

```
virtual void hide();
```

Does nothing. The *hide* member function is called automatically by GDKapp after the *Scene* has given up control. *Hide* can be overridden to perform cleanup tasks, such as stopping any sound clips that are playing.

KeyDown

```
UINT KeyDown(int key);
```

The *KeyDown* function inquires about a key's state. *key* can be any of the VK_ codes that Windows provides (see "Keyboard Codes" later in this chapter). If the key specified by the *key* parameter is not being pressed, *KeyDown* returns 0. Otherwise, *KeyDown* returns the number of times that the key has been checked since the key was last pressed. *KeyDown* returns 1 if there is a new keystroke. The Windows type-matic rate has no effect on this function.

RunNextScene

```
void RunNextScene();
```

Signals the *Scene* created after the current *Scene* to take over. If the current *Scene* was the last to be created, the application terminates.

RunScene

```
void RunScene(int Scene);
```

Signals the *scene* indicated by the *scene* parameter to take over. The *scene*s are ordered according to their creation in the *App* constructor. The index starts at 1.

RunScene

```
void RunScene(const type_info& sceneid);
```

Signals the *Scene* indicated by the *sceneid* parameter to take over. The parameter is a runtime type information (RTTI) class reference that uniquely identifies a class. If GDKapp cannot find the requested scene, a message box is displayed and the application terminates. Here is an example:

```
RunScene(typeid(MyMenuScene));
```

RunPrevScene

```
void RunPrevScene();
```

Signals the *Scene* created before the current *Scene* to take over. If the current *Scene* was the first to be created, the application terminates.

SaveScreen

```
void Scene::SaveScreen()
```

Saves the current screen image to disk. The *SaveScreen* function produces BMP files in the current directory that are named **screen??.bmp,** starting with **screen01.bmp.**

Show

```
virtual void show();
```

The *show* member function is called automatically by GDKapp when the *Scene* is about to take over. *Show* can be overridden to initialize variables and reset object states.

StopApp

```
void StopApp();
```

Signals the application to terminate.

Update

```
virtual void Update();
```

Does nothing. *Update* is called once per frame for the active scene and is designed to be overridden. The *Update* function is typically used to check for user input, launch scenes, and terminate applications.

SoundDevice (sound.h)

The *SoundDevice* class supports sound effects and voices by maintaining and playing sound clips. It is possible to derive a class from *SoundDevice* and use the derived class to produce all the sounds for the game. Or you can have each object that makes a sound instantiate its own *SoundDevice* object.

Constructor

```
SoundDevice(const char* soundlist);
```

Creates a *SoundDevice* object. The *soundlist* parameter is the name of a text file that contains a list of **.WAV** files. Each *SoundDevice* instance loads its own copy of each **.WAV** file.

GetFreq

```
void GetFreq(short index,DWORD& freq);
```

Retrieves the frequency setting for the specified buffer. The buffer frequency setting determines how fast the sound is played. The *index* parameter specifies which buffer the inquiry targets. The *freq* parameter is a reference to a DWORD that will contain the frequency. Frequency settings are expressed in Hz and range from 100 to 100,000 Hz.

GetPan

```
void GetPan(short index,long& pan);
```

Retrieves the buffer pan setting. The *index* parameter is the sound clip index. The *pan* parameter is a reference to the variable where the setting is to be stored. Values range from –10,000 to 10,000, where –10,000 is left channel only, and 10,000 is right channel only. The default pan of 0 means that the output in the left and right channels is equal.

GetVol

```
void GetVol(short index,long& vol);
```

Retrieves the volume setting for a specified buffer. The *index* parameter determines which buffer will be adjusted. The *vol* parameter is a reference to the variable where the setting is to be stored. The returned value is the volume adjustment. If the sound has not been adjusted, this function will return 0. Negative numbers mean that the volume has been reduced. At this time, the Games SDK does not support buffer amplification, so only zero and negative numbers will be returned.

isLooping

```
BOOL isLooping(short index);
```

Returns TRUE if the sound clip specified by *index* is currently being played repeatedly. The index values start at 1.

isPlaying

```
BOOL isPlaying(short index);
```

Returns TRUE if the sound clip specified by *index* is currently being played. The index values start at 1.

Loop

```
void Loop(short index);
```

Starts to play the sound clip specified by *index*. The sound will play repeatedly until you specify that the looping stop or until the application terminates. The index values start at 1.

Play

```
void Play(short index);
```

Starts to play the sound clip specified by *index*. If the sound is already playing, then the sound clip is restarted. The index values start at 1.

SetFreq

```
void SetFreq(short index,DWORD freq);
```

Adjusts the frequency (playback speed) for the specified buffer. The *index* parameter specifies the buffer to be adjusted. The *freq* parameter is the desired frequency. Valid frequencies range from 100 to 100,000.

SetPan

```
void SetPan(short index,long pan);
```

Adjusts the pan setting for the sound clip specified by *index*. *Panning* means adjusting the amount of sound that is coming out of the left and right speakers. The *pan* value ranges from –10,000 to 10,000, where –10,000 is left channel only, and 10,000 is right channel only. The default pan of 0 means that the output in the left and right channels is equal.

SetVol

```
void SetVol(short index,long vol);
```

Adjusts the volume setting for the sound clip specified by *index*. The *vol* parameter is the volume adjustment. Sending 0 leaves the volume unchanged. Sending negative numbers reduces the volume. The lowest volume setting is –10,000. At this time, the Games SDK does not support buffer amplification, so sending positive numbers causes an error.

Stop

```
void Stop(short index);
```

Stops the sound clip specified by *index*. If the sound was already stopped, the function has no effect. The index values start at 1.

StopAll

```
void StopAll();
```

Stops all of the sound clips being played by the *SoundDevice*. This function has no effect on sound clips being played by other instances of *SoundDevice*.

Sprite (sprite.h)

Sprite provides support for the display and animation of complex shapes. With the exception of backgrounds, all the graphical portions of GDKapp games are instances of the *Sprite* class.

Constructor

```
Sprite(const char* gfx);
```

Creates a *Sprite* object. The *gfx* parameter is the name of the **.GFX** file that contains the sprite's bitmaps.

AnyKeyDown

```
BOOL AnyKeyDown();
```

Returns TRUE if the user is pressing any key (or a detectable key at least), otherwise FALSE. This function has a higher performance overhead than the *Sprite::KeyDown* member function, so it is best for use with intro and exit screens.

GetZ

```
int GetZ();
```

Returns the sprite's Z-order setting. GDKapp uses this value to determine the order in which the sprites are drawn. The value can be any value that an *int* can represent.

KeyDown

```
UINT KeyDown(int key);
```

The *KeyDown* function inquires about a key's state. *key* can be any of the VK_ codes that Windows provides (see "Keyboard Codes" later in this chapter). If the key specified by the *key* parameter is not being pressed, *KeyDown* returns 0. Otherwise, *KeyDown* returns the number of times that the key has been checked since the key was last pressed. *KeyDown* returns 1 if there is a new keystroke. The Windows type-matic rate has no effect on this function.

OnSpriteHit

```
virtual void OnSpriteHit(Sprite* sprite);
```

Indicates that the sprite has come into contact with another sprite. The *sprite* parameter is a pointer to the other sprite and can be used to query the other sprite. The framework notifies both sprites when a hit occurs, so it is not necessary to inform the other sprite of the collision.

OnTileHit

```
virtual void OnTileHit(Sprite* tile);
```

Indicates that the sprite has come into contact with a background tile that has a solid attribute. The *tile* parameter is a pointer to the tile. The parameter can be used to query the tile about its location or Z-order.

SetHitDetection

```
void SetHitDetection(short hdlevel);
```

Specifies the hit-detection level for the sprite. The *hdlevel* parameter should be set to HD_NONE, HD_RECT, or HD_FULL. The default setting is HD_FULL. This function has no effect unless the sprite's background object enables hit detection for tiles, sprites, or both.

SetZ

```
void SetZ(int z);
```

Sets the sprite's Z-order. The function causes GDKapp to relocate the sprite in the internal list that is used to compose each display frame. The changes do not take place on the screen until the next frame is generated.

Update

```
virtual void Update();
```

Does nothing. The *Sprite::Update* function is called once per screen update. The function can be overloaded to adjust the sprite's characteristics, such as location, visibility, Z-order, and frame number.

Macros

GDKapp provides macros that are designed to aid in error detection and debugging. These macros are used in the framework implementation and should also be used for error checking in your game code.

CHECK

```
CHECK(condition);
```

The CHECK macro works just like the Standard C *assert* macro. CHECK allows an assertion to find its way to the functions that make an orderly shutdown of the game runtime environment, including the release of Windows resources.

If the condition evaluates to zero, GDKapp displays a message box that lists the source code file name and line number where the error occurred. If the condition evaluates to any number other than zero, CHECK does nothing.

The CHECK macro evaluates the condition only when the application is compiled in debug mode. In release mode, the CHECK macro produces no code, thereby eliminating any overhead.

FATAL

```
FATAL(message);
```

The FATAL macro terminates the program after displaying the *message* parameter in a message box. Unlike the CHECK macro, FATAL produces code in release mode. FATAL should be used to report conditions such as missing files or disk space shortages.

Adjusting GDKapp (gdkconst.h)

The following constant values define ranges and operating limits for the library. For most games, the values assigned to these settings suffice, but a large or unusual game may need to change one or more of these values. In this case, modify the value and recompile GDKapp. The constants discussed next are defined in **gdkconst.h**.

MODEWIDTH

GDKapp uses 640x480 mode. The MODEWIDTH constant is used to initialize the video mode and to check whether sprites are on the screen.

MODEHEIGHT

GDKapp uses 640x480 video mode. The MODEHEIGHT constant is used to initialize the video mode and to check whether sprites are on the screen.

MAXTILEINDEX

By default, GDKapp limits the number of tiles to 256. This limit does not refer to the size of the tile map but rather to the highest legal tile entry in the map. A limit of 256 means that the **.GFX** file that is used for the background shouldn't contain more than 256 tiles.

MAXSPRITES

GDKapp manages several lists of sprites internally. This constant specifies the size of some of these lists. By default, a value of 500 is used.

Keyboard Codes

The symbols shown in Table 15.1 are values that can be used with the *KeyDown* member functions of *Scene* and *Sprite*. The codes prefixed with VK_ are defined in **winuser.h** (usually located in **\MSDEV\INCLUDE**). The rest of the codes are from **keys.h**.

Table 15.1 Keyboard constants

DEL	DN	DOWNARROW
END	ENTER	ESC
ESCAPE	HOME	INS
INSERT	LEFTARROW	LF
PGDN	PGUP	RIGHTARROW
RT	SPACE	SPACEBAR
UP	UPARROW	VK_ADD
VK_BACK	VK_CAPITAL	VK_CLEAR
VK_CONTROL	VK_DECIMAL	VK_DELETE
VK_DIVIDE	VK_DOWN	VK_EXECUTE
VK_END	VK_ESCAPE	VK_F1
VK_F10	VK_F11	VK_F12
VK_F2	VK_F3	VK_F4
VK_F5	VK_F6	VK_F7
VK_F8	VK_F9	VK_HOME
VK_INSERT	VK_LCONTROL	VK_LEFT
VK_LSHIFT	VK_MENU	VK_MULTIPLY
VK_NET	VK_NUMLOCK	VK_NUMPAD0
VK_NUMPAD1	VK_NUMPAD2	VK_NUMPAD3
VK_NUMPAD4	VK_NUMPAD5	VK_NUMPAD6
VK_NUMPAD7	VK_NUMPAD8	VK_NUMPAD9
VK_PAUSE	VK_PRINT	VK_PRIOR
VK_RCONTROL	VK_RETURN	VK_RIGHT
VK_RSHIFT	VK_SCROLL	VK_SELECT
VK_SEPARATOR	VK_SHIFT	VK_SNAPSHOT
VK_SPACE	VK_SUBTRACT	VK_TAB
VK_UP		

THE GDKAPP DEMOS

The best way to learn a new framework is to study examples of it in use. The GDKapp framework includes seven demos: Skeleton, Sprite, Scroll, Scene, Sound, Collide and TankTop. This chapter discusses each demo, starting with Skeleton (the simplest demo), and finishing with TankTop (the most complex). Each framework feature, such as animation, sound, or hit detection is exercised in at least one of the demos. In this chapter you will learn about:

- Animation
- Scrolling
- Sound support
- Multiple scenes
- Hit detection

The Skeleton Demo

The Skeleton demo is an example of the smallest possible GDKapp application; it displays a single background until the user presses a key. The demo is a good starting place because it provides all the necessary elements of a GDKapp application without introducing unneeded code. Skeleton does not include sprites, scrolling, or sound. Figure 16.1 is the Skeleton demo.

Figure 16.1 The Skeleton demo

The Skeleton demo project is in the **\gdkapp\demos\skeleton** directory, and all the code for the demo is in **main.cpp**. The first class that **main.cpp** defines is *SampleScene*:

```
class SampleScene : public Scene
{
public:
     SampleScene() : Scene("demo.pal")
     {
          background=new BackGround("bg.gfx");
     }
     ~SampleScene()
     {
```

```
                        delete background;
                }
                void Update()
                {
                        if (AnyKeyDown())
                                StopApp();
                }
        private:
                BackGround* background;
        };
```

The constructor passes the name of a palette file to the *Scene* constructor. You create palette files using the GENPAL or GETPAL utility. The *SampleScene* constructor then creates an instance of *BackGround*, passing to the *BackGround* constructor the name of the **.GFX** file that contains the background image. The *SampleScene* destructor deletes the *BackGround* instance. The *Scene::Update* function checks to see whether the user has pressed any keys and stops the application if a key has been pressed.

The *SampleApp* class is responsible for creating an instance of the *SampleScene* class. *SampleApp* looks like this:

```
class SampleApp : public App
{
public:
        SampleApp(HINSTANCE h,int show) : App(h,show,"Skeleton Demo")
        {
                scene=new SampleScene;
        }
        ~SampleApp()
        {
                delete scene;
        }
private:
        Scene* scene;
};
```

SampleApp is derived from the *App* class. The constructor sends three arguments to the *App* constructor, including the name of the application.

An instance of *SampleApp* is created and run by the *WinMain* function:

```
int PASCAL WinMain(HINSTANCE hInstance,HINSTANCE,LPSTR,int show)
{
      SampleApp* app=new SampleApp(hInstance,show);
      int r=app->Run();
      delete app;
      return r;
}
```

The *Run* member launches the application. When *Run* returns, the application has terminated, and the *SampleApp* object is deleted.

The Sprite Demo

The Sprite demo, an enhanced version of the Skeleton demo, animates a single sprite across a nonscrolling background. Pressing the **Esc** key terminates the demo. Figure 16.2 is the Sprite demo.

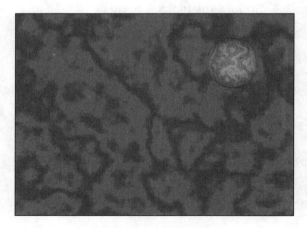

Figure 16.2 The Sprite demo

The Sprite demo project is in the **\gdkapp\demos\sprite** directory. As with the Skeleton demo, two classes are defined: *SampleScene* and *SampleApp*. *SampleScene* is modified to add animation; the *SampleApp* class and the *WinMain* function remain like their counterparts in the Skeleton demo. The *SampleScene* constructor looks like this:

```
SampleScene() : Scene("demo.pal")
{
        background=new BackGround("bg.gfx");
        sprite=new Sprite("sprite.gfx");
        short halfwidth=sprite->GetWidth()/2;
        short halfheight=sprite->GetHeight()/2;
        sprite->SetLoc(320-halfwidth,240-halfheight);
        xinc=NextIncrement(0);
        yinc=NextIncrement(0);
        minx=-halfwidth;
        miny=-halfheight;
        maxx=640-halfwidth;
        maxy=480-halfheight;
        srand((unsigned)time(NULL));}
}
```

The *SampleScene* constructor begins by creating *BackGround* and *Sprite* objects. Both objects are supplied with the names of **.GFX** files. The *SetLoc* member of *Sprite* is used to place the sprite in the middle of the screen. The *xinc* and *yinc* variables determine the direction of the sprite, and the *minx*, *miny*, *maxx*, and *maxy* variables determine the area that the sprite can bounce around in. The *srand* function is used to seed the random generator, because the sprite's movement and speed are randomly decided.

The *SampleScene::Update* function calculates the sprite's location for each frame. *Update* is defined this way:

```
void Update()
{
    short x,y;
    sprite->GetLoc(x,y);
    x+=xinc;
    y+=yinc;
    if (x<minx || x>maxx)
    {
        x-=xinc;
        xinc=NextIncrement(xinc);
    }
    if (y<miny || y>maxy)
    {
        y-=yinc;
        yinc=NextIncrement(yinc);
    }
    sprite->SetLoc(x,y);
    if (KeyDown(ENTER) || KeyDown(ESCAPE))
        StopApp();
}
```

The *GetLoc* function is used to determine the sprite's current location. The x and y coordinates are then incremented by the increment that has been determined for each axis. The new location is then checked against the sprite's limits. When the sprite reaches the limit for an axis, its previous location is restored, and its direction is reversed. The *SetLoc* function is used to notify the sprite of its new location. Finally, the keyboard is checked for input. Pressing **Enter** or **Esc** causes the demo to terminate.

The Scroll Demo

The Scroll demo enhances the Sprite demo by adding a scrolling background. Tiles are used instead of a single background image. A text file, called a *map file*, is used to define a map that determines the placement of the tiles. The Scroll demo uses a sprite that spins in addition to bouncing around the screen. Pressing **Esc** terminates the demo. Figure 16.3 is the Scroll demo.

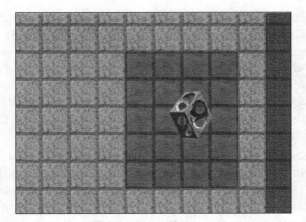

Figure 16.3 The Scroll demo

The Scroll demo project is in the **\gdkapp\demos\scroll** directory. The *SampleScene* constructor looks like this:

```
SampleScene() : Scene("demo.pal")
{
        background=new BackGround("tiles.gfx","map.txt");
        sprite=new Sprite("sprite.gfx");
        sprite->SetLoc(320,240);
        sprite->SetZ(100);
        background->FocusOn(sprite);
        short bgwidth,bgheight;
        background->GetSize(bgwidth,bgheight);
        short halfwidth=sprite->GetWidth()/2;
        short halfheight=sprite->GetHeight()/2;
        xinc=NextIncrement(0);
        yinc=NextIncrement(0);
        minx=-halfwidth;
        miny=-halfheight;
        maxx=bgwidth-halfwidth;
        maxy=bgheight-halfheight;
        frame=1;
        numframes=sprite->GetNumFrames();
        srand((unsigned)time(NULL));
}
```

The *SampleScene* class passes the names of the **.GFX** file and the map file to the *BackGround* constructor. An instance of the *Sprite* class is constructed, and its position is assigned. The sprite is placed with its upper-left corner in the middle of the screen. The sprite's Z-order is set using the *SetZ* function. We use the value 100 so that the sprite will appear in front of the tiles on the background (the tile Z-order value defaults to zero). If a background tile has a Z-order value greater than a sprite's value, the tile will appear in front of the sprite.

The *BackGround::FocusOn* function is used to determine which sprite the background will follow. The framework attempts to keep the sprite that has the focus in the center of the screen. The *minx, miny, maxx,* and *maxy* variables are assigned according to the size of the background. The values returned by *GetSize* depend on the size of the tiles and the number of columns and rows that are defined in the map file.

The Scroll demo uses a multiframe sprite. This means that the sprite can represent itself using any one of a set of bitmaps. The Scroll sprite uses 60 frames, each showing the sprite at a different rotation. The *frame* and *numframes* variables are used to determine the frame to be used for each screen update. All 60 frames are supplied in the **sprite.gfx** file.

The map file that is sent to the *BackGround* object is a text file that defines a map of index values. Each index specifies a tile within the **.GFX** file. Because the **.GFX** file is treated as a set of tiles, the file should contain bitmaps that are all the same size. The map file also determines the Z-order value for each tile. The **map.txt** file used by the Scroll demo looks like this:

```
20 20
2 2 2 2 2 2 2 2 2 2 2 2 2 2 2 2 2 2 2 2
2 1 1 1 1 1 1 1 1 1 1 1 3 3 4 4 4 4 4 2
2 1 7 7 7 1 1 1 1 1 1 1 3 3 4 4 4 4 4 2
2 1 7 7 7 1 1 1 1 1 1 1 3 3 4 4 4 4 4 2
2 1 7 7 7 1 1 1 1 1 1 1 3 3 4 4 4 4 4 2
2 1 1 1 1 1 1 1 1 1 1 1 3 3 4 4 4 4 4 2
2 1 1 1 1 1 1 1 1 1 1 1 3 3 4 4 4 4 4 2
2 1 1 1 1 1 1 1 1 1 1 1 3 3 4 4 4 4 4 2
2 1 1 1 1 1 1 1 1 1 1 1 3 3 3 3 3 3 3 2
2 1 1 1 1 1 1 1 1 1 1 1 3 3 3 3 3 3 3 2
2 1 1 1 1 1 1 1 1 1 1 1 1 1 1 1 1 1 1 2
2 1 1 1 1 1 1 1 1 1 1 1 1 1 1 1 1 1 1 2
2 1 6 6 6 6 1 1 1 1 1 1 1 1 1 1 1 1 1 2
2 1 6 1 1 6 1 1 1 1 1 1 1 5 5 5 5 1 1 2
2 1 6 1 1 6 1 1 1 1 1 1 1 5 5 5 5 1 1 2
2 1 6 6 6 6 1 1 1 1 1 1 1 5 5 5 5 1 1 2
2 1 1 1 1 1 1 1 1 1 1 1 1 5 5 5 5 1 1 2
2 1 1 1 1 1 1 1 1 1 1 1 1 5 5 5 5 1 1 2
2 1 1 1 1 1 1 1 1 1 1 1 1 1 1 1 1 1 1 2
2 2 2 2 2 2 2 2 2 2 2 2 2 2 2 2 2 2 2 2

1 e 0
2 e 150
3 e 150
4 e 0
5 e 0
6 e 150
7 e 150
```

The file defines a map that is 20 by 20 tiles in size and uses seven different tiles. Some of the tiles are defined with Z-order values that are higher than those of the sprite created in the *SampleScene* constructor. These tiles appear in front of the sprite. Map files are discussed in detail in Chapter 14.

The Scene Demo

Few games throw a player directly into the action. Most games provide an introduction and a menu before the game begins. The Scene demo illustrates how intro screens and menus are implemented with GDKapp. The demo contains four scenes: an intro, a menu, a game scene, and a trailer or credits scene. There are no sprites or sounds in the Scene demo. Figure 16.4 is the intro scene from the Scene demo.

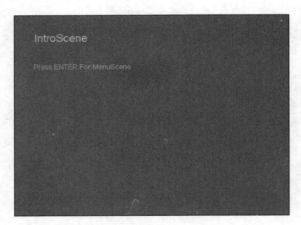

Figure 16.4 The first scene in the Scene demo

Each scene displays an identifying label and one or more instructions. The intro scene provides a connection, or link, to the menu scene. The menu scene allows you to view the trailer scene or proceed to the game scene.

The Scene demo project is in the **\gdkapp\demos\scene** directory. The code for the Scene demo defines four Scene derived classes: *IntroScene*, *MenuScene*, *GameScene*, and *TrailerScene*. The code for *IntroScene* looks like this:

```
class IntroScene : public Scene
{
public:
    IntroScene() : Scene("intro.pal")
    {
        background=new BackGround("intro.gfx");
    }
    ~IntroScene()
    {
        delete background;
    }
    void Update()
    {
        if (KeyDown(ENTER))
            RunScene(typeid(MenuScene));
    }
private:
    BackGround* background;
};
```

The *IntroScene* constructor creates a *BackGround* instance and supplies it with the name of the **.GFX** file. The destructor deletes the instance. The *Update* function checks to see whether the user has pressed **Enter**. If **Enter** has been pressed, the *RunScene* member function is used to indicate to GDKapp that the *MenuScene* class should be executed. The *typeid* operator creates a *type_info* instance that uniquely identifies the *MenuScene* class.

The other scenes in the Scene demo are similar to *IntroScene*. The *MenuScene* class looks like this:

```
class MenuScene : public Scene
{
public:
      MenuScene() : Scene("menu.pal")
      {
             background=new BackGround("menu.gfx");
      }
      ~MenuScene()
      {
             delete background;
      }
      void Update()
      {
             if (KeyDown('G'))
                   RunScene(typeid(GameScene));
             if (KeyDown(VK_ESCAPE))
                   RunScene(typeid(TrailerScene));
      }
private:
      BackGround* background;
};
```

The *MenuScene::Update* member checks for two keys and runs two different scenes depending on the input.

The Sound Demo

The Sound demo showcases the *SoundDevice* class. The demo displays a menu of sound effects and the keys to press in order to play them. Pressing **Esc** terminates the demo. Figure 16.5 is the Sound demo.

```
            GDKapp SoundDevice Demo


                    1        glass
        Group1      2        pistol
                    3        shotgun
                    4        applause (looping)

                    0        silence Group 1


                    F1       click
        Group2      F2       thump
                    F3       jaildoor (looping)

                    F10      silence Group 2
```

Figure 16.5 The Sound demo

The Sound demo project is in the **\gdkapp\demos\sound** directory. The *SampleScene* class constructor prepares the application by creating one *BackGround* and two *SoundDevice* objects:

```
SampleScene() : Scene("bg.pal")
{
        background=new BackGround("bg.gfx");
        sounddevice1=new SoundDevice("group1.txt");
        sounddevice2=new SoundDevice("group2.txt");
}
```

The text files that are passed to each *SoundDevice* instance contain a list of **.WAV** files that make up the **.WAV** file collection for each instance. The **group1.txt** file looks like this:

```
glass.wav
gun.wav
shotgun.wav
applause.wav
```

The remainder of the work occurs in the *SampleScene::Update* function:

```
void Update()
{
        if (KeyDown('1')==1)
                sounddevice1->Play(1);
        if (KeyDown('2')==1)
                sounddevice1->Play(2);
        if (KeyDown('3')==1)
                sounddevice1->Play(3);
        if (KeyDown('4')==1)
                sounddevice1->Loop(4);
        if (KeyDown('0')==1)
                sounddevice1->StopAll();
        if (KeyDown(VK_F1)==1)
                sounddevice2->Play(1);
        if (KeyDown(VK_F2)==1)
                sounddevice2->Play(2);
        if (KeyDown(VK_F3)==1)
                sounddevice2->Loop(3);
        if (KeyDown(VK_F10)==1)
                sounddevice2->StopAll();
        if (KeyDown(ESCAPE))
                StopApp();
}
```

Compare the *Update* member function with the menu in Figure 16.5. Each key press causes a *SoundDevice* function to be executed. Two of the sound effects loop continuously, because the *Loop* member function is used instead of *Play*. The *StopAll* member function stops all the sound clips that are currently being played by *SoundDevice*. The **Esc** key causes the demo to terminate. The return values from the *KeyDown* member functions are compared to 1 so that the condition is TRUE only once for each keystroke. Refer to Chapter 15 for more about the *KeyDown* member function.

The Collide Demo

The Sprite and Scroll demos animate sprites. The sprites in these demos float over static backgrounds or scrolling tiles but are not affected by other objects in the scene. The Collide demo illustrates the use of GDKapp's hit-detection support. Collide displays a set of sprites, each of which can be moved using the arrow keys. When two or more of the sprites collide, an annoying sound is played. Pressing **Esc** terminates the demo. Figure 16.6 is the Collide demo.

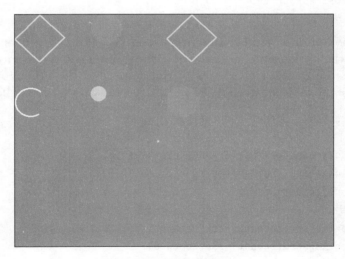

Figure 16.6 The Collide demo

Six sprites are displayed. Each sprite can be moved using the arrow keys. Pressing the **Tab** key changes the active (movable) sprite. When two sprites collide, each of them is notified of the collision. A collision occurs when two nontransparent pixels are drawn at the same location. Notice that the diamond-shaped sprite is transparent in the center. If you maneuver a sprite into the center of the diamond so that the edge of the diamond does not make contact with the sprite, no collision occurs. The Collide *SampleScene* class is defined this way:

```
class SampleScene : public Scene
{
public:
      SampleScene();
      ~SampleScene();
      void Update();
private:
      BackGround* background;
      DemoSprite* sprite[MAXSPRITES];
      short spritecount;
      short cursprite;
};
```

We will look at the member functions soon. The data members include a pointer to the background, an array of sprite pointers, and two integers: one for storing the number of sprites in the demo and the other for keeping track of the movable sprite. The *SampleScene* constructor looks like this:

```
SampleScene() : Scene("demo.pal")
{
      background=new BackGround("blank.gfx");
      background->SetSpriteHitDetection(TRUE);
      spritecount=0;

      sprite[spritecount]=new DemoSprite(1,"diamond.gfx");
      sprite[spritecount]->SetLoc(0,0);
      spritecount++;

      sprite[spritecount]=new DemoSprite(8,"circle.gfx");
      sprite[spritecount]->SetLoc(150,0);
      spritecount++;

      sprite[spritecount]=new DemoSprite(2,"c.gfx");
      sprite[spritecount]->SetLoc(0,150);
      spritecount++;
```

```
sprite[spritecount]=new DemoSprite(2,"small.gfx");
sprite[spritecount]->SetLoc(150,150);
spritecount++;

sprite[spritecount]=new DemoSprite(2,"diamond.gfx");
sprite[spritecount]->SetLoc(300,0);
spritecount++;

sprite[spritecount]=new DemoSprite(2,"circle.gfx");
sprite[spritecount]->SetLoc(300,150);
spritecount++;

cursprite=0;
sprite[cursprite]->SetActive();
}
```

After the *BackGround* object is created, the *SetSpriteHitDetection* member function is called with TRUE as an argument. This activates the sprite-to-sprite hit detection. Once the hit detection is activated, the default hit-detection method for each sprite is HD_FULL, indicating that pixel-level detection is to be used. The hit-detection settings are discussed in Chapter 14.

The *SampleScene* constructor creates six sprites and places each one in a different section of the screen. The first *Sprite* is made active using the *SetActive* member function. *SetActive* is a *DemoSprite* member function that causes the sprite in question to respond to the arrow keys only when it is active. The active *Sprite* is determined by the *SampleScene::Update* function:

```
void Update()
{
    if (KeyDown(ESCAPE))
        StopApp();
    if (KeyDown(VK_TAB)==1)
    {
        sprite[cursprite]->SetInActive();
        cursprite=(cursprite+1)%spritecount;
        sprite[cursprite]->SetActive();
    }
}
```

The *Update* member function terminates the application if the user has pressed **Esc**. If **Tab** is pressed, the currently active sprite is deactivated and the next sprite in the *sprite* array is activated.

The *DemoSprite* class is defined this way:

```
class DemoSprite : public Sprite
{
public:
    DemoSprite(short i,const char* gfx) : Sprite(gfx)
    {
        inc=i;
        active=FALSE;
    }
    void SetActive()    { active=TRUE; }
    void SetInActive()  { active=FALSE; }
    void Update()
    {
        if (!active)
            return;
        short x,y;
        GetLoc(x,y);
        if (KeyDown(LEFT))
            x-=inc;
        if (KeyDown(UP))
            y-=inc;
        if (KeyDown(RIGHT))
            x+=inc;
        if (KeyDown(DOWN))
            y+=inc;
        SetLoc(x,y);
    }
    void OnSpriteHit(Sprite* s)
    {
        sounddevice->Play(1);
    }
private:
```

```
        short inc;
        BOOL active;
};
```

The *DemoSprite* constructor accepts two arguments. The first argument is the increment by which the sprite is moved, and the second is the **.GFX** file that contains the sprite's bitmap. The constructor sets the *active* flag to FALSE. The *Update* function checks the *active* flag and returns immediately if the flag is not set to TRUE. If the *DemoSprite* is active, then the keyboard is checked for arrow keys and the *x* and *y* variables are updated.

The *OnSpriteHit* member function is called by GDKapp whenever the sprite collides with another sprite. *DemoSprite* plays a sound whenever a hit is detected by the framework. The *OnSpriteHit* function supplies a pointer to the *Sprite* involved in the collision. This pointer is useful if you want to determine the location or Z-order value of the offending sprite.

Because the Collide demo uses sound to indicate collisions, a *SoundDevice* instance must be created. The *SampleApp* class creates an instance and stores a pointer in a global variable. The *SampleApp* class is defined this way:

```
class SampleApp : public App
{
public:
        SampleApp(HINSTANCE hInstance,int show) :
App(hInstance,show,"Collide Demo")
        {
                sounddevice=new SoundDevice("sounds.txt");
                scene=new SampleScene;
        }
        ~SampleApp()
        {
                delete scene;
                delete sounddevice;
        }
private:
        Scene* scene;
};
```

The TankTop Demo

In this chapter we've looked at demos that feature animation, scrolling, sound playback, and hit detection. The TankTop demo uses all these features. TankTop is a simple tank simulation. The tank includes a rotating turret and can fire bullets. Use the arrow keys to control the tank, the **Spacebar** to fire the gun, and the **Q** and **W** keys to rotate the turret. Pressing **Esc** terminates the demo. Figure 16.7 is the TankTop demo.

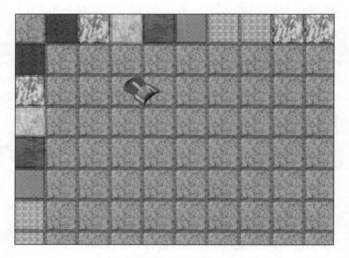

Figure 16.7 The TankTop demo

The demo is implemented with the following classes: *TankTopApp*, *TankTopScene*, *Tank*, *UserTank*, *Bullet*, and *Gun*. The *TankTopApp* and *TankTopScene* classes are similar to the *App-* and *Scene*-derived classes that we've seen in the other demos. The *Tank* class is defined this way:

```
class Tank : public Sprite
{
public:
    Tank();
    ~Tank();
    short GetSpeed()  { return speed; }
```

```
protected:
      void  ShiftUp();
      void  ShiftDown();
      void  Stop();
      void  Shoot();
      void  TurnLeft();
      void  TurnRight();
      void  TurnGunLeft();
      void  TurnGunRight();
      void  Update();
      void  OnTileHit(Sprite* s);
private:
      short speed;
      short rot,oldrot;
      double x,y;
      double oldx,oldy;
      short halfwidth,halfheight;
      short gunrot,oldgunrot;
      short halfgunwidth,halfgunheight;
      Gun* gun;
};
```

The tank can be controlled using functions such as *ShiftUp*, *ShiftDown*, *Stop*, *TurnLeft*, and so on. The *Tank* class manages the tank location, speed, and rotation as well as the rotation of the turret. The tank has 60 rotation angles, three forward speeds, and three backward speeds.

The *UserTank* class is derived from *Tank*. The *UserTank* class overrides the *Update* member function to modify the tank's behavior. The *UserTank* class looks like this:

```
class UserTank : public Tank
{
public:
      void Update();
};
```

The *UserTank::Update* member function interprets keystrokes and uses the *Tank* member functions to control the tank:

```
void UserTank::Update()
{
        if (KeyDown(UP)==1)
                ShiftUp();
        if (KeyDown(DOWN)==1)
                ShiftDown();
        if (KeyDown(LEFT)%2)
                TurnLeft();
        if (KeyDown(RIGHT)%2)
                TurnRight();
        if (KeyDown('Q')%2)
                TurnGunLeft();
        if (KeyDown('W')%2)
                TurnGunRight();
        if (KeyDown(VK_CLEAR)==1)
                Stop();
        if (KeyDown(VK_SPACE)==1)
                Shoot();
        Tank::Update();
}
```

Notice that some of the keyboard checks use the modulus operator on the *KeyDown* return value. Using a value of 2 causes the condition to fail if *KeyDown* returns an even number. The rate of the tank rotation is slowed using this technique. After the keyboard has been checked, the *Tank::Update* member function is called. *Update* calculates the location and rotation for each frame:

```
void Tank::Update()
{
    oldx=x;
    oldy=y;
    if (speed>0)
    {
        x+=inctable[rot][speed-1].x;
        y+=inctable[rot][speed-1].y;
    }
    else if (speed<0)
    {
        short r=ADD_DEG(rot,NDEGREES/2);
        short s=abs(speed)-1;
        x+=inctable[r][s].x;
        y+=inctable[r][s].y;
    }
    SetLoc((short)x-halfwidth,(short)y-halfheight);
    gun->SetLoc((short)x-halfgunwidth,(short)y-halfgunheight);

    SetCurFrame(rot+1);
    gun->SetCurFrame(ADD_DEG(rot,gunrot)+1);
}
```

The x and y variables are incremented with values from the *inctable* array, a table of acceleration values. The speed and rotation of the tank are used to index into the table and retrieve the increment values. The *Bullet* class uses the same table to propel bullets. The TankTop demo project is in the **\gdkapp\demos\tanktop** directory on the CD-ROM.

THE GAMES TOOLSET
ON THE **CD-ROM**

This appendix describes the tools that a games programmer uses to construct the graphical, musical, and sound components of a game. All but one of the programs described in this appendix are either a part of Windows 95 or included on the CD-ROM that accompanies this book. The one that we omitted (VFD, listed last) is readily available for download from on-line sources. This appendix lists the tools and gives brief descriptions of their operations. For complete documentation, refer to the documentation and help files that accompany the tools on the CD-ROM.

In this appendix you will learn about:

- Paint programs
- 3-D modelers
- Ray-tracers
- Ray-tracing utility programs
- MIDI sequencers
- Image conversion and utility programs
- Animation programs

About Freeware and Shareware

Some of the tool programs on the CD-ROM are what is generally referred to as *freeware*, although the vendor of a particular program may not consider the program to be such. The term *freeware* has no legal connotation as far as we know. Some of these programs are copyrighted, which means that you may use the programs without charge, but you may not redistribute them except as specified in their documentation, usually in a nonprofit medium. Some are in the *public domain*, which means that you can do anything you want with them. Some of the programs are not supported, although their authors may be found on CompuServe and may be willing to answer questions.

Other tool programs on the CD-ROM are *shareware*, which means that you may use them to try them out. If you decide that one of them is useful enough to continue using, you must *register* with the program's vendor for a license to use the program. Registration involves paying a small fee, which reimburses the vendor for the development of the program. By distributing the program as shareware, the vendor avoids expensive advertising, packaging, and commercial distribution and therefore keeps the cost down. When you register, you become eligible for support and upgrades. Each shareware program's documentation files include instructions for registration.

Paint Programs

Paint programs permit you to create and modify bitmap image files. A *bitmap image* file is one that stores a picture as an array of picture elements (pixels). Each pixel can represent one of some number of colors, depending on the format of the file. The pixel values are offsets into a palette table. Each entry in the palette table represents one color from those available in the current display mode.

Windows 95 supports the **.BMP** bitmap format. There are many other formats.

NeoPaint

NeoPaint is a shareware DOS paint program. It is among the best of the DOS shareware paint programs, and we used it extensively to build the scenery for the arcade-style games and sprites that demonstrate our frameworks.

The strengths of NeoPaint are found in its use of texture patterns, stamps, and text fonts. These tools greatly ease the task of creating complex pictures. Figure A.1 is a screen shot from NeoPaint showing the town scene from the Shootout game under construction. The signs, shingles, windows, bricks, and siding are all built from standard NeoPaint components.

Figure A.1 NeoPaint screen shot

NeoPaint does not run well in a Windows 95 DOS box. You will find it easier to use if you boot your system with an earlier version of DOS. Later versions of NeoPaint may correct this problem.

Paint Shop Pro

Paint Shop Pro is a professional shareware paint and image processing program that runs under Windows 95 and supports 26 raster image formats and nine meta and vector image formats. You can process bitmap image files in all these formats, and you can readily convert a file from any one of the formats to a file of any of the others. The program includes image processing tools that rival the best of the paint programs. Figure A.2 shows Paint Shop Pro being used to enhance Figure 11.2 from Chapter 11.

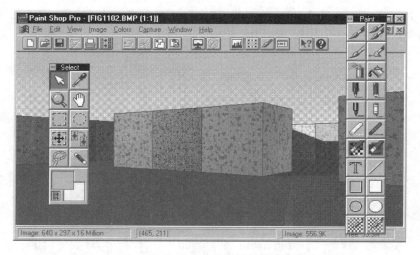

Figure A.2 Paint Shop Pro

Windows 95 Paint

Windows 95 comes with its own paint program. The feature list of Windows 95 Paint is not as comprehensive as those of NeoPaint and Paint Shop Pro, but its price is right. Figure A.3 shows Windows 95 Paint being used to view the Pond scene from the Skater demo.

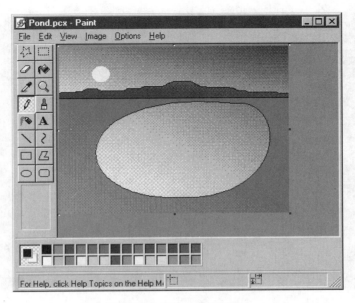

Figure A.3 Windows 95 Paint

3-D Modelers

3-D modelers are programs that allow you to build a wire-frame model of scenes and sprites. When the wire-frame image is combined with surfaces and textures, the resulting file is ready to be rendered by a ray-tracer. The three modelers discussed here can produce source code for POV-Ray and Polyray ray-tracers.

MORAY

MORAY is the 3-D modeler program that we used to build the scenes for the Town game. Figure A.4 is a screen shot of MORAY with a scene from the Town game.

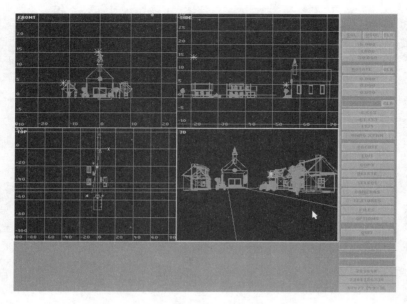

Figure A.4 MORAY

The screen shot in Figure A.4 is from a version of MORAY that predates the one included on the CD-ROM. The new version runs properly in a full-screen Windows 95 DOS box but does not permit the use of **Alt+Print Screen** to capture its graphical image to the Windows 95 clipboard. Consequently, we cannot show a screen shot in this appendix. You need a VESA-compliant video adapter in order to run MORAY.

MORAY displays the model in four views: side, top, front, and isometric. You can view them together or dedicate the viewing area entirely to one of them. You can pan and zoom any portion of the flat view. The isometric view represents what the ray-tracer's camera sees. You can move the camera around and change its aperture. As you change the model, all four views change. MORAY records the model in an MDL file of its own format. It exports the model to the ray-tracer's source code format and can launch execution of the ray-tracer to render the scene.

POVCAD

POVCAD is a Windows 95–hosted 3-D modeler. POVCAD shows the same four views that MORAY shows but only one of them at a time. Figure A.5 is a screen shot of POVCAD building a simple model.

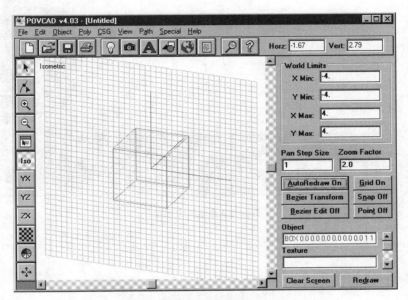

Figure A.5 POVCAD

WinModeller

WinModeller is a Windows 95–hosted 3-D modeler. It supports multiple views of the model, so you can configure it to show the three side views and the isometric view simultaneously. Figure A.6 is a screen shot of WinModeller building a simple model.

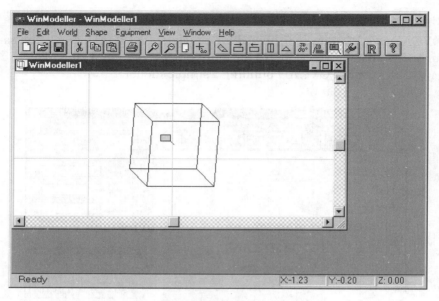

Figure A.6 WinModeller

Ray-Tracers

Ray-tracers process a form of source code into images. The source code represents a three-dimensional space that contains shapes, light sources, and a camera. Each shape is assigned a texture, which identifies the reactions of the shape's surfaces to light with respect to color, reflection, refraction, diffusion, and so on. Each light source is assigned a position. The camera is configured to represent the position and viewing angle of the person viewing the image. From each light source, the program then traces pseudo light rays reflected from the shapes onto the image at each pixel position. Creating an image this way is called *rendering* the image. Ray-traced images exhibit photo-realistic effects.

Polyray and POV-Ray

Polyray is a shareware ray-tracer. POV-Ray is copyrighted freeware. The two programs are similar in what they do and how they work. Both programs run from the DOS command line. They compile the source code into an image and render an image file in the **.TGA** format. Both programs can display the image on a VGA monitor as the image is being rendered.

POV-Ray is the result of a team effort. The team is coordinated in the CompuServe Graphdev forum, and support for the program is strong. There are many utility programs that enhance a POV-Ray environment, and some of them are included on the CD-ROM with this book.

The POV-Ray program, along with complete documentation and many sample model files, is included on the CD-ROM with this book. So is the complete source code to POV-Ray. It is written in C and has been ported to many platforms. The source code reflects these ports.

Although POV-Ray is distributed freely, there are restrictions on how you may use it. You may not incorporate the C source code from POV-Ray into other programs. You may use the standard textures and shapes to render your own scenes, but you may not use entire objects or scenes from the sample scenes. You are free to do whatever you like with the scenes that you render.

WinPOV32

There are several unofficial versions of POV-Ray. One of them is WinPOV32, a 32-bit version of the program that has been compiled to run under the Windows 95 DOS box. We included it with this book because it renders scenes significantly faster than the official executable version does. WinPOV32 is the version that we use routinely. The CD-ROM includes source code modifications that implement the Win32 version.

Ray-Tracing Utility Programs

These utility programs support ray tracing. Of the ones that are readily available, we selected just a few based on what we perceive to be the requirements for a games developer. Many more utilities are available in many on-line services. As you become more familiar with the operation and potential of a ray-tracer, your own requirements will become clearer. You should explore the on-line resources to see what is available.

Polyray and POV-Ray Preprocessor

This program, called PPP or P-cubed, preprocesses structured source code into Polyray and POV-Ray source code. The PPP syntax supports variable declarations and loops, making it possible to create complex animation sequences from a single source code file. You embed the ray-tracer source code in the PPP source code. PPP passes the embedded ray-tracer code through to the ray-tracer.

Poly Win

Poly Win is a Windows 95–hosted front end to the Polyray ray-tracer. Figure A.7 shows the Poly Win application. Poly Win accepts information about an image to be rendered and then launches the image from within Windows 95.

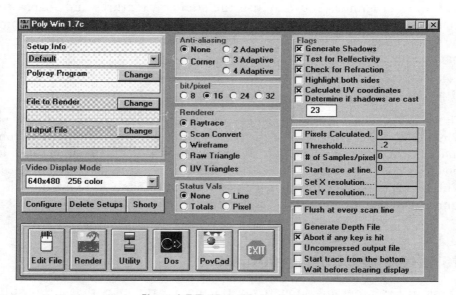

Figure A.7 The Poly Win application

POVNET

POVNET implements a rendering server in a network. Developers build POV-Ray source code in their workstations, and the server renders the images.

Ray tracing is a processor-intensive and time-consuming operation. Depending on the processor speed, the target resolution, and the number of shapes and light sources in the scene, rendering an image can take several hours. The process works well in a Windows 95 background DOS box, but you must be careful not to do anything else that might bring the system down, lest you lose the rendering work in progress.

No matter how bulletproof the operating system, we programmers frequently do things that require a reboot. Often we simply lock up the system. It is our right and duty to do so, and we do not want to be constrained in that activity by the fact that a long background task is running. We'd prefer to offload those tasks to a less susceptible computer.

For that reason, we developed POVNET, which involved writing two programs and modifying POV-Ray to accommodate the environment. Using a text editor or a 3-D modeler, you build your POV-Ray source code at your workstation. Then you upload the source code to the server. The server is constantly watching for new source code files. When the server receives a new source code file, the server launches POV-Ray to render the file into an image. From the workstation you periodically check for your file's progress by examining the expected output from the ray-tracer. When the image has been rendered, you download it from the server.

WRAW to POV-Ray Converter for Windows (WRAW2POV)

WRAW2POV is a Windows 95–hosted program that converts ASCII files of triangle vertices into ray-tracing source code. To smooth the rendered object, WRAW2POV also calculates normals for the vertices. WRAW2POV supports the formats of Polyray, POV-Ray, and Vivid, another ray-tracer (not discussed in this book). Figure A.9 shows the WRAW2POV application.

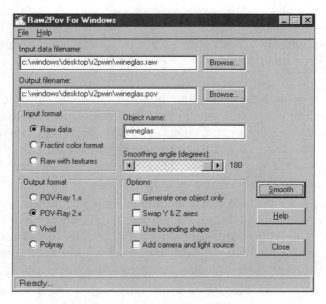

Figure A.8 The WRAW2POV application

MIDI Sequencers

A *MIDI sequencer* lets you create and modify MIDI music files from either a MIDI keyboard or your computer's keyboard and mouse. By assigning different tracks to different instruments, you can create the effect of a complete orchestra in a single file. This file, when played through the Windows 95 MIDI sound system, adds a musical score to your game program.

WinJammer

WinJammer is a Windows 95–hosted MIDI sequencer. You can assign an instrument to each MIDI channel and record the channels individually. You can view the sequence's notes for a given track in a display called the *piano roll*. This display is not a musical score with musical notation; instead, it represents each note as a horizontal bar in a time-based display. You can use the mouse and keyboard to change the properties of each note. Figure A.9 shows the WinJammer application.

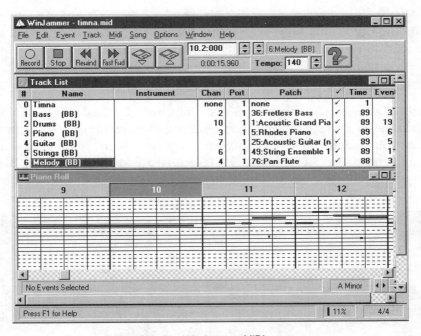

Figure A.9 The WinJammer MIDI sequencer

MT - Multi-Track Sequencer/Editor

In 1989, M&T books published *MIDI Sequencing in C*, by Jim Conger. The MT software was included with the book. MT is a multiple-track sequencer program that runs under DOS and interfaces with MPU-401 MIDI devices. You can use the program along with a compatible MIDI interface card and a MIDI keyboard to record MIDI songs such as the ones that accompany our demo games.

When the book went out of print, Conger released MT as unsupported freeware. The software, including the source code, is on the CD-ROM that accompanies this book.

Sound Effects Recorders/Editors

Games programs use **.WAV** files to play sound effects. You can use canned **.WAV** files from public-domain sources, and you can record your own. Recording the sound, however, is only part of the process. You need to be able to edit and enhance the sound clip with different effects.

Blaster Master

Blaster Master is a complete DOS system for recording, editing, and playing sound files on a Creative Labs Sound Blaster. The program is useful for fine-tuning your sound effects and converting between sound file formats, and it has an impressive set of features. Figure A.10 is a screen shot of Blaster Master in operation.

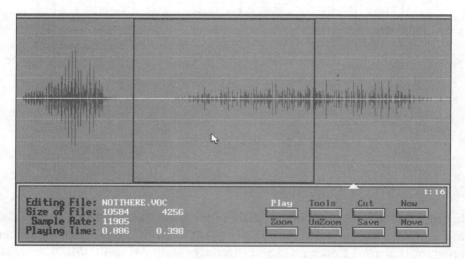

Figure A.10 Blaster Master

Windows 95 Sound Recorder

The Windows 95 Sound Recorder applet is included with Windows 95. You use it to convert audio input or MIDI or CD audio playbacks into **.WAV** files. Sound Recorder supports limited editing. You can edit a sound clip by removing either end to eliminate dead space and by changing volume, pitch, and reverberation. Figure A.11 shows the Sound Recorder applet.

Figure A.11 The Sound Recorder applet

Image Conversion and Utility Programs

Ray-tracers produce **.TGA** files. Windows 95 programs typically support **.BMP** files. Paint programs support files of most formats. There are many automated utilities that convert and enhance the images recorded by these files. We have included two such utility programs on the CD-ROM that accompanies this book.

Image Alchemy

Image Alchemy is an impressive and reliable bitmapped graphical file format converter. Its sole purpose is to convert between formats, and it is probably the most comprehensive of such programs. The demo version included on the CD-ROM converts images that are 640 by 480 pixels and smaller. To work with images at higher resolutions, you must register the product and receive the registered version. Image Alchemy supports virtually every graphical file format. The documentation is in a file called **alchemy.doc**, which must be decompressed using the **manual.exe** program.

Piclab

Piclab is a powerful public-domain DOS image-processing program based on a text command language. Piclab can convert between image file formats; it can also change the colors and resolution of a file to a different format. Piclab can generate a new palette and map the image onto the new palette. The program has commands to change the brightness and contrast of an image, smooth the rough spots in an image, and much more. Piclab can also display the transformed image on a VGA screen.

Animation Programs

Contemporary hardware supports animation more effectively than before, and animated games are more popular than ever. Traditional animation renders frames in real time by selecting sequential sprite frames, specific screen coordinates, and a background scene on which to render the frames. The newer form of animation plays a movie clip in which the frames have been captured or rendered in advance. The clip can consist of a sequence of ray-traced or hand-painted scenes or frames of live-action video captured by a video recorder.

There are several formats for recording video clips.

Dave's .TGA Animation (DTA)

The DTA utility is designed to generate video **.FLI** or **.FLC** files from sets of graphical images. This tool allows you to create video files from sets of **.PCX** or **.TGA** frame images. The set is processed by DTA into a **.FLC** file, which can be shown by video player software or used in a game. One of the strengths of DTA is that it can decompress its frame image files from any of several compression archive formats.

The DTA program comes with documentation, but the best DTA reference is the book, *Morphing on Your PC*, written by DTA's author, David Mason.

AniBatch for Windows

AniBatch is a Windows 95–hosted utility program that generates animation sequences in source code format for POV-Ray. AniBatch creates a batch command file that runs POV-Ray enough times to create the animation and then launches DTA to create the animation file. Figure A.12 shows the AniBatch utility.

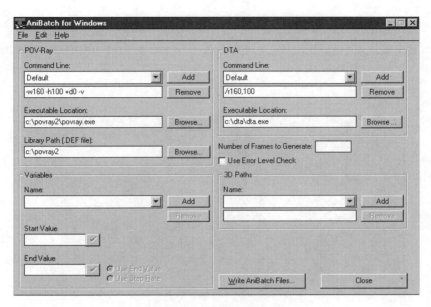

Figure A.12 AniBatch for Windows

Video for DOS (VFD)

VFD is a useful utility program for creating animation files and converting between the animation files of various formats. We have not included VFD on the CD-ROM for two reasons: First, its documentation specifically prohibits such distribution without written permission from the author. Second, its author has dropped out of sight, so we have been unable to request, much less receive, the required permission. Nonetheless, VFD is useful enough to be mentioned as a likely tool for a games programmer's toolset. You can download VFD from the CompuServe graphical forums. Search for a file named **VFD.ZIP**. If you can find the author, please register the program. The registration fee is $39.

VFD is a DOS utility that builds animation files from sequences of graphical images. VFD includes a simple scripting language that allows you to specify the order of frames along with effects such as pingponging and CD-ROM padding. Unlike DTA, VFD will not read its image files from compressed archives. Uncompressed image files can consume a lot of space, so we often use DTA to build a **.FLC** file and VFD to convert that file to the **.AVI** format that Windows 95 supports.

Truespace

Truespace is a complete 3D modeling, rendering, and animation package. Truespace has a remarkably innovative user interface, and is easier to learn than most other 3D packages. Figure A.14 shows truespace.

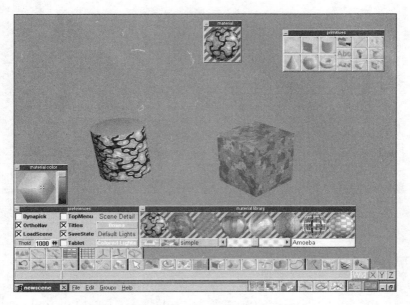

Figure A.13 The TrueSpace Application Window

A 30 day trial version of Truespace is included on the CD-ROM. With the exception of a few features, the trial version is fully functional. After 30 days, the application will stop running.

BIBLIOGRAPHY

Abrash, Michael. *Zen of Code Optimization.* Coriolis Group Books, 1994.

Abrash, Michael. *Zen of Graphics Programming.* Coriolis Group Books, 1995.

Conger, Jim. *C Programming for MIDI.* M&T Books, 1988.

Conger, Jim. *Microsoft Foundation Class Primer.* Waite Group Press, 1993.

Conger, Jim. *MIDI Sequencing in C.* M&T Books, 1989.

Ferraro, Richard E. *Programmer's Guide to the EGA and VGA Cards,* Second Edition. Addison-Wesley, 1990.

Gruber, Diana. *Action Arcade Adventure Set.* Coriolis Group Books, 1994.

Holzner, Steve. *Heavy Metal Visual C++ Programming.* IDG Books, 1994.

LaMothe, André, John Ratcliff, Mark Seminatore, and Denise Tyler. *Tricks of the Game Programming Gurus.* Sams Publishing, 1994.

Lampton, Christopher. *Flights of Fantasy.* Waite Group Press, 1993.

Lampton. Christopher. *Gardens of Imagination.* Waite Group Press, 1994.

Levy, Steven. *Hackers.* Dell, 1984.

Luse, Marv. *Bitmapped Graphics Programming in C++.* Addison-Wesley, 1993.

Mason, David K. *Morphing on Your PC.* Waite Group Press, 1994.

Roberts, Dave. *PC Game Programming Explorer.* Coriolis Group Books, 1994.

Thompson, Nigel. *Animation Techniques in Win32.* Microsoft Press, 1995.

Watkins, Christopher, and Stephen Marenka. *Taking Flight.* M&T Books, 1994.

Wilton, Richard. *Programmer's Guide to PC & PS/2 Video Systems.* Microsoft Press, 1987.

Young, Chris, and Drew Wells, *Ray Tracing Creations,* Second Edition. Waite Group Press, 1994.

GLOSSARY

3-D model

A computer data structure with data values that represent an image in terms of its component objects positioned and scaled in a three-dimensional coordinate system.

abstraction, level of

The working level of detail and knowledge at which a programmer writes code. At higher levels of abstraction, the underlying system encapsulates and hides more of the lower-level details.

active video page

The video page that the program reads from and writes to. The active video page can be visible or hidden.

analog signal

A waveform represented in its true, continuous form.

animation

The rapid display of a sequence of pictures that, when viewed, depicts a moving object.

API

Application program interface.

ASCII

The American Standard Code for Information Interchange, which associates integer values to numbers, letters, and special characters. Standard ASCII ranges from 0 to 127 and assigns values to digits, upper- and lowercase letters, punctuation marks, form control characters, and special transmission characters. Extended ASCII ranges from 128 to 255 and, on the PC architecture, assigns these values to foreign (non-English) language characters and graphics characters.

background

The image that occupies the full screen in a game and that represents the scenery in a scene.

baud rate

The speed in approximate bits per second at which a serial port transmits and receives data.

bitmapped graphics

The format that represents an image as an array of pixel values. There are several such formats for bitmapped graphics data files. The most common ones are **.PCX**, **.BMP**, TIFF, and **.GIF**. Each format is distinguished by the way it compresses image data and the format of the header data.

.BMP

The bitmapped graphics file format used in Microsoft Windows.

callback function

A user-defined function that the system calls when an event occurs. The game program registers for event notification by requesting that specific callback functions be called for specific events.

controller

A device that the game player uses to control the game. The keyboard, mouse, and joystick are controllers.

conventional memory

The computer memory in the first megabyte of address space.

coordinates

The addressing system that specifies screen pixels in a column/row scheme. The X axis is from zero to the highest horizontal resolution of the screen. The Y axis is from zero to the highest vertical resolution of the screen. Zero/zero addresses the upper-left pixel. 320/240 addresses the lower-right pixel when the display is operating in Mode X.

cue

An event that causes a callback function to be called.

digital signal

A waveform represented by digital values sampled at fixed intervals.

event

Something that happens outside of and asynchronous to the game program. Clock ticks, keystrokes, mouse movements, mouse clicks, joystick motion, joystick button presses, and receptions of network packets are events.

.FLC

A video clip file format originated by Autodesk Animator Pro.

flight simulator

A program that simulates aircraft flight. The program's user is the pilot. The program displays an instrument panel and scenery through the windshield of the simulated aircraft.

game console

A game-specific computer unit such as a coin video machine. The term also applies to home game units.

GDK

Games Development Kit.

.GIF

Graphics Interchange Format. A proprietary bitmapped graphics file format copyrighted by the CompuServe Information Service.

hackability

A contrived term used to describe the ease with which an application can be modified.

hardware acceleration

The use of hardware for tasks that traditionally are performed in software.

hidden video page

One of the video pages that contains display data that the user does not see.

interrupt

The interruption of a program's normal procedure of instruction execution, usually caused by an event—such as a key or button press—associated with a device, such as a controller or system timer.

loadable driver

A program that is read into memory as if it were a data file. The host program executes the driver by calling memory offsets from the beginning of the loaded module or by issuing software interrupts.

message

A function call that the system makes to registered member functions of the game program. Messages report events to the game program.

MIDI

Musical instrument digital interface. A standard for recording and reproducing musical performances as packets of digital information. Each packet represents a note or event. Packets address channels, which are assigned to instrument sounds.

Mode X

The VGA graphics mode with a resolution of 320 by 240 and with 256 distinct colors selected from a palette of 256KB possible colors.

modem

Modulator/demodulator. A device that allows two computers to communicate over voice-quality telephone lines. Each computer connects to its modem through the computer's serial port. Both modems are connected to the telephone lines at their respective sites. One computer originates a call, and the other computer answers. After the connection is completed, the two computers communicate as if they were directly connected at their serial ports with a null modem cable.

mouse cursor

The graphical display that represents where the mouse is pointing. A program can specify custom mouse cursor shapes, and it can select from a standard set of mouse cursor shapes.

paint program

A program that allows you to construct graphical images by using interactive tools to create and manipulate shapes, lines, colors, and textures.

palette

A table of red, green, and blue values. Each table entry represents a color. Each VGA screen display has an associated palette. The data bytes in video memory are vectors into the palette. Each data byte represents a pixel. The pixel's color is determined by its corresponding palette value.

palette normalization (or correction)

The process whereby several bitmapped images are modified so that they all use a common palette and can be displayed on the screen at the same time.

patch

The sound assigned to a MIDI instrument. This term is also used by the *VideoDirector* class (from the Theatrix framework) to indicate rectangular areas of the display pages.

.PCX

A bitmapped graphics file format associated with ZSoft's PC Paintbrush program and supported by the Windows Paintbrush program in Windows versions prior to Windows 95.

perspective

The visual property of sprite image components wherein more-distant images are rendered smaller and higher on the screen's Y coordinate than closer ones.

photo-realism

The quality of a computer-generated image that makes it almost seem to be a photograph. Often associated with ray-traced images.

pixel

Picture element. One dot on a video screen.

quantize

To smooth the pattern of notes played by a MIDI sequencer to a lowest common resolution, such as the eighth note. The term is also used to describe the process of modifying images to use fewer colors.

ray casting

Building an image of a scene by casting rays from the viewing position until they intersect objects, at which time the pixel values of vertical strips are computed. Ray casting depends on computer models of symmetrical and perpendicular geometric shapes such as walls and corridors.

ray tracing

Building an image from a 3-D model that includes light sources and a viewing position. The model specifies shapes, textures, and surfaces. The shapes can have logical and hierarchical relationships with one another. The ray-tracing program computes the color value of each screen pixel by tracing from the light sources through transparent objects to the first opaque object that the ray intersects and then back to the viewing position.

render

To produce a displayable image from a 3-D computer model.

resolution

In video displays, the number of horizontal and vertical pixels that a video mode can display. In digital waveform recording, the minimum and maximum values that a sample can represent expressed as the number of bits in a sample.

RTTI

Runtime type information.

sample

In digital signal processing, the single value of a point on a waveform. In music reproduction, a note played by an instrument and recorded to be combined with other recorded samples in the electronic reproduction of a musical selection.

sampling rate

The rate, expressed in samples per second, at which samples are made during the recording of a digital waveform.

scan code

The eight-bit value that the keyboard transmits to the computer when the user presses a key.

scanner

A device that scans a drawing, photograph, or other image into a bitmapped graphics format in the PC.

scenery

See "background."

SDK

Software Development Kit.

sequencer

A device that reads files of MIDI data and transmits the packets to synthesizers. A sequencer can also record MIDI files by reading the notes played on a synthesizer.

serial port

The communications port that connects one PC with another either directly or indirectly through a modem. Programs in two computers can communicate through the machines' serial ports.

simulation

A computer model of a real-world object, event, place, or combination of the three.

sound clip

A binary stream that represents the recording of a voice or sound effect. The stream includes a header block that defines the sampling rate and resolution of the sound clip.

sprite

An animated character in a game.

super VGA

A video controller card, compatible with VGA, that is capable of displaying more colors and higher resolution than VGA.

synthesizer

A device that produces musical sounds electronically.

system clock

The hardware interrupt that occurs at approximately 18.2 times per second.

texture mapping

Creating the image of an object's surface by covering the surface of the object with repetitions of a single tile that contains an image of the texture.

.TGA

Targa. A bitmapped graphics file format developed by AT&T.

TIFF

Tagged Image File Format. A bitmapped graphics file format developed by Aldus.

timer

A software counter that counts down from a programmed value to zero or from zero to the value of the timer. Timers can increment or decrement at each click of the system clock or as a function of the processor speed.

transpose

Change the key signature of a musical composition, adjusting all the notes appropriately.

VGA

Virtual Graphics Array. The video controller card used in most PCs.

video buffer

A contiguous area of memory that holds video display information.

video clip

A sequence of still frame images that can be displayed as a motion picture. The program does not alter the sequence or position of any of the frames while the video clip plays.

video mode

The way that the video controller displays data. The mode specifies pixel resolution and number of colors. Modes are associated with the video controllers. The VGA can use all the modes of earlier PC video controllers and adds several modes of its own. Some modes are graphics modes. Others are text modes. In graphics modes, the value of a byte of video memory specifies the color at a pixel location. In text modes, the value of a word of video memory specifies an ASCII value to be displayed and its color attributes.

video page

One of several video buffers that the program can address. Only one video page at a time is visible to the user. The others are hidden.

visible video page

The video page that contains the display data that the user sees.

.VOC

A sound clip file format originated by Creative Labs' Sound Blaster.

.WAV

A sound clip file format defined by Microsoft.

wire frame model

A computer model built of vectors that connect to represent the edges of shapes.

Z-Order

The order of a sprite relative to the other sprites in the Z coordinate, which defines which sprites will display on top of—and, therefore, in front of—which other sprites when sprite images intersect.

INDEX

C

ABOUT THE CD-ROM

See Appendix A for a full description of the CD-ROM,
and installation details.

The Theatrix framework, demos, and tools are located in the **\Theatrix**
directory.

The RayCast framework, demos, and tools are located in the **\RayCaster**
directory.

The GDKapp framework, demos, and tools are located in the **\GDKapp**
directory.

The **\Executables** directory contains ready-to-run versions of all of the
demos in the book. These demos can be run directory off of the CD-ROM,
or copied to your hard drive.

The **\Tools** directory contains the freeware and shareware tools. See
Appendix A for information on each tool.

The **\Extras** directory contains some shareware and freeware games, such
as AstroFire and Relentless.

To install each framework, use the **xcopy** command to copy the directory
tree to your hard drive. For example, if your CD-ROM drive is drive D, and
you want to install the Theatrix framework on drive C, use the following
command:

```
xcopy /s /e d:\Theatrix c:\Theatrix\*.*
```

The files on the CD-ROM each have a read-only attribute (because a CD-
ROM is a read-only device). Once you copy a directory from the CD-ROM
drive to your hard drive, you will need to remove these attributes before
you can modify the files. This can be done with the **attrib** command. To
modify the files in the Theatrix directory on your hard drive, use these
commands:

```
c:
cd \Theatrix
attrib /s -r
```